# IT Tactics

## IT Strategy Execution
## Tactics and the Individual

# IT Tactics

## IT Strategy Execution
## Tactics and the Individual

Richard P. Skinner

Library of Congress Number:     2006905744

ISBN # 1-4196-3999-4

**To order additional copies, please contact us.**
BookSurge, LLC
www.booksurge.com
1-866-308-6235
orders@booksurge.com

# Dedication

This book is dedicated to the Information Technology (IT)
managers who assisted me in developing these strategies and tactics:
Doug Fraser, Bob Mayes, and Ray Valentine.

# Preface

This book is meant to be the second in a series of guidebooks for small to medium sized businesses (SMBs) who face challenges with their IT departments. The first book in the series is titled *IT is about the Strategy* and is available through xlibris.com, ITisaboutStrategy.com, Borders, Amazon, and other major book sellers.

## A Word From The Author

I have written this book to assist IT departments in strategy execution.
The challenge in IT is to think strategically and execute tactically.
Strategic execution requires cohesive tactics. In my experience most SMBs
never get past the tactical thinking stage. Not only do they not think
strategically but they frequently don't even think in terms of cohesive tactics.
Most SMBs just react to internal pressures.

## Definitions

IT is simply Information Technology.

IS is simply Information Systems or Information Services.

SMB and SMBs are abbreviations for small to medium sized businesses and are the target audience for this book.

# IT Tactics
# Table of Contents

# Introduction

The purpose of this book is to build on the work titled *IT is about the Strategy* by providing tactical tools, techniques and templates for strategic execution. Tactics are the steps taken to execute strategy. IT is about the strategy. This tactics book also provides recommendations and guidelines for management of IT individuals. Please refer to Appendix I-1 which is both a blueprint for the requisite tools and techniques as well as an overview of the approach used in this book. This book is a guidebook for execution so it will contain numerous templates. These will be included as appendices or embedded in the text where possible. These templates are also available for distribution without charge from the website ITisaboutStrategy.com.

The format of the book is based on the three IT strategies I recommended in my first book:

- Business Layer
- Business Model
- Business Process

The work consists of mapping these strategies to the required tactics within the three technology layers (infrastructure, back office, and customer facing) and to the three components of personnel management (the organization structure, the management team and the individual employee).

The audience for this book is both the business leadership (CEO, CFO, or any executive tasked with reporting responsibility for the IT department) and the IT leadership. The premise of the book is that IT is not about the technology, but rather the strategy and that the IT strategy must be developed, owned and executed by business leadership.

The three strategies I recommend in my previous book grow more complex in nature as the business grows and matures. The business layer strategy is the first strategy that the SMB should consider and is a straightforward basic approach. It recommends dividing technology into three layers and addressing the layers individually with different tactics. The business model strategy is the next logical strategy and is more complex. It recommends establishing strategic areas of focus and using these to decide which technologies and projects are needed to drive the business. The business process strategy is the most complex of the three strategies and follows the business model strategy. The business process strategy focuses on process and the need to identify the IT processes and organize the IT department around those processes. All of these strategies are meant to remove those barriers that the IT department will encounter as the SMB grows and changes.

The general approach I recommend throughout this book is one of iterative improvements over time. One of the primary flaws I see in both corporations and society in general is the search for a quick fix. There is always a quick fix or a band-aid that can be applied to any problem but in my experience it seldom lasts. I keep preaching to any business leader that will listen that these initiatives take time. It is frustrating to see SMBs pursue quick fixes in technologies and processes when permanent resolution takes time and repetition. You must put some process in place no matter how crude and build on and improve it over time. I think this key observation is one of the reasons for the sad state of affairs in most IT organizations in most SMBs. You cannot fix it once with a quick fix and walk away. As the business grows the SMB must return to each process to enhance and improve it. This is both a strategic and tactical exercise.

# Infrastructure

## A. Infrastructure Strategy

As defined in the book *IT is about the Strategy*, the first strategy any SMB should embrace should be the business layer strategy. The business layer strategy entails categorizing the existing technology solutions into one of three technology layers and addressing each of these layers in a different fashion. Please refer to Appendix 1-1 for a pictorial view of this strategy.

The first layer, Infrastructure, is the base layer of technology comprised of the underlying technology architecture components on which all other functionality is built. It is the technology foundation. It includes components like local and wide area networks, telephone systems, work stations, PC desktops, processors and servers, printers and other miscellaneous hardware. This layer is a surprisingly common layer that will not differ substantially from SMB to SMB.

The output of this strategic exercise should be a written report. Please refer to the first tab on Appendix 1-2 for an abbreviated sample of the infrastructure report. This report should follow a standard format and have the three technology layers firmly defined and categorized. Using this report the business can describe the current infrastructure situation and have a plan for solving issues and problems. Using this strategy the business can define tactics, which in this case are specific activities and projects required to execute the strategy.

## B. Infrastructure Tactics

Here are the recommended infrastructure tactics. First and foremost please keep the following infrastructure tactics in mind and do not deviate from them.

- **Buy instead of building**

    The SMB should not construct the infrastructure using internal staff but should instead outsource the work to independent external integrators. Do not outsource to specific hardware vendors. Hardware vendors are in the market to sell products. External integrators are paid for service and to integrate products from multiple vendors. External integrators can choose products from various hardware vendors most suitable to the challenge at hand. The business should not ask or allow the IT department to build infrastructure. For example, the IT department should never build the local area network using internal staff. Instead hire an independent integrator and use internal staff for vendor relationship management and executing the vision. There is no value and no competitive advantage in this technology layer. The IT department should not need or want to get good at building infrastructure. Nothing the business can do here will provide it with a competitive edge. Infrastructure outsourcing can now even include the desktop and remote desktop support. If the external integrator is willing to own the entire infrastructure then the desktop and other personal devices may be included. This solves a broad range of issues that usually plague a small IT department. These issues include configuration management, change management, virus protection, standard images and individual customization of the desktop.

- **Adopt industry standards**

    This is very important! Nothing is more expensive than replacing infrastructure components. Infrastructure replacement may be dictated for several reasons. The technology vendor may go out of business. The business may not be getting adequate maintenance and support. Support may even get so expensive it is cheaper to replace the technology. To prevent infrastructure replacement pick the right solutions the first time. The ultimate goal is to do solid market research, identify the industry leaders and make safe choices. I would recommend the business stay the middle ground. It is dangerous to get ahead of the technology curve and buy "bleeding" edge technology. Make every effort to select a vendor who will be in the market for the long haul. The chosen external integrator should be able to make strong recommendations and the SMB should intelligently follow their advice. I am not recommending a carte blanche approach but the integrator has a vested interest in providing both the requisite functionality and a supportable environment. It will be important to follow the integrator's lead but retain final approval.

- **Think connectivity and interfaces**

    It is important that each technology component in each of the infrastructure areas (networks, servers, telephony) connect seamlessly and communicate with each other. This can only be accomplished with like technologies of similar generations and where components are basically compatible. The best example I can provide is in call center technologies where the various components of PBX, automatic call distributor (ACD), interactive voice response (IVR) and other voice technologies must coexist in the same environment. The IT department can spend a substantial amount of time trying to build these interfaces after purchase or they can be accommodated during the planning phase. It is important to define connectivity as an upfront requirement in dealing with integrators. The integrators can meet this need through appropriate product selection and by adhering to sound, well defined architecture principles. Outsourcing does not absolve the business of making choices. If anything, it requires that the business defines the requirements more closely and that it has a clearer picture when it starts. This external integrator should be able to provide solutions that work seamlessly together. Some of the value that an integrator brings should include industry know-how, product knowledge and the ability to choose compatible components that connect.

## C. Infrastructure Tactics Execution

In order to execute the infrastructure vision for this strategy, perform the following tactical steps:

**1.  Develop the infrastructure list**

Again refer to the first tab of Appendix 1-2. This is a fairly exhaustive list of basic infrastructure components. If you have something unique please add it to this list. You will find that infrastructure components are remarkably common among SMBs.

**2.  Attach any identified problems and issues**

During the strategic exercise the SMB identified problems and issues with existing infrastructure. Merely slot these in the space provided. I have given a few examples on the first tab of Appendix 1-2 which includes issues like the following:
- Slow or off-brand servers need replaced
- Connectivity to network too slow
- PCs outdated and need replaced
- PBX behind on firmware releases
- Connectivity between servers too slow

**3.  Identify the projects**

Each identified problem or issue should be resolved by an activity or a project. If an issue can be resolved by a simple act or a simple activity, then schedule and execute it. If not, identify the series of activities or steps required to remedy the issue and establish a project. Each infrastructure component where installation and support now falls to internal staff needs to be outsourced to the appropriate independent external integrator. Each component could also have other issues and problems that must be addressed. The composite of these two broad areas will be the infrastructure project list. It is important to assure that all identified problems and issues are considered project requirements and that the project addresses them satisfactorily. Please refer to Appendix 1-3 for a recommended infrastructure (as well as back office and customer facing) project list format.

My overriding recommendation for infrastructure in this strategy is to find a reliable outsourcing vendor and have them not only host the applications but provide a total infrastructure outsourcing solution. If this is not a feasible approach, for whatever reason, then the other two alternatives are to continue to self-host the infrastructure or to find a vendor who provides simple hosting facilities. External hosting is preferable to self-hosting and either option should only be considered in the short term not the long term. The ultimate goal is to stay out of the computer hosting business and avoid time and effort expended on infrastructure construction and support.

## 4. Sequence the projects

Now, sequence the projects. Strategy execution is not instantaneous, nor immediate. This is the real world. A strategy is by necessity a blueprint for action over time. The business should not seek to do wholesale outsourcing or immediately rush to push everything out the door to whatever outsourcers are known to be available. The SMB does need to solve the infrastructure problems and issues that are affecting the business. The goal of any strategy is to have a way to make specific tactical decisions on a day-to-day basis. While the business should look for some quick wins, the business also needs to develop a sequence of execution that makes sense based on a combination of the following criteria:

- **Available personnel** - Has the business hired the right individuals to manage both the execution and support of these projects? Recruiting is a critical factor for executing the projects.
- **Pain points** - Which infrastructure components are either having the most negative impact on the business or conversely will have the most positive impact on the business when fixed? Fix the highest pain points first.
- **Funding** - Each project will require project expenses and funding. Each project should also have a positive return on investment (ROI). Funding may dictate the sequencing.
- **Messages** - Which projects will gain the most positive publicity within the company and with customers? Which will send the most positive messages to the interested stakeholders? IT often forgets that they need to market themselves to the rest of the organization. Some projects will carry a larger marketing impact than others.
- **Risk** - Which projects carry a low risk and can be implemented knowing there will be some minor problems? Some projects will be high profile and high risk and need to be executed slowly and carefully.

## 5.  Measure cost effectiveness

Each project will require project expenses for execution. Each project should also have a positive ROI. Perform a quick cost benefit analysis to identify the biggest winners. The easiest calculation can be:
-   Define your current costs and expenditures. Include ongoing manpower, maintenance and support costs.
-   Define current losses or missed opportunities due to current problems or issues. There must be lost revenue or other lost opportunities that are causing concerns with the existing infrastructure.
-   Calculate anticipated new costs and expenditures. Include one time and ongoing costs.
-   Calculate anticipated pay back (increased revenue, decreased expenses, lowered headcount) per month.
-   Calculate the amount of time it will take to recover the expenditure.

Please see Appendix 1-4 for a sample ROI (cost benefit) calculation template.

## 6.  Execute the projects

Deploy an abbreviated basic and concise project management methodology. Please refer to the project management methodology found in Chapter 10 titled "Simplified Project Management". In instances where outsourcing is not an issue, continue directly to Chapter 2. For outsourcing activities please read on.

## 7.  Finding and selecting the external integrators

There may not be a single vendor available that will provide for your entire infrastructure. For example, there may well be one voice integrator and one data integrator despite the fact that these two technologies are converging. The vendors should be relied upon to both assist in the infrastructure selection and then provide the hosting, maintenance and support. This is not to be confused with simple data center hosting which simply provides a place to host your processors outside of your physical locations. While these vendors do provide tangible value and this may be considered as an interim step, the business should be looking for a comprehensive, long-term solution. Vendors have been slow to catch onto this strategic approach as have SMBs so it may be difficult to find the proper providers. However, I am encouraged by the number of new players entering this market and particularly impressed by vendors who have built entire infrastructure and support capabilities. The SMB may still have to find several vendors but there should be a stated goal to use as few as possible. The greater the number of integrators that is required the more difficult it is to manage. The process for vendor evaluation and selection is described below.

### a.  Develop an initial vendor list

The business should first compile a list of known external integrators. This can be initiated by talking to existing and known vendors who provide this service.

The list can be supplemented by contacting various business and technical associations, by research on the internet and by contacting the local chamber of commerce or other local government organizations. The CEO, CFO and other executives should also use their informal networks and affiliations to secure recommendations. The list may at this time be small but the business still needs to use a structured approach to selection and not jump to a solution. This is simply good business practice in the form of comparison shopping.

### b. Develop requirements and selection criteria

The project requirements for the integrators will consist of providing the required infrastructure components including the resolution of the issues and problems associated with the list. In addition to meeting these more basic requirements the integration vendor selection criteria should also contain any or all of the following:

- Service offered (the more comprehensive the better)
- Price (cost to the business, do ROI calculations)
- Length of contract required and escape clauses (should that become necessary)
- Performance based on SLAs (poll the integrator's existing clients for the satisfaction of those clients)
- Integrator facilities (number, size, location, proximity)
- Disaster recovery capability (backup generators, redundancy, power grids utilized and so on)
- Years in business (experience)
- Viability and healthiness of the vendor (ask to see financial statements or accountant's opinions)
- The growth plans and estimated needs of the SMB (can the vendor grow with the SMB?)

### c. Conduct the selection process

The selection process needs to be structured and methodical. I have included a vendor selection and management chapter (14) and a package evaluation and selection chapter (13). Neither will be exactly what needs to be done but both are useful in this exercise. Immediately eliminate all but the most viable vendors based on the criteria. Prepare and submit a very brief request for information or request for proposal to the candidate vendors. Be sure to structure your relationships with the vendors to maintain control of the relationships. Using the information or proposal that the vendors returned, the SMB can plot the responses against the requirement criteria. You can build a simple matrix mapping the requirements to the vendors. Visit the vendor's existing customers and look for comparisons. The selection process can be numerical and the top two or three vendors can be taken into the negotiation and contract process. Do not hesitate to allow the vendors to compete. Pricing here can be soft and competition is healthy. Have a firm idea in mind of what the business expects from the vendor in terms of availability and performance. Get as much of that as possible into the contract.

## 8.  Managing the external integrators

Per this strategy, once the vendor or vendors (integrators) have been selected, the challenge now becomes how to manage and control the infrastructure even though it has been moved and outsourced. The business obviously still owns the infrastructure and must manage it to assure that it meets all of the business requirements. Below are the considerations for managing the integrators.

### a.  Service level agreements (SLAs)

The purpose of a SLA is to assure maximum infrastructure availability by managing and measuring that availability. The watch phrase is you cannot manage what you cannot measure. The first step should be to establish the SLAs themselves. These are simply the IT and external integrator's commitment and agreement with the business as to what is an acceptable level of service. Defined in this SLA are the measurements the business will use to evaluate the service provided. SLAs for technology are cumulative in nature. The final goal is the availability of the back office or customer facing application as infrastructure in and of itself provides no inherent value to the business. Here are some areas of focus which require SLAs:

- The application hardware server needs to be available and capable of processing the workload.
- The local area network (LAN) needs to be available and carrying traffic.
- For remote delivery of applications the network across the wide area network (WAN) has to be available.
- Any orders or data from the clients must arrive and be processed to provide daily products or services.
- The website needs to be up and functioning properly to handle service and orders.
- The telephone system (PBX) needs to function to communicate with clients.
- The system response time needs to be acceptable with no prolonged waits or halts between screens.

Failure of any one of these components above effectively renders the business user down. The purpose of measuring availability is to provide the maximum opportunity for the business to function properly!

### b.  Measuring availability

If any customer facing application is narrowly defined as a service being offered to the company, then IT can create a score card that would summarize the availability of this service. Please see Appendix 1-5 for a sample scorecard.

This scorecard would include all of the SLA items above in terms of the measurements below:

- What percentage of time was the server available during scheduled published service times?
- What percentage of time was the server reachable from the LAN during scheduled published service times?
- What percentage of time was the server reachable from the WAN during scheduled published service times?
- What percentage of time did nightly processing complete in time?
- What percentage of time was the web site available and functioning?
- What percentage of time was the PBX available?

Measuring all of these items together gives a better view of the user experience and allows IT to trend progress over time. Armed with this information, IT and the external integrator will know where to apply resources to reach SLA goals. IT can then say with confidence what kind of service they are providing to the business.

### c. Measuring responsiveness

Even when the service is available it is also important to measure the responsiveness of the applications. It does little good to have the application up but have long wait periods between screen prompts or when painting screens. I recommend establishing response time measures with length of time for system responses on the major applications. These should be in single digit seconds unless the user is doing a complex query.

## D. Infrastructure and Personnel

There are no special requirements for IT management with this tactical execution. There are no complicated organizational requirements. The organization is basically flat with one senior leader and one or more relationship managers.

At the individual level in infrastructure for managing projects and activities the business needs a technical relationship manager with skills to manage the vision, direction, vendors, solutions, projects, consultants and relationships. The IT department will need one or more of these relationship management employees. The skill set depends on a sound and thorough understanding of the technology but not the ability to work with it. It requires excellent organization and communication skills. It requires an understanding of vendor relationship management. It requires knowledge of the business and the internal and external business processes. The position will also be performing project management duties so an understanding and experience with a simplified methodology is important. This position requires a combination of strategic and tactical skill sets.

The responsibilities of this position will be to manage the vendor relationships and the SLAs. This position requires no small amount of diplomacy and a degree of tact. Long term vendor relationships must be cultivated but it must not bleed over into a personal relationship.

## Back Office Applications

> **WISDOM to work by:**
>
> 1. <u>*Back office applications are a commodity.*</u>
>    *The back office applications offer no competitive advantages for the SMB. A poor set of back office applications may well ruin the business but an outstanding back office merely allows you to begin to compete.*
>
> 2. <u>*Back office applications...don't do it yourself.*</u>
>    *Buy software applications or use Application Service Providers (ASPs). Use independent application software integrators if possible. Never build back office software applications.*
>
> 3. <u>*Change your internal business processes to meet the requirements of the software.*</u>
>    *Do not change the software to fit your internal processes.*
>
> 4. <u>*Process, process, process.*</u>
>    *Use a structured process to find the back office software applications. There is a better way.*
>
> 5. <u>*You cannot manage what you do not measure.*</u>
>    *Manage external integrators through SLAs that track technology availability and responsiveness.*

## A. Back Office Applications Strategy

As defined in *IT is about the Strategy,* the first strategy any SMB should embrace should be the business layer strategy. The business layer strategy entails categorizing the existing technology solutions into one of three technology layers and addressing each of these layers in a different fashion. Please refer to Appendix 1-1 for a pictorial view of this strategy.

The second layer, Back Office, is the middle layer of technology critical to the day to day running of the company and provides the applications and functionality that nearly all SMBs cannot live without. It resides and functions on top of the infrastructure layer. It consists of applications that provide managerial support, administrative support and office systems. It includes accounting packages, financial packages, human resource systems, email capabilities, voicemail functionality, document faxing and handling, and most other internally focused software and application systems. These are the applications that must be dealt with no matter what product or service the SMB provides. This layer is also a surprisingly common layer (not unlike infrastructure) that will not differ much from SMB to SMB.

The output of this strategic exercise should be a written report. Please refer to the second tab on Appendix 1-2 for an abbreviated sample of the back office report. Using this framework, the business should describe the current back office situation and have a blueprint for resolving issues. Using the strategy the business can define tactics which in this case are specific activities and projects required to execute the strategy. As with infrastructure, the strategic plan will provide the blueprint for this strategic layer. As with infrastructure, replacing or converting back office applications is a very difficult thing to do and needs to be approached in a structured and tightly controlled fashion. Ideally all back office applications should be housed on outsourced infrastructure so this adds a layer of complexity as far as timing is concerned. Timing should be one of the key factors for sequencing both the infrastructure and the back office projects due to their interdependencies.

## B. Back Office Applications Tactics

To begin, almost everything discussed in addressing the base or infrastructure layer holds true for the middle or back office layer. Instead of hardware infrastructure, the back office deals primarily with software and application systems with a smattering of hardware components as well.

Surprisingly the middle or back office layer in one SMB will also not differ substantially from most other SMBs. The same components are required for all businesses since all businesses have the same or similar accounting, payroll, human resource and communication requirements. As with the base layer there are three simple tactics that are nearly the same.

- **Buy instead of building**
  The SMB should not build back office applications but should outsource the work to independent external integrators. Do not outsource to specific software vendors without considering all options. You may also make an exception to this rule if you are seeking an application service provider (ASP) solution. Software vendors are in the business to sell software while software integrators can be vendor independent and choose from the many available solutions. More importantly, the IT department should not be allowed to build back office applications themselves or to buy a software package and internally make modifications. The business should buy and use the functionality provided. I recommend changing the business processes to meet the demands of the software and not the reverse. If the business collected the requirements properly, the purchased package should suffice. If not, consider starting over and redoing requirements. Reinstallation is preferable to continual unbridled modification. I have personally seen back office modification projects go on for months and months and even years. This is a mistake of focus. There is no value and no competitive advantage in this strategic layer. The business and the IT department should not want or need to get good at building the back office layer. Use internal staff wisely for vendor relationship management and executing the vision. Nothing the business can do here will provide a competitive edge. If not done properly, however, poor handling of the back office functionality can seriously hamper the business.

- **Adopt industry standards**

  As with infrastructure, this tactic is extremely important. Do proper market research and identify the industry leaders. Make safe choices. The goal is to buy safe, reliable back office functionality and the safest way to do this is to stick with industry leaders who follow industry standards. It is important to define the business requirements and use a structured selection process. See Chapter 13 for a solid approach to package evaluation and selection. The business should also not allow any one person to drive any one selection process. Please try to avoid buying based on sales people or sales relationships or buying packages used by existing employees at other companies. Select a vendor based on the requirements of your SMB and of your current technology model. Select a vendor who will be in the market for the long term and who can support and enhance their products.

- **Think connectivity and interfaces**

  It is critical that the back office systems connect seamlessly and "talk" or communicate with each other. The IT department can spend a substantial amount of time trying to construct these interfaces after the applications have been installed or these can be accommodated in the planning phase. It is important to define connectivity as an upfront requirement in dealing with integrators. The integrators can meet the need if the business can adequately define it. Outsourcing of back office applications does not absolve the business of making these connectivity choices. If anything, it requires that the business define the requirements more closely and that it has a clearer picture when it starts. Keying data from system to system is a very bad practice. There is usually an inverse relationship between the number of ad hoc databases or spreadsheets and the upfront work done on connectivity and interfaces. Every manual interface is an opportunity for a mistake. Every informal step added to the process is an unneeded risk and complication. Buying a suite of products that do not integrate can ultimately be as expensive as building solutions internally.

## C. Back Office Applications Tactics Execution

### 1. Develop the back office applications list

Please refer again to the second tab on Appendix 1-2. This is a full list of back office application components. Modify it to suit your particular situation.

### 2. Attach the identified problems and issues

During this strategic exercise the SMB identified problems and issues with existing back office applications components. Merely slot these in the space provided. I have given a few examples on the second tab of Appendix 1-2 but it should include issues like the following:
  - Running on internal servers, need to move to outsourced infrastructure
  - Homegrown package needs replaced

- Homegrown package that has been internally modified and has become a maintenance problem
- Does not interface easily to any other system
- Company has outgrown the package and replacement is required

## 3.   Identify the projects

Each identified issue should be resolved by an activity or a project. If an issue can be resolved by a simple act or a simple activity, then schedule and execute it. If not, identify the series of activities or steps required to remedy the issue and conduct a project. Projects will take the form of resolving each of the problems and issues identified above as well as the move of the applications to the outsourced infrastructure. Each back office application component where development or internal modification has taken place should also be considered as a candidate for replacement. Each component could also have other issues and problems that must be addressed. The composite of these broad areas will be the back office project list. It is important to assure that all identified problems and issues are considered project requirements and that the project addresses them satisfactorily. Please refer to Appendix 1-3 for a recommended back office (as well as infrastructure and customer facing) project list format.

## 4.   Scope the projects

The first tactical challenge is how to combine the required functionality requirements or systems into groups of applications that can and should be addressed by a given vendor solution set. This is the challenge of scope. One example is that accounts payable, accounts receivable, general ledger, financial reporting and fixed assets will likely come to the business as an integrated suite. Based on the vendor and applications provided, the SMB should also investigate all other vendor offerings as a complement to this suite. Integration of back office components is a primary challenge when solutions come from multiple vendors. In this example any commission software, inventory control software or sales force management software should also be considered. The SMB is looking for solid core functionality and vendors generally offer a suite of tools and seldom just one package. The trick is to consider the suite as a whole and avoid the interface challenge. The external integrator should be able to assist greatly with the scoping exercise. The scope and number of solutions considered can play a major role in the vendor and applications selection process so the business should not underestimate or ignore the scoping exercise.

## 5.   Give consideration to purchasing software or purchasing service

There are always two realistic options for software applications. The business can purchase the application and have it run on the outsourced infrastructure or the business can employ an ASP where the vendor not only provides the software but hosts and manages the software as well. In the latter case, the business merely enters data into the system provided and the vendor worries about everything else. Proper consideration should be given to both solutions. Again, avoid the software development trap and avoid modifying purchased applications.

## 6. Finalize the project list

The goal of back office tactics is to rely on external resources to host and run the applications on the infrastructure that has been provided from the infrastructure layer strategy or rely on ASP services. The tactical result will be a back office application project list. It is important that all identified problems and issues are considered project requirements and that the project addresses them satisfactorily.

## 7. Sequence the projects

Next sequence the projects. Strategy execution is seldom instantaneous and imme-diate. While the business should look for some quick wins, the business needs to develop a sequence of execution that makes sense for the business based on the criteria listed below. Prioritize these projects based on the strongest positive business impact, the cost to the business and the available manpower. Remember these are business projects and not technology projects. A project can be a single application or a suite of applications as dictated by the scoping exercise performed above. Again, the scoping exercise is pivotal.
- **Available personnel** - Has the business hired the right individual or individuals to manage both the execution and support of these projects? Recruiting is critical to execute the projects.
- **Pain points** - Which back office components are either having the most negative impact on the business or conversely will have the most positive impact on the business? Fix the highest pain points first.
- **Funding** - Each project will require project expenses. Each project should also have a positive ROI. Perform the quick cost benefit analysis to identify the biggest winners. See Appendix 1-4 for a sample format.
- **Messages** - Which projects will gain the most positive publicity within the company and with customers? Which will send the most positive messages to the interested stakeholders? IT often forgets that they need to market themselves to the rest of the organization and some projects will carry a larger marketing impact than others.
- **Risk** - Which projects carry a low risk and can be implemented knowing there will be some minor problems? Some projects will be high profile and high risk and need to be executed slowly and carefully.

## 8. Execute the projects

Deploy an abbreviated basic and concise project management methodology to execute the projects. Please refer to the project management methodology found later in this book in Chapter 10 under Common Tactics. The most difficult part of project execution will be application package selection. There is a well defined way to do package selection that will go a long way to insure success. Please refer to the package selection methodology found later in this book in Chapter 13 under Common Tactics.

A summary of that process is as follows:
- Define business and technical requirements.
- Define scope (here we are talking both about scope in broad, general terms and also the specific project scope as well).
- Conduct research. Identify four to six potential solutions for each application area.
- Interview vendors in a structured way.
- Narrow the solution set to three to four vendors.
- Develop selection criteria in addition to the requirements.
- Map vendors to selection criteria and weight the results.
- Conduct customer visits.
- Develop a one page matrix with the vendors scored against the criteria to make your selection.
- Please refer to Appendix 13-1 for an entire package selection process example.

Once the package selection process has been completed the SMB moves on to package installation. This also requires a solid project management methodology. From here the business moves into day-to-day management of the application and the vendor. These issues are addressed below.

**9.   Manage the application service providers**

Once an application is brought into production, the SMB must turn their attention to managing the application service providers and assuring that the contracted service is delivered. The focus moves from projects to day-to-day administration and management. These are very different skills sets.

**a. SLAs**

Applications when compared to infrastructure have the following service level considerations or performance related components:
- Availability
- Cost effectiveness
- Accuracy

These factors must be managed and measured.

**b   Manage availability, cost effectiveness and accuracy**

Please reference the discussion on managing availability and cost effectiveness in the infrastructure section. There are measurements spelled out there that must be developed in order to manage delivery of services to the business. The same factors and considerations apply in the back office.

For accuracy there is a different and discreet approach. It will take diligence and solid record keeping to track the accuracy and performance of a back office software application. The overriding goal is to document and manage every problem or issue with the software application. Begin by developing a back office applications issue log in the form of an Excel spreadsheet. Include the following information:

- Problem or issue number
- Problem or issue description
- Date identified
- Identified by
- Assigned to (IT owner)
- Date assigned
- Department or area affected
- Business owner
- Due date
- Date completed
- Current status (open, active, closed)
- Status detail

This is a simple, straightforward way of documenting the issues that will arise with any application. The vendor relationship manager from IT is responsible for this tracking. The relationship manager will then need to conduct periodic performance review sessions with both the business and the independent outsourcer or ASP. I recommend starting with a weekly meeting shortly after installation and then moving to a biweekly or monthly meeting over time as the installation issues are addressed. The volume of issues should naturally diminish. The format of the meeting should be to review the issues log, discuss availability and cost effectiveness, discuss releases and upgrades to the products, and provide feedback from both the vendor and the business. The more structured approach that can be taken the better. Please do not forget to take and publish meeting minutes as you will be surprised how often participants forget about past resolutions and agreements. The goal is that performance needs to be measurable and these measurements need to be accurate. A structured approach is best.

## D. Back Office Applications and Personnel

There are no special requirements for IT management with this tactical execution. There are no organizational requirements. The organization is basically flat.

At the individual level in the back office for managing projects and activities, the business needs an applications relationship manager with skills to manage the vision, direction, vendors, solutions, projects, consultants and relationships. The IT department will need one or more of these relationship management employees. The skill set depends on an understanding of application software but not the ability to program or code. It requires excellent organization and communication skills. It requires an understanding of vendor relationship management. It requires a thorough knowledge of the business and the internal and external business processes. This position requires a combination of strategic and tactical skill sets. A mix of accounting/finance and IT experience with strong business knowledge is a plus.

## Customer Facing Applications

> ### WISDOM to work by:
>
> 1. *<u>Focus, focus, focus!</u>*
>    *Customer facing applications should be your primary IT focus. Pull out all the stops. These software applications are the differentiators for your business. Be creative.*
> 2. *<u>Customer facing applications...don't build it from scratch.</u>*
>    *There is almost never a good reason to build software from scratch anymore. Practice component and tool kit integration instead. Roughly eighty percent of all software development projects fail. Don't reinvent the wheel.*
> 3. *<u>Process, process, process.</u>*
>    *Use a structured process to select and integrate customer facing software applications. There is a better way.*

## A. Customer Facing Applications Strategy

As defined in *IT is about the Strategy*, the first strategy any SMB should embrace after their first period of growth should be the business layer strategy. It is time to halt the mad rush to implement new technologies which resulted in daily service and support issues and a mishmash of technology solutions. The business layer strategy entails categorizing the existing technology solutions into one of three technology layers and addressing each of these layers in a different strategic fashion. Please refer to Appendix 1-1 for a pictorial view of this strategy.

The third layer, or customer facing, is the top layer of technology and consists of the systems that touch the customer and support the delivery of products or services, whatever the core reason for being in business. Like the back office layer, this layer resides and functions on top of the infrastructure layer. These are the systems that support the existing client base or enable the business to secure new markets or new clients. This customer facing layer is where the business can and should differentiate itself. While outsourcing, standardizing, and basically homogenizing the first two layers (infrastructure and back office), the solutions here need to be unique and creative.

The result of this strategic exercise should be a written report. Please refer to the third tab on Appendix 1-2 for an abbreviated sample of a customer facing report. Using this framework, the business should describe the current customer facing situation and have a blueprint for resolving issues and growing the capability. Using this strategy, the business can define tactics which in this case are specific activities and projects required to execute the strategy. As with the back office the strategic plan will provide the blueprint for this strategic layer. Much like infrastructure and similar to back office applications replacing or converting customer facing applications is a very difficult thing to do and needs to be approached in a structured and tightly controlled fashion. All customer facing applications should be housed on the outsourced infrastructure or with an ASP. This adds a layer of complexity as far as timing is concerned. Timing should be one of the key factors for sequencing customer facing projects.

## B. Customer Facing Applications Tactics

Customer facing applications can truly be unique. While every SMB seems to believe they are unique in all aspects of their business, I contend that each should only be unique in their customer facing applications and not in infrastructure or the back office. Customer facing applications are the only place where the business should even consider custom development due to the need for creative solutions. Custom development does not have to mean software development. The IT department does not have to build systems. In some cases there are packaged applications that do what needs to be done and fully meet the business requirements. If packages do not suffice, then component development should be examined. If the business is looking for competitive advantages in the market place it may well be found in new software component applications. If at all possible, avoid having the IT team sit down and start coding. Coding systems from scratch should almost never be done anymore. The IT department needs to be systems facilitators and systems integrators who select existing applications, components and tool kits and make them work together in new and unusual ways. Shareware and freeware may even be considered. Most likely the business cannot afford the time frames required for simple custom software development anyway. The tactical approach is as follows:

- **Consider building**

    The IT department may well be able to find products and services in the market place to provide basic functionality but here they may consider building before buying. Still try to avoid total custom development. Custom development is very expensive and historically eighty percent of all software development projects fail. Try constructing systems with components or building blocks instead of coding. Try developing custom applications with tool kits like work flow, document management, messaging tools and other engines or components. The business can still find a competitive edge in the creative use and application of some of these products.

- **Remember the interfaces to the back office applications but emphasize customer facing functionality**

    Consider the flow of data out of customer facing systems into back office systems like billing, receivables, and other accounting and financial systems. These interfaces could become customer issues if the interfaces fail or otherwise become inaccurate or unreliable. Do not let these become overriding concerns but document them as requirements and address them. The focus of the customer facing layer is functionality and the goal is to provide a competitive advantage to the business in the market place.

- **In-source by developing internal support capabilities**
Here is where the IT department can turn the creative members of the department loose. Here is where creativity and technology savvy will pay dividends. The business has avoided committing the internal IT department's time, energy and effort to the first two layers of infrastructure and back office. Now the business and the IT department can commit to distinguishing itself from the competition in this, the customer facing layer. While structured techniques are still required, the technology people can be cut loose to explore and create. The challenge is to create functionality in new and creative ways to meet current and anticipated business needs.

## C.　Customer Facing Applications Tactics Execution

### 1.　Develop the customer facing vision and scope

This is more difficult than it may initially seem. If the business is certain that they have identified the right customer facing projects, and that the choices are clear, please skip down to Section 2 below. Many businesses, however, are doing the wrong customer facing projects and are thereby working on the wrong things. This could be due to getting off on the wrong track initially or due to improper or inadequate scoping. Often times the need for immediate functionality by operations management forces "one off" and point solution installation. Business leaders involved in the day to day running of the business do not have the luxury of thinking strategically and will always pressure for a quick "one off" solution to meet their immediate needs. Individually these are not bad decisions but these tactics ultimately lead to an unsupportable non-cohesive mess.

The best way to view this scoping or vision challenge is to define the customer facing challenge from a process and functionality perspective. It may be a worthwhile exercise at this point to review the business model strategy for applicability. A summary is found in Chapter 6 and the book *IT is about the Strategy* discusses it in detail. Use the vision to examine existing package applications, solution sets and tool kits that are available for purchase. From a package application perspective, every vendor for every package starts with one core product focus and inevitably expands in scope as the product matures in the market place. An application may start out as a sales force management tool but then broadens to include functionality like time scheduling, or commission calculation, or even customer relationship management. Consequently, the business can solve one or many problems with any vendor's package solution. The challenge becomes one of scope. The trick is to determine how much functionality you should buy from any one vendor. You must determine how the product offerings fit with your view of the required functionality. This is no small feat. You can buy twenty point solutions or you can buy a single solution that attempts to do twenty different things. The real world situation will be that you will buy several solutions to garner the requisite functionality and what remains in question is where the functionality provided from one solution begins and ends.

This scoping challenge is a good reason to consider buying components instead of buying specific package solutions. Components can be used across the organization to provide functionality in different customer facing applications while purchased applications are generally requirement specific. Still, purchasing applications is recommended before coding anything. To summarize, the customer facing applications list needs to be developed in terms of processes and functionality, not specific products. Once the processes are identified, write requirements for each process. Only then can application products and solution sets be evaluated.

## 2.   Attach the identified problems and issues

During your strategic exercise you identified problems and issues with existing customer facing applications components. You should have identified the additional functionality that you need to provide with application solutions. You merely relate these to the customer facing applications list. Again, express problems and issues in terms of processes, not products. Please refer to the third tab in Appendix 1-2 for an example of a problems and issues application list which should include issues like the following:
  - Running on internal servers, need to move to outsourced infrastructure
  - Homegrown package needs replaced
  - Homegrown package that has been internally modified and has become a maintenance problem
  - Does not interface easily to any other system
  - Company has outgrown the package and replacement is required

## 3.   Identify the projects

Identify the required projects by using the vision, scope and identified problems and issues. The customer facing suite needs to be fully scoped as described above and the entire solution suite needs defined at a high level before project work begins. Franklin Covey teaches "Begin with the end in mind". This is true for defining the customer facing vision and identifying the projects required to fulfill that vision. It is important for the business to define the processes in detail for customer interaction. These must be used in selecting the products and services that are in essence the business capabilities. This process flow will allow for selecting technology components that can be configured and specified to provide customer facing business functionality. The result of this exercise will be the project list.

## 4.   Sequence the projects

Strategy execution is not instantaneous and immediate. This is the real world. While the business should look for some quick wins, the business needs to develop a sequence of execution that makes sense based on the criteria below. The goal is to prioritize projects based on the strongest positive business impact, the cost to the business and the available manpower. Remember, these are business projects and not technology projects.

- **Prerequisites** - Projects have prerequisites and the scope of the solution often dictates the project sequence. The projects may have to be built sequentially according to the process flow. Completed projects will have to coexist in an environment where legacy applications prevail so automated interfaces as opposed to manual will have to be considered.
- **Project components** - Which components being in place will enable the realization of the most functionality? Will the work flow component enable the business to fast track immediate functionality?
- **Affected business users** - Whether installing applications or component functionality, the impact on the business for their project participation must be scheduled.
- **Available personnel** - Has the business hired the right individual or individuals to manage the execution of these projects?
- **Pain points** - Determine which customer facing components are either having the most negative impact on the business or conversely will have the most positive impact on the business.
- **Funding** - Each project will require project expenses. Each project should also have a positive ROI. Perform the quick cost benefit analysis to identify the biggest winners.
- **Messages** - Which projects will gain the most positive publicity within the company and with customers? Which will send the most positive messages to the interested parties?
- **Risk** - Which projects carry a low risk and can be implemented knowing there will be some problems? Some projects will be high profile and high risk and need to be executed slowly and carefully.

5. **Execute the construction or acquisition projects**

Projects for customer facing applications will be one of two varieties based on your solution approach. The first is where the functionality is to be realized by buying applications or applications suites. This approach is consistent with purchasing back office functionality and a review of that chapter will provide basic guidelines. The second is where the functionality is to be realized by buying components or tool kits and the projects will consist of the following three activities:

- **Scoping and vision** - Scope the process flow, required functionality and vision. Identify the required components. This is discussed above in developing the applications list.
- **Component selection** - Review and select the components from the candidate suites. Conduct component evaluation and selection.
- **Integration of components** - Integrate the components to deliver the required functionality and build the applications.

There should be one project for the general scoping and vision exercise and two projects for each application or component. There will be one project for selection and one for installation and integration. Deploy an abbreviated basic and concise project management methodology. Please refer to the project management methodology in Chapter 10 under Common Tactics. Project execution for customer facing applications is much more difficult than for back office applications. It is easier to buy back office applications than it is to select components and integrate them for functionality. The most difficult part of project execution will be application and component selection. There is a well defined way to do this selection that will go a long way to insure success. Please refer to the package evaluation and selection methodology in Chapter 13 under Common Tactics. A summary of that process is described as follows:

- Define the customer facing application process flow (vision).
- Define the business and technical requirements.
- Define the scope (please see the relevant discussion above).
- Identify the applications or component tool kits required.
- Match the applications or components to the requirements and define the final solution in terms of which components will be used.
- Conduct product research.
- Identify the two to three potential solutions for each application or component requirement.
- Interview the vendors in a structured way.
- Develop the selection criteria in addition to the requirements.
- Map the vendors to the selection criteria and weight the results.
- Conduct customer visits.
- Develop a one page matrix with the vendors scored against the criteria to make the selection.
- Please see Appendix 13-1 for an entire package selection process example.

Once the application or component selection process has been completed the SMB moves on to package installation. This also requires a good project management methodology. From here the business moves on to day-to-day management of the application and the vendor. These issues are addressed below.

## 6.  Execute the installation or integration projects.

Once the components or set of application systems have been selected, the work of installation and integration begins. These are also full projects and need to be managed in much the same way you would manage a software development effort. It requires the same amount of communication, testing and user interaction. Please refer to Chapter 6 for a discussion of projects, project capacity and project planning.

## 7.  Managing the customer facing applications

If the route of purchasing customer facing applications was taken, please refer to Chapter 2 and follow the guidelines for managing back office applications. The same tools and techniques are required.

If the route of purchasing and assembling components was taken, please skip to Chapter 12 to address change management activities. Building from components moves the resulting applications into an internally built status and the day-to-day management of the application falls to internal staff. You will need a robust problem tracking and management system to adequately manage the application.

## D. Customer Facing Applications and Personnel

IT leadership needs to take the lead on the vision and the selection process for applications and components. This is a very difficult undertaking and will require some solid organization and process skills. There may be some real value gained in getting outside consulting assistance to help manage and control these efforts. The visioning and scoping exercises themselves require an experienced and steady hand. The business needs to combine the creativity of the existing staff with structure and controls not often found in smaller SMBs. I recommend establishing a solid business partner relationship to assist with the vision, the application or component selection, installation and integration. It is important to use a blend of internal and external staff since support of the customer facing applications will need to stay with the SMB.

At the individual level for customer facing applications, the business needs creative technical skills to research, design, develop, project manage and support customer solutions. The skill sets here are mostly tactical. They require an excellent technical understanding and more than a little creativity. The hacker mentality is important but needs to be tempered with market awareness and the ability to evaluate and select software solutions. Once installed, the applications and solutions need to be supported while problems need to be tracked and resolved. The beginning of a service desk approach is required.

## Hardware/Platform/Network

---

**WISDOM to work by:**

1. *Infrastructure must keep pace.*
   *Every business model project will have an impact on infrastructure.*
2. *Manage change!*
   *Every change to infrastructure must go through a solid change management process. Manage change or it will manage you.*
3. *Process, process, process.*
   *Enhancements, upgrades and improvements need to follow a solid repeatable process.*
4. *IT is a service organization.*
   *The purpose of infrastructure is to service the organization.*

---

## A. Infrastructure Strategy

As defined in *IT is about the Strategy*, the next or second strategy that the SMB should embrace is the business model strategy. In general, the business model strategy identifies the customer facing applications that are either key components or critical impediments to business growth. These applications are arrived at through use of a business model which is a document that shows how the product or service provided by the business is delivered. This business process generally begins with a sale or order and proceeds through the internal business processes culminating in order fulfillment for the customer and revenue to the business. The goal of the business model is to define and document a description of the core business processes with accompanying business parameters. It provides a process view of the business. Please refer to Appendix 4-1 for a pictorial view of this strategy.

This business model strategy at the base level for infrastructure assumes that the business layer strategy has been enacted and that the business layer tactics have been successfully completed. If this is not a valid assumption and infrastructure is still an issue, please refer to Chapter 1. Remember that infrastructure is the base layer of technology that consists of the underlying technology infrastructure on which all other functionality is built. It is the foundation. The focus in the business model strategy is decidedly not on infrastructure. However, since infrastructure is foundational, there are hardware, platform and network issues that must be continually addressed. As the business model strategy is implemented, the infrastructure will grow and change along with the newly installed or upgraded customer facing software application components. In addition to following and complying with the business layer strategy the strategy here is necessarily an expansion and enhancement of that initial strategy with an additional focus on service.

## 1.  The Technology model

In preparation for tactical execution, develop and document the technology model. The technology model is a multi-page document (views) showing how IT has constructed the various technology systems in support of the business system. A technology model lists the hardware and network components assembled in support of the business. The technology model defines the service delivery configuration in generic process terms and in specific hardware and network terms.

## 2.  Technology model views

There are two model views for infrastructure in the technology model.

### a. View 1 - Hardware/Platform view

The hardware or platform view will simply list the existing hardware configuration. It is best depicted in a network style diagram that should relate closely to the software and business model views. Please refer to Appendix 4-2 for a sample hardware/platform view.

### b. View 2 - Network view

This network view will show the LAN, WAN and Internet connectivity components. It should also be depicted in a network style diagram and be easy to relate to previously developed views. These two views are specific in terms of defining the specific technology components including such things as make and model numbers. This view is commonly done in all IT organizations and should be kept current and made available for this kind of exercise. Please refer to Appendix 4-3 for a sample network view.

## B. Infrastructure Tactics

The tactical approach to the business model strategy for the infrastructure components of hardware, platform and network is to focus on two executables or deliverables.
- Infrastructure enhancements and improvements in support of the business model strategy enactment
- IT service definition and improvements

These tactics are designed to enable the SMB to keep the infrastructure components aligned with the back office and customer facing software applications.

# C. Infrastructure Tactics Execution

## 1.  Enhancements and improvements

The focus of the business model strategy in general is to identify and select those enabling software application technologies that will remove the technology barriers to business growth. The strategy will be defined as a set of broad strategic areas of focus by using the technology vision models. From these broad strategic areas of focus, the business will develop customer facing projects to implement the strategy.

The goal in infrastructure is to basically keep up. That is all. But it is easier said than done. As part of each application project the infrastructure will need to be considered and evaluated. With each project there will be an infrastructure impact that must be identified and quantified. The IT infrastructure relationship person or team will have to document the anticipated impacts on the infrastructure components and work with either internal staff or the independent external integrators to address them. It is important to have any external integrators deeply involved in all planning and design sessions. Project execution will involve constant and ongoing upgrades and enhancements. These will have to be managed as discreet events since each incident is also a risk to the stability and availability of infrastructure. Adopt the following approach:
- Define the infrastructure component for every new project or major project enhancement.
- Upgrade the hardware/platform and network views.
- Develop an implementation plan for adding or enhancing the infrastructure component. Work closely with the independent external integrator.
- Execute the implementation plan.
- Publish the results and the new configurations.

## 2.  Service

The second component of infrastructure tactics is to define and adopt a service mentality and to provide documented service improvements. Remember that infra-structure in and of itself provides no value. Only the addition of back office and customer facing applications allows you to leverage infrastructure. This approach builds on the SLAs and other performance measurements defined in the business layer strategy. Adopt the following approach:
- Define and publish the service pyramid. See Appendix 4-4. The focus of the service pyramid is to prioritize infrastructure work in terms of the impact on the business. All three components of the pyramid are important but IT must first and foremost take care of the base of the pyramid. Once that is done, then tactical and strategic improvements can be undertaken. When given a choice and forced to prioritize among options, the service pyramid is both a visual guide and a way to communicate this approach to the infrastructure team.
- Define and publish the service statement. See Appendix 4-5. This is an actual organ-ization announcement that I have used to tell the business what the IT department is all about. I find that clear, concise communication with the rest of the business

goes a long way in getting them to understand how IT operates. The messages on the appendix are designed to open a dialogue with the business about service and to begin to build the bridges to solid communication. This must be followed shortly thereafter by implementing the following processes and measurements.

- Develop or purchase a technology dashboard component. Every business executive has a few key measurements that they would like to track on a daily basis. One of the best ways to get these directives is to do one-on-one interviews with business leadership. Another way is to prepare and present a canned set of operational measurements in the form of a dashboard to the executive team and allow them to request specific modifications. In either case the important point is to provide the daily information that allows the business management team to better do their jobs. A couple of easy-to-generate and maintain examples are given next, but these may take any form so long as the key information is provided. Purchasing dashboard software is definitely not required until such time that the organization has grown to the point it can justify the purchase. Simple emails and reports work well as long as they are easy to access and read. Try using a simple traffic signal on the intranet homepage to designate key system availability. Have two lights, one for the nightly batch processing and one for the daily systems availability. The MS product Sharepoint is another option that is a function rich and reasonably priced alternative.
- Define and publish SLAs (Appendix 1-5) and those system availability messages (stop light approach, Appendix 4-6). These are samples of various ways to show the business that IT has developed measurements to track their own performance and the performance of the IT infrastructure. There are numerous ways to approach this style of reporting but the goal is to answer the questions about availability and performance before they are asked, and to do this in a standard structured way. By defining the messages that can be sent ahead of time and establishing a communication plan for these messages, nothing is left to chance.

## 3.  Architectural re-evaluation

It is conceivable that the demands of the business model strategy will place such high demands on the infrastructure that simple enhancements and improvements will not be enough to meet the business needs. In that case, the architectural effort will have to begin anew. The best examples of this might include the following situations:

- Server and storage requirements might become so large that existing solutions do not work. Maybe newer, faster server technology will be required to handle processing loads. Storage area networks may now be required to replace attached storage.
- Movement from legacy to web based applications may force the SMB out of the mainframe and into the web world.
- Increased connectivity requirements for clients or branch offices could force a change in network product solutions or force a change in network protocols.
- Growth in the areas of networking or file sharing may require changes to security and protection. Growth may force new product selection or even architectural re-evaluation of products and solutions.

Please reference the following chapters when performing an architecture evaluation since there are numerous common tactics involved in properly meeting this challenge:
- Chapter 7 - Architecture
- Chapter 10 - Simplified Project Management
- Chapter 14 - Vendor Selection and Management

The tactics deployed will be as follows. First, document the new infrastructure requirements in a narrative form. Then develop the "to be" hardware/platform views showing how the infrastructure must change to meet the new requirements. Then spend some time understanding the overriding architectural concerns and the need to view infrastructure in an architectural light. Please read Chapter 7. Work with the existing vendors on a series of projects to bring the new infrastructure into production and realize the vision. Then reevaluate the vendors to assure that the existing business partners are the ones that can deliver the new functionality and support. This structured approach will go a long way to insure that infrastructure will support the business model and the various back office and customer facing applications.

## D. Hardware/Platform/Network and Personnel

The infrastructure person or persons generally evolve into a team here. In non-strategic environments, the business would see the evolution of several teams. Traditionally, the IT department would generally have a network team, a server team, a systems administration team, a telecom team and so on. With the strategic approach of using independent external systems integrators and/or application service providers, the number of IT employees should be considerably fewer. While you may have an employee dedicated to each (or several) technology areas, you do not need a team of technologists. If one IT employee can handle the vision, direction, vendors, solutions, projects, consultants and relationships for several technology focus areas, then staffing may be kept even more reasonably low. The organizational structure of the department becomes one layer deeper with a managerial role required for each of the strategic areas:
- Infrastructure
- Back office applications
- Customer facing applications

The manager of each strategic area will not be a true manager who does solely management activities. The manager will also be a worker and a participant and have project and support responsibilities as well. The management role will be one of communication, administration and single point of contact. The strongest of each team in terms of organization skills, business knowledge and technology understanding will be a logical leadership choice.

The IT manager will need to be a visionary. There are numerous mistakes to be made in terms of infrastructure. Risks include choosing the wrong external integrator, letting the integrator run the relationship, thinking too small or too large, spending too much or too little or not understanding the impacts of the projects on infrastructure.

## Back Office Software/Database

> **WISDOM** to work by:
>
> 1. *Back office applications must keep up.*
>    There must be enhancements and improvements in support of
>    growth and change.
> 2. *Process, process, process.*
>    Follow a standard process for enhancements and improvements
>    to back office applications.
> 3. *Manage change!*
>    Every enhancement, improvement, release or upgrade must go
>    through a solid change management process.

## A. Back Office Applications Software/Database Strategy

As defined in *IT is about the Strategy*, the next or second strategy that the SMB should embrace is the business model strategy. In general the business model strategy identifies the customer facing applications that are either key components or critical impediments to business growth. The applications are arrived at through use of a business model which is a document that shows how the product or service provided by the business is delivered. This business process generally begins with a sale or order and proceeds through the internal business processes culminating in order fulfillment for the customer and revenue to the business. The goal of this business model is to define and document a description of the core business processes with accompanying business parameters. It provides a process view of the business. Please refer to Appendix 4-1 for a pictorial view of this strategy.

The business model strategy assumes that the business layer strategy has been enacted and that the back office tactics have been successfully completed. If this is not the case and back office applications are still an issue, please refer to Chapter 2. Remember the back office applications are the middle or second layer of technology critical to the day-to-day running of the company. They provide the business functionality that nearly all SMBs cannot live without. Back office applications reside and function on top of the infrastructure layer. They consist of applications that provide managerial support, administrative support and office systems. They include accounting packages, financial packages, human resource systems, email capabilities, voicemail functionality, document faxing, and most other internal software and application systems. The focus in the business model strategy is decidedly not on back office applications. However, since the business is growing and changing, there are back office application issues that must be continually addressed. As the business model strategy is implemented the back office applications will also grow and change. In addition to following and complying with the business layer strategy, the business model strategy is necessarily an expansion of that initial strategy with a focus on service.

1. **The technology model**

In preparation for tactical execution, develop and document the back office application component of the technology model. For the first two components (hardware/platform and network) see the infrastructure strategy. As a reminder the technology model is a multi-page document (views) showing how IT has constructed the various technology systems in support of the business system. A technology model in this case lists the software and database components assembled in support of the back office processes of the business.

2. **Technology model view**

There is only one relevant model view for back office applications in the technology model. It is the back office software/database view excluding customer facing applications. This view shows the software and applications that are currently used to support the back office processes. It is easiest to depict in a flowchart form. Please refer to Appendix 5-1 for an example. Also, provide a narrative appendix that lists the various back office application solutions that have been deployed to support the business model. An example of this can be found in the second tab of Appendix 1-2.

## B. Back Office Applications Software/Database Tactics

The tactical approach is to focus on two executables or deliverables.
- Back office application changes like enhancements, improvements, releases, upgrades and replacements in support of growth and change
- IT service definition and improvements

## C. Back Office Applications Software/Database Tactics Execution

As with infrastructure each back office application change has to be handled as a risk event. Each has to be managed and administered in such a way as to reduce the risk to the business. The goals are to increase functionality without negatively impacting the production environment. If those two goals are served the tactics are a success.

1. **Enhancements, improvements, releases and upgrades**

To manage releases and upgrades there are two tools that are very valuable. These are the change management plan and the communication plan. Please refer to the change management Appendices in Chapter 12 and the project management communication plan Appendix in Chapter 10 for examples. For releases and upgrades the following steps should be taken.

- Study, understand and summarize the release or upgrade.
- Install the upgrade in a test environment and test.
- Communicate the nature and risks associated with the release or upgrade to both IT and the business.
- Schedule the release or upgrade.
- Conduct any required training.
- Execute the release or upgrade.
- Monitor the results and take corrective action if necessary.

Every release or upgrade should come with release notes from the vendor. Handling vendor releases is a balancing act. You do not want to upgrade too soon or too late. It is critical that the business understands the importance of staying current with the vendor in terms of releases and upgrades. There is great risk in falling behind and not keeping up. This risk includes having to jump several releases or upgrades at some point in time and the results of such an action are often unpredictable. The business should also not be an early adopter and take every release or upgrade and install immediately. Unless the release or upgrade fixes a specific pressing problem for the business, do not rush to install it. Insure the release or upgrade has been out for a reasonable period of time and that the vendor has resolved any issues. Nothing is more disruptive than a release or upgrade that the vendor has to fix on the fly.

Many businesses balk at having a full blown test environment. Servers and storage are getting more reasonably priced every day. Dedicated test systems are cost justifiable and should be considered. If this option is rejected, the back office application external integrators should be able to secure occasional use of a test environment for use by all of their customers. This privilege should be negotiated with the vendor from the beginning of the relationship. The vendor should be able to make shared resources available or be able to deploy resources normally set aside for disaster recovery services.

It is important to involve the users of each back office application with the testing. There should be a basic test plan developed that allows for testing each of the major functions of the system. Since each system is unique it is not possible to provide a sample test plan but it should include the following at a minimum:

- Reads of every file.
- Writes to every file.
- Navigation of every screen.
- Running samples of selected reports.
- Test areas of known changes and enhancements using the release or upgrade notes as a guide.

The IT relationship management person in charge of back office needs to develop a communication plan using a fixed format. The questions are as follows. Who needs to know what? When do they need to know it? What is the best way to tell them? The answer is the communication plan. The communication plan needs to be in an appealing format as an incentive for the business to read it. This will take some work. Please again refer to the project management communication plan Appendices in Chapter 10 (10-11 and 10-12) for a suggested format.

The release or upgrade should be scheduled with the business and by the business. It is assumed that this will take place during non-business hours during an evening or a weekend. Care must be taken to install releases or upgrades during non-critical times of the month so that should problems occur they will have minimal impact on the business. For example, accounting and finance package upgrades need to occur after one month end and well before the next so that any issues will be resolved before impacting the monthly financial closing.

Once the upgrade is accomplished it is important to monitor and record all issues and problems. In my experience two interesting things can happen. Often the business users will assist so well in problem identification that they find even old problems that have been in the system for an extended period of time. Alternately the business users will question the system even more than usual and identify problems that are not even there. In both cases use of the tracking log for applications issues becomes most important. Track and resolve all issues and keep the issues logs for future reference. Writing a post-mortem or release/upgrade summary report, even if not generally distributed, is a very good idea. Please refer to Appendix 5-2 for a sample.

## 2. Replacing systems

It will become necessary at some point to replace back office solutions. These instances should be few. Replacing back office systems should be approached with extreme caution because they carry huge risks. The business must be able to justify a replacement system with a good business case, a supportable ROI or due to some unforeseen circumstance like the vendor going out of business. In nearly all cases, no matter how well managed and executed, there will be disruptions to the business.

As with an initial application installation follow the tactics recommended in selecting and deploying new back office applications. These are duplicated below. There is no reason why a replacement system should not be even better than the original. The business should strive to retain all existing functionally and to solve any and all shortcomings from the first install.

Deploy an abbreviated basic and concise project management methodology. Please refer to the project management methodology found in Chapter 10. The most difficult part of project execution will be application package selection. This topic is included in great detail in Chapter 13. There is a well defined way to do package selection that will go a long way to insure success. The process is summarized as follows:
- Define business and technical requirements (this is critical).
- Define scope.
- Conduct research. This includes reading periodicals, researching potential solutions and buying product comparisons from companies like Doculabs. These reports compare functions and features of all products in an application space but do not make recommendations. The business must match their requirements to the strengths and weaknesses of the solutions to select the most appropriate product.
- Identify four to six potential solutions.
- Send out an RFI or an RFP.
- Interview vendors in a structured way. The business must control the vendors and

the vendor interactions. Here is where many SMBs get off track. They get enamored with a sales person or a given product before the selection criteria is applied. Allow vendors to make an initial fixed duration presentation. Allow them to submit a limited number of follow up questions in writing. Set rigid time frames and allow no exceptions. This is critical!

- Develop selection criteria in addition to the requirements. The first goal should be to meet the written requirements but other factors must be considered as well. Please see Appendix 13-4 for other examples.
- Map vendors to the selection criteria and weight the results. Some criteria are more important than others.
- Conduct customer visits. Try to find vendor's customers who are using the product like you plan to use it. Force the vendor to provide several references and do the visit selection yourself.
- Develop a one page matrix with the vendors scored against the criteria to make your selection.
- Please see Appendix 13-1 for an entire package selection process example.

**3. Service**

Service for the back office applications uses the same approach as is used for infrastructure. Please reference the section on service in Chapter 4.

## D. Back Office Applications Software/Database and Personnel

The back office application person or persons generally becomes a team of associates here. In traditional environments, the business would see the evolution of the large software development team or teams. The IT department would generally have a team of systems analysts, programmer analysts, programmers, database administrators, business analysts and so on. With the strategic approach of using independent, external systems integrators the number of IT employees should be considerably less. You do not need a team of development technologists. While one IT employee may not be able to handle the vision, direction, vendors, solutions, projects, consultants and relationships for this entire technology focus area, a large team is not required. It may take several employees and possibly one for each business process area like finance/accounting or administrative systems. The organizational structure of the department becomes one layer deeper with a managerial role required for this strategic area.

The IT manager will need to be a visionary. There are numerous mistakes to be made in terms of back office applications. Risks include choosing the wrong external integrator, letting the integrator run the relationship, misusing the application, falling behind in releases and upgrades, and failing vendors and applications that come to the end of their life cycle without handling new requirements like Sarbanes-Oxley.

## Customer Facing Software/Database

> ### WISDOM to work by:
>
> 1. <u>*Know your strategic areas of focus.*</u>
>    *This will enable the SMB to work on the right stuff.*
> 2. <u>*Know your strategic drivers.*</u>
>    *Know what is important when selecting technology.*
> 3. <u>*Remember there is almost never a good reason to build software from scratch anymore.*</u>
>    *Practice component and tool kit integration. Roughly eighty percent of all software development projects fail.*
> 4. <u>*Make someone responsible.*</u>
>    *Establish IT strategic teams to own and execute the strategy. Establish one team per strategic area of focus.*
> 5. <u>*There is no way to manage what you do not measure.*</u>
>    *Time reporting is the key to knowing project capacity and one of the keys to project execution. Know the three simple time measures that need to be tracked.*
> 6. <u>*The business owns the IT strategy.*</u>
>    *Establish an IT council and conduct regular meetings.*
> 7. <u>*Make them participate.*</u>
>    *Hold regular meetings with the business. Make standardized reporting a part of your project management arsenal.*

## A. Customer Facing Applications Software/Database Strategy

### 1.    Introduction

As defined in *IT is about the Strategy*, the next or second strategy that the SMB should embrace is the business model strategy. In general, the business model strategy identifies the customer facing applications that are either key components or critical impediments to business growth. The applications are arrived at through the use of a business model, which is a document that shows how the product or service provided by the business is delivered. This business process generally begins with a sale or order and proceeds through the internal business processes culminating in order fulfillment for the customer and revenue to the business. The goal of the business model is to define and document a description of the core business processes with accompanying business parameters. It provides a process view of the business. Please refer to Appendix 4-1 for a pictorial view of this strategy.

The business model strategy assumes that the business layer strategy has been enacted and that the business layer tactics have been successfully completed. If this is not the case please refer to Chapter 3. The primary focus of the business model strategy is on customer facing applications. This is the most important aspect of the business model strategy. This is the layer of software applications that are used to interact with customers. This third layer, like the back office or second layer resides on and runs on top of the infrastructure. It consists of applications that enable the SMB to do business with their customers no matter what their reason for being in business.

Strategically, this is where the business can differentiate itself and develop a competitive edge. While outsourcing, standardizing and basically homogenizing the first two layers, the solutions here need to be unique and creative. These are the systems that are customer facing and support the delivery of product or services whatever the core reason for being in business. These are the systems that support the existing client base or enable the business to secure new markets or new clients.

## 2.   The technology model

In preparation for tactical execution, develop and document the customer facing application component of the technology model. For the first two components (hardware/platform and network) see the infrastructure strategy. As a reminder, the technology model is a multi-page document (views) showing how IT has constructed the various technology systems in support of the business system. A technology model in this case lists the software and database components assembled in support of the customer facing processes of the business. The relevant technology model view is the customer facing software/database view excluding back office applications. It is easiest to depict in a flow chart form. Please refer to Appendix 6-1 for an example. Also provide a narrative appendix that lists the various customer facing application solutions that have been deployed to support the business model. An example of this can be found in the third tab of Appendix 1-2.

The customer facing component of the strategy should be completed in the form of a written report. It needs to first contain the strategic areas of focus. These are the broad strategic technology areas where the IT department should be working. Please refer to Appendix 6-2 for a pictorial description of how the entire customer facing strategy builds and fits together. Examples of strategic areas of focus from this strategic exercise include broad technology areas like the following:
-   Document management
-   Call center management
-   Distribution management
-   Customer profiles and touches management
-   Financial information gathering management
-   Insurance handling management

The strategy is also comprised of the strategic drivers. These are the governing parameters for making tactical decisions. Examples of some sample strategic drivers are attached as Appendix 6-3. Based on the strategic areas of focus and tempered by the strategic drivers the SMB can make practical decisions about projects by getting the projects identified and initiated.

## 3.    Strategic areas of focus

In *IT is about the Strategy*, I focused on how to use the business and technology models to select the strategic areas of focus. I would like to take the opportunity to expound on that here. Every business seems to think that they are unique. I would submit that if the SMB is able to take a step back from what it feels makes it unique, and objectively view the core business processes through the business model, they might come to a startling revelation. The uniqueness the business feels may be in the product or service being offered, as well it should be, but the commonality of core business process functions are strikingly similar from business to business. That is to say the product or service may be unique but the other processes are the same. Those processes include marketing, sales, billing, revenue recognition, shipping, inventory control, accounts receivable and handling, and so on. This commonality is the primary reason that the infrastructure and back office should be standardized, homogenized and outsourced. I would like to take that thought even further and submit that in customer facing applications as well there are common processes for things like touching customers (call centers, web applications), handling orders (order processing, web orders), or providing services (service delivery, service tracking, quality assurance, work flow). These like processes allow for like solutions. The key is to understand the business at a process level and seek functionality at a process level. The tools and techniques are available as long as the business looks for the process commonalities and not at the uniqueness of their business. Many businesses seem to be fooled into thinking that the uniqueness of their product or service leaves no choice but to build custom applications from scratch through line by line coding. They fail to look instead for a general set of tools that can be customized and combined in unique ways.

## 4.    Strategic drivers

I would like to expound on strategic drivers as well. These are the governing principles used during tactical execution for making decisions on tools and technologies. Please refer to Appendix 6-3 for some sample strategic drivers. Technology selection is very difficult to begin with. If there are no guiding principles or restraints, no guidebook or restrictions, the decisions made will be the wrong ones. I believe many businesses will attempt to ignore this step because it has a slight academic tinge. I strongly recommend against ignoring this step. The important determining factors for solution selection could, and does often come down to, strategic drivers.

Please allow me to use an example. I think a common question in many SMBs is whether to customize their services. Let's use a financial example. The SMB is performing a financial service for a group of other companies and the performance results are sent back to the customer in the form of printed or electronic reports. If the SMB does not make a decision early to not customize their reporting, then every customer will insist on having the data in their own particular format. Without a standard the sales people could also fill the void by offering to provide whatever the customer wishes. Financial reporting is likely to become a nightmare. Instead of maintaining a dozen standard reports selected by the SMB themselves, the IT department will eventually have to handle hundreds of custom reports that vary only slightly by a field here or a heading there. Also, the IT department will be stuck with either coding the many reports or purchasing a report or data generator and spending hours and hours developing, configuring, and maintaining this custom reporting capability. This could prove to be expensive and negatively impact the cost of offering the service. The SMB can make a conscious decision about customization by discussing, developing and using a customization strategic driver. If the SMB feels they have enough clout and leverage to offer only a set number of standard reports then the cost of doing business is greatly reduced. If customization is selected as a strategic driver then the SMB has made a business decision. They should then try to leverage this customization in data reporting as a competitive advantage by investing in the best tools and technologies available. Using this way of thinking about strategic drivers the business makes a business decision instead of leaving the decision to chance.

One of the key differentiators between IT organizations that have been successful and those that have not is the selection and adherence to not only the strategic drivers but to the right strategic drivers.

## B. Customer Facing Applications Software/Database Tactics

As a reminder, execution (or tactics) consists of converting IT strategic areas of focus into projects and executing these projects. The strategic exercise is now complete. The business has a blueprint for changing the technology backbone of the company. Execution now becomes the key. The amount of change that will be required should not be underestimated. I recommend the following sequence of events:

- Establish IT strategic teams (one for each strategic area of focus)
- Identify the projects (within each strategic area of focus)
- Sequence the projects (based on business drivers)
- Execute the projects (using a structured project management methodology)

*IT is about the Strategy* goes deeply into business model tactics so please refer to that book for overall guidance here. To supplement, that work there are additional tactical tools and techniques that can be deployed to enhance and improve customer facing application selection. This methodology will also be discussed in detail below and in Chapter 13.

## C. Customer Facing Applications Software/Database Tactics Execution

### 1. Introduction

Before discussion about specific steps to tactical execution it is important to understand the wealth of options available to construct a software application. Besides the number of pre-built software applications, there are numerous component and tool kit options available to the SMB for constructing needed functionality. Remember that there is almost never a case for developing software from scratch anymore. Most software development projects fail. Most software development projects take long periods of time to accomplish even in the unlikely event that they do succeed. I recommend building applications from components or tool kits and avoiding the custom software development nightmare. Below are a few examples of tools and products from which an SMB can craft an application without resorting to coding. This only scratches the surface of the numerous available options. By the way, I offer these only as an interested third party and have had no contact or affiliation with these companies.

- Adobe Acrobat and associated document and data handling tools. Adobe is doing some very strong things with their product offerings.
- Document repositories for a document database (in contrast to a data database). I have personal experience with OnBase but the business needs to map their requirements to the available tools on this market.
- Web hosting and web building tools and services. These offerings are getting more robust every day.
- Shopping carts and payment handing systems for web shopping and web purchasing.
- Work flow tools which are the enablers for the various tool kits. Work flow is the glue that will hold the set of application components together. Do a simple web search on work flow tools and you will be overwhelmed by the options and the maturity of these products.
- Document scanning, bar coding, imaging, and handling. Document management is a large part of nearly every SMB.
- Microsoft suites like Share Point, CRM, Excel and Access. Microsoft tools should not be overlooked. Coupled with an Exchange Server, Outlook and the Office Suite, there is powerful functionality that can be exploited.
- Web application and database building products like Alpha 5.
- Tracking software like Track It and other tools.
- Fax servers like Right Fax or even outsourced fax server services.
- Full service back office applications like Exact (formerly Macola) These companies market a comprehensive set of packages including things like accounting, finance, inventory control, warehousing, manufacturing, work flow and so on.
- PBX based applications for inbound call handling and management.
- Predictive Dialing applications for outbound call handling and management.
- Shipping software from the various shipping vendors.
- Shipping rate software like Rate Shopper.
- Application generators like Ten Fold, Synopsis and Skyway Software. These are software products that go from requirements to a completed application without coding line by line solutions.
- Portfolio management tools like those from 3 Olive that allow you to track and monitor your project portfolio.
- There are now even full service providers like TraverseIT that offer IT operations and back office components in a bundled solution. This will allow any SMB to treat the first two layers like simple utilities and focus on differentiating the business in the customer facing arena.

I firmly believe that any business can construct a customer facing application suite using these kinds of products without resorting to coding. I have advocated avoiding software development at all costs and I would like to elaborate on this a bit. I am not saying that some organizations will not successfully code and implement a customer facing application. I am saying that for any business the chances are about two out of ten that they will succeed. Historically, roughly eighty percent of all software development projects are deemed failures. The business may roll the dice and prove me wrong. In that case for that twenty percent of the time the business has my congratulations. But in the long term and given the odds, would any business offer a new product or service or otherwise take on an endeavor that has a historical fail rate of eighty percent? I would guess not. So avoid the software development trap. Get good at component and package selection. Research the various solution components. It will be safer and much cheaper in the short and long term.

## 2.   IT strategic teams

As we have learned, developing the IT strategic areas of focus allows the business to develop broad technology focus areas. These will be guided and governed by the strategic drivers. The strategic areas of focus will need to be further broken down into components that will ultimately translate into a series of projects. These projects will need to be owned and executed to enact the strategy. The best method I have found to achieve ownership is through a team effort and something I call the IT strategic teams. These teams are a joint effort between IT and the business created specifically to execute the strategies. IT strategic teams can be tasked with the definition, development and installation of the strategic area of focus through a series of projects. The team needs to be comprised of members from the following groups:
-   Senior business management (VP, directors, managers)
-   Affected business groups (leads, supervisors)
-   IT technology infrastructure team (engineers)
-   IT software applications team (relationship managers)
-   Independent external integrators and partners (technology experts)

Selecting leadership for each of the strategic teams is the most critical step in determining the success or failure of the team. Leadership translates to ownership and ownership for a particular strategy is serious business. Choose the leadership wisely. The higher up the individual serves in the organization the better.

## 3.   Identify the projects

Using the vehicle of the IT strategic teams this is the creative step of turning all work to date into actionable projects. It requires a series of brainstorming and workshop sessions with the IT strategic team. It should take a number of days. The business members of the team will contribute the current and future anticipated business requirements. This is the required business knowledge. The IT team members will contribute all technology knowledge and previous technology research as well as a structured way to deal with the requirements. This includes application package research, industry technology knowledge, as well as a range of approaches and solutions that should be analyzed. This is the technology knowledge. The IT team members should also be responsible for bringing in various independent external integrators to make technology presentations and conduct informal educational seminars. Please exercise care here that the business does not jump to the stage of buying. The business should stay at the analysis stage of the process. The business should not be vendor sold or vendor controlled. The outcome of this exercise will be a solidified vision within each strategic area of focus and a series of projects to realize that vision.

## 4.   Sequence the projects

Next the projects need to be sequenced. This can be done in any number of ways or by one of the following exercises:
- Start at the beginning process of the business model and work toward the end process in a linear fashion.
- Understand the dependencies between the projects and schedule the projects based on the interdependencies and sequencing requirements. This means installing foundation tools and technologies first and building on these.
- When dependencies and sequencing are not an impediment, let the budget dictate the sequence. Do the projects when the business can afford them.
- Make sure the projects with the largest pay back are done first or at least early in the strategy. This generates momentum and reinforces the value of the strategy.

Once the projects are sequenced the business can turn to project execution.

## 5. Execute the projects

The IT team members will begin to execute the projects. The efforts will be managed and guided by the IT strategic teams. The team will use the appropriate project management methodology detailed in Chapter 10. Project management is but one challenge. Project and time reporting is another.

### a.  Project and time reporting

The IT strategic team has translated the strategic area of focus into projects and sequenced these projects into a project list. IT must now execute. It is critical that IT develops a time reporting methodology that adequately summarizes activity.

Project planning and project reporting begins with time tracking. There is no way to manage what you can't measure. My experience is that time tracking measurements generally suffer from trying to measure too many things or trying to measure the wrong things. Time reporting like project management is generally viewed in the SMB as a time wasting bureaucratic exercise. I believe that is because time reporting gets bogged down in trying to measure too much and trying to measure at too granular a level. Speaking as an IT manager there are three

broad categories that need to be measured. These measures need to explain how much time is spent in the following areas:
- Daily operational support (break/fix, move/add/change, questions)
- New project work (formal project tasks only)
- Administrative and all other lost time

Basically that is all IT management needs to know to manage the department. Tracking more than this can be a waste of time. Knowing at a high level the hours in each of these categories allows IT management to plan projects, track activities and provide costs back to the business. IT management can show how time is spent and justify those expenditures. They can develop meaningful project estimates and provide a more accurate schedule of activities to the business. If IT management has a time tracking system that can provide these simple measurements they are poised to make use of the tools provided below. If not, IT management needs to buy and implement something immediately or modify their current time reporting to make these measurements immediately available. Time tracking is a critical component of project execution.

## b. Project estimates

Using the list of identified projects and the desired sequence of project execution IT management must now establish the project estimates. These project estimates are developed in man hours at the project task level and in the aggregate. Project estimates establish from the onset what can be realistically expected of IT and determine what IT should realistically accomplish. The goal here is to identify the required IT project resources, decide where they will be deployed and select the projects that can be undertaken. This is done by mapping the project estimates to the available project resources thereby establishing a schedule of projects for a given time period. At a minimum IT management needs to develop rough project estimates for each identified project in terms of broad man hour estimates. This will support the high level planning and scheduling.

For a schedule I recommend quarterly scheduling. Monthly is too short and anything longer than a quarter quickly becomes irrelevant. I recommend that IT conduct this exercise at the beginning of each quarter. Establish the quarterly schedule to coincide with the fiscal calendar and number the quarters as simply Q1 through Q4. The following three components comprise the project estimating exercise:
- IT development capacity
- Project estimates
- Map estimates to capacity

## c. Available development hours - capacity

At the beginning of each quarter IT management should begin by identifying the available development man hours. This is simply put the project capacity for the quarter. If IT management has a time reporting methodology in place, begin with how much time was devoted to new project development in the previous quarter. Let's use an example of 2,880 hours meaning IT reported 2,880 man hours of time to new development projects the previous quarter. Next factor in any adjustments that must be made for the upcoming quarter. Use known impacts such as staffing deletions, vacations, known support problems eating into development time or anything else affecting capacity for the coming quarter. These adjustments reduce or enhance the available capacity. Let's assume we lose 180 man hours to vacations and that we add a development resource and can expect an additional 360 hours from that person. Based on the previous quarter, known impacts and extrapolation calculate the estimated time that can be spent on new development projects in the coming quarter. In our example that would be roughly 3,060 man hours. This is the IT development capacity from a planning perspective. Please refer to Appendix 6-4 for an example of project capacity and planning.

This exercise underscores the importance of tracking the time spent each quarter on the broad service categories. For the initial quarter or when other data is not available IT leadership may be forced to use an estimated number. I would use no more than sixty five percent of the total available manpower hours for application integration and no more than twenty five percent for technology infrastructure installation projects.

### d. Project delivery schedules

The IT strategic team may now establish the project delivery schedule using the available capacity in man hours, the proper sequencing of the projects and the project estimates that have been developed. IT management may simply schedule the projects selected by the IT strategic team in sequence until their capacity is exhausted. Once this is accomplished the IT strategic team needs to finalize the schedule with the IT council to get their buy in and support. I recommend an initial meeting at the beginning of each quarter. The outcome of that meeting should be a list of projects that can realistically be completed in the upcoming quarter. This project delivery schedule is the schedule that IT will now track and report against. Please refer to Appendix 6-5 for a capacity analysis and project delivery schedule.

## 6. IT council meetings

In order to communicate effectively with the business on project activity IT leadership needs to establish a forum. I recommend establishment of an IT council with regularly scheduled weekly review meetings. The IT council will serve as the project governing and reporting body as well as the broker for the IT strategic teams. They will resolve any priority or sequencing conflicts. The IT council will be comprised of the top business executives who are the primary stakeholders in the company. The IT council should include all project sponsors as well as any business project managers. Most small organizations do not have dedicated project managers who just manage projects so may get their project management personnel from among the business management. Project management should have the highest interest in the project activity.

I recommend a weekly meeting. Establish a regular time for the meetings. Take great pains to schedule the meeting at a time where IT can expect the most participation. Feed them if you must. The more participation the better chance IT has of working on what is most important to the business. Limit the discussion to a half hour if at all possible. Instead of a typical meeting, one company I worked with held "huddles" where the participants stood up instead of sitting. Naturally, these meetings were brief.

Deal only with project exceptions and not projects on schedule. I have seen these meetings become poorly attended and eventually become irrelevant. This is a major danger signal. It implies that the projects have become unimportant to the business and that the technology focus is being centered outside of the endorsed projects and outside of IT.

## 7. Project reporting

Once the initial kickoff meeting is completed and the project schedule is defined the real work begins. In addition to actually doing the projects IT management needs to develop and publish the detailed project delivery schedule based on previously defined project milestones. To create a milestone plan take the major milestones and the project identification information and create an Excel spreadsheet. This becomes the detailed project reporting information for each project. It should provide for anyone interested in the project a detailed snapshot of how the project is being conducted. Please refer to Appendix 6-6 for an example.

Issue the spreadsheet weekly as the IT status report. The focus of the IT council meeting should be on project exceptions. Projects that are going well and meeting milestones should not be discussed. The meeting must not become a general discussion or a complaint session but a progress reporting session. Identify any projects that are slipping and discuss the reasons for slippage. Discuss steps IT leadership is taking to get the project back on schedule. Provide the re-forecasted completion dates. Don't allow for regular project slippage or IT loses credibility. Reforecast dates for a project no more than once during a quarter. Do not reforecast dates for more than one project at a meeting or IT credibility again comes into question. The goal here is to communicate early and often. Do not let projects meander down to a deadline before they become discussion topics and get corrective attention.

As a coversheet for the detailed report develop a one page summary of the project progress. At a glance, this summary will convey the progress throughout the quarter. It might be color coded with red and green codes to depict all is well or the project is off track. This report should be viewed as a status reporting document that can be shared with anyone in the business to reveal project status.

# D. Customer Facing Applications Software/Database and Personnel

The customer facing application personnel generally evolve into a team here. In traditional environments the business would see the evolution of the software development team or teams. The IT department would generally have a team of systems analysts, programmer analysts, programmers, database administrators, business analysts and so on. With the strategic approach of using independent external systems integrators the number of IT employees should be considerably fewer and you do not need a team of development technologists. One IT employee probably cannot handle the vision, direction, vendors, solutions, projects, consultants and relationships for this entire technology focus area. It will take several and possibly one for each strategic area of focus. The organizational structure of the department becomes one layer deeper with a managerial role required for this strategic area.

The IT manager will need to be a visionary. There are numerous mistakes to be made in terms of customer facing applications. Risks include choosing the wrong external integrator, letting the integrator run the relationship, misusing the application, falling behind in releases and upgrades, failing vendors and applications that come to the end of their lifecycle or do not handle new requirements like Sarbanes-Oxley. Another risk is that the SMB will be tempted to take the software development plunge and begin developing applications from scratch. The IT manager needs to be vigilant to prevent this.

## Architecture

## A. Architecture Strategy

As defined in *IT is about the Strategy*, the third strategy the SMB will need to embrace is the business process strategy. The focus of this strategy is to define the IT and business processes, align them and improve upon them thereby improving the overall performance of IT and the SMB. Please refer to Appendix 7-1 for a pictorial view of this strategy.

The purpose of the architecture component of the strategy is to define the architecture planning process and to provide the overall architecture vision for the SMB. IT management will then be able to use the technology architecture vision to execute the tactics and realize that vision. The power of this strategy is that IT is no longer focusing on individual technologies but on the bigger picture of overriding architecture. This includes the vision and principles needed to guide IT through the tough technology terrain. Making technology decisions without the benefit of an architecture strategy will most likely result in a hodge-podge of solutions. These solutions may well become throw-away because they do not work well with the entire solution set. Technology decisions should not be made in a "one off" manner but as part of a cohesive vision dictated by the architecture strategy.

The goals surrounding technology architecture strategy are to define a set of boundaries and guidelines against which technologies can be analyzed and fitted into a cohesive solution set. Architecture is a framework or structure against which individual technologies, tools, languages and other attributes can be weighed. Using the analogy of a house the technology architecture is the blueprint and the exterior framing. The individual technologies that are selected are the interior choices and the furniture.

The infrastructure or architecture engineering group within IT generally owns the architecture and must continually refine and update it. They do this through a series of exercises and technology statements. To define the strategy IT management and the IT infrastructure engineering group must prepare technology statements for each of the following components of the architecture. These are standard components identified by everyone from Meta to Gartner and can be used to comprehensively describe your architecture.

- Data
- Platform
- Network
- Application
- Security
- Enterprise Management

These technology statements will be comprised of the following sections:

- An introduction (what component is being described and what are the major areas within that component?)
- An executive summary
- Key issues and observations (including technology issues and business drivers)
- Assessment of the current situation (background, gap analysis, migration planning)
- Architecture design principles (just like strategic drivers but for the architecture component itself)
- Strategies (describe your go forward approach to selecting technology solutions)
- Projects (identified to execute the vision)
- Standards and products (further clarification of the strategic drivers and specific products that need evaluated)
- Summary (what are you trying to accomplish and the direction taken?)

The output of this strategic exercise will be a technology architecture document. This should be a document that is kept current and frequently updated. IT infrastructure engineering has responsibility for these documents and should make them available to the rest of the department.

## B. Architecture Tactics

Execution of technology architecture tactics consists of using the architecture strategy and guidelines to add to and expand the existing infrastructure and applications technology. IT management should use the written technology statements when they are selecting technology. They should follow these guidelines. Complying with the direction and limitations developed in the strategy will allow IT to build a cohesive infrastructure and application solution set to fully support the business. IT must leverage this strategy they have developed. This is a cohesive way to operate and it will save both time and money. It will allow IT to avoid costly technology mistakes.

## C. Architecture Tactics Execution

Tactics execution is comprised of two major components. The first is to use the architecture strategy to select the appropriate technology components. Simply write the statements and use them to select technology. The second is to acquire and install the selected technologies through a proper project management methodology. Simply do the project right. This will complete the tactics.

## 1. Technology selection

As with any strategy it provides no value until you begin to execute the tactics. Tactical execution takes the form of writing the strategic architecture statements and then using these statements (and the information gathered to write them) to identify actionable projects and activities. These projects and activities will fall naturally out of the strategic exercise. You have now developed a vision and an end-state that you will work toward. I have summarized these statements below through a narrative approach to show how projects will be identified. These are examples of abbreviated technology statements for each of the components of the architecture showing how they will be used to do technology selection and to make technology decisions.

### a. Data

The component of data architecture will supply a framework for consistent data storage, development standards, data access, data presentation and data security.

The business drivers that surround data include an unforgiving need for data accuracy in the form of names, addresses and telephone numbers. Data in these fields are provided by our clients but are not always up-to-date or accurate. Since we mail and contact by telephone any increase in data accuracy is reflected in an increase in profitability. Consequently we must find cost effective ways to improve on this data. We need to provide ongoing vendor evaluation and selection to assure the highest accuracy at the lowest cost.

An analysis of the existing situation reveals a mixture of database technologies and disparate databases. We need a concerted effort to standardize on a given database management system and to integrate and link the existing data into a smaller number of data stores. This will measurably reduce our support costs.

Our architecture principles include data definition standards for length, format, naming and security. All new development must pass through the data steward committee who will manage data administration from an enterprise ownership perspective.

Our architecture principles also include component architecture definition for data design. All data design for all databases will include steps like comprehensive storage, distribution and retrieval techniques.

Our data lifecycles are documented so all projects will include archiving and retention parameters.

Identified projects and activities include the following examples:
- Conduct vendor evaluation for improving addresses and telephone numbers
- Pick standard database architecture
- Integrate and link existing data store into a smaller number
- Pass each project design through the data steward committee

## b. Platform

The platform component of architecture will supply a framework for selecting the base infrastructure including hardware server platforms, operating systems, storage and peripherals. The need for a platform architecture strategy becomes increasingly important since platform technologies have evolved from host/dumb terminal to server/PC and maybe even to thick server/thin client.

The business drivers include reducing the maintenance and support costs for the server environment while eliminating downtime and still providing adequate support. It is well known that as servers age they cost more to maintain and become inherently less reliable. For that reason we will replace all servers at the end of their recommended life cycles and before maintenance costs sharply escalate.

We have a variety of device attached storage and need to investigate and justify the cost of storage area network (SAN) technology. We must document the costs and benefits for our environment.

We have a variety of servers from various manufacturers. We need to complete a study to determine best manufacturer and best vendor for our environment. We need to standardize our configuration and our purchasing.

Our desktops and laptops are also aging and maintenance costs are rising. Reliability is decreasing. We need a retirement policy for desktops and laptops as well as a way to dispose of or redeploy aged equipment.

Other standards and products that must be defined and implemented include connectivity to clients and the outside world at large, a single enterprise wide operating system environment, server scalability and use of multi-processors and total cost of ownership (TCO) considerations.

Identified projects and activities include the following examples:
- Write server retirement policy
- SAN project
- Select best server manufacturer and vendor
- Standardize on single operating system environment

## c. Network

The component of network architecture will supply a framework for the local and wide area networks and internet connectivity.

We are a virtual company comprised of numerous branch offices in numerous locations in the U.S. and abroad. We will be serving up software applications including back office and customer facing functionality around the world. The business drivers include application availability, application response time and security of applications and data.

Our challenges include establishing a common set of connectivity, topology and data transfer technologies to create a homogenous fault-tolerant service.

Our local area network will currently support a limited number of inter-network transport service connections. We have an active project to minimize these to a single service.

Our voice technology services are a critical component of our network services. The integration of voice transmissions must be a primary component of our network planning and should be factored into all technology decisions.

Identified projects and activities include the following examples:
- Design new network
- Standardize transport service
- Integrate voice and data over a single carrier
- Investigate and select voice technologies

### d. Application

The component of application architecture will encompass the structure of the organization's business applications. It defines the major kinds of applications needed to manage the back office and customer facing functions of the business. It defines how they will be evaluated, selected and integrated. It defines where they will reside and when they will be accessed. Additional factors will be considered at the application level itself and will include system components, ownership, scaling and performance issues.

A key component of this strategy is the current "buy before build" philosophy where custom development is to be avoided at all costs.

As in most organizations, the application architecture is currently comprised of a complex array of systems that don't provide for standard interfaces or application program interfaces (APIs). These standards need to be provided for and included in future application evaluation and selection.

We need to develop a list of the existing applications and complete an evaluation of their strengths and weaknesses. We can use this to identify the role they play in the current enterprise application suite. We can identify the factors that must be considered in enhancements or replacements as the application ages.

The design principles that we should include in all purchased or composite (built with toolkits or components) applications include use of component architecture, three tiered architecture, loosely coupled tiers where changes in one tier does not affect the others, location transparency, use of object technology, scalability considerations and use of industry standards.

Identified projects and activities include the following examples:
- Standardize buy versus build methodology
- Replace key back office applications
- Replace key customer facing applications
- Evaluation of work flow tools

### e. Security

This component of the architecture strategy applies to strategies, design principles and standards in support of security of data and underlying software applications as presented through the enterprise infrastructure. We have farther defined three sub-components to include the following:

- Authentication and firewalls
- Internet security
- Intrusion detection and remote access technologies

The business drivers include our client's desire to audit our security and the large amount of private financial and personal data that we must carry within our applications to do our business. This dictates a Fortune 500 style solution that will stand up to scrutiny from our financial services clients and that will withstand attacks against our networks.

It begins with user access and user authentication and forces us to improve our user identification and password approach.

It continues through our use of the appropriate firewall technologies and the requisite investment in software to manage intrusion detection. At the same time we must balance the business need for remote access. Many of our executives must work while traveling and many of our technology contributors must work from home.

We have established a secure site for file transfers to and from our clients. This must be managed in the most secure fashion. Data transmissions must now include encryption. We need a project to evaluate encryption technologies and choose an industry standard solution that we can quickly install and incorporate.

The guiding principle will include the statement that security is not an end state but a constant journey that must be undertaken as technology grows and changes.

Identified projects and activities include the following examples:
- Audits by our three largest clients
- Evaluate and select user authentication software
- Evaluate and select intrusion detection software
- Evaluate and select data encryption software

## f. Enterprise management

This technology architecture component establishes the functions, processes and services used to manage and monitor the enterprise. It is further comprised of four sub-components:
- Service level management
- Fault management
- Configuration management
- Accounting management

We were not concerned about these sub-components during the previous two strategies. We will certainly need to address them now as we have grown enough to use the business process strategy. These are the products and services used to manage the various segments of the enterprise and how they interact with each other.

Service level management involves establishing service level agreements regarding application availability. It involves developing measurements in support of these agreements.

Fault management involves evaluating and selecting tools to monitor and manage infrastructure service delivery.

Configuration management involves managing and administering, among other things, our desktops and laptops. It speaks to how we must seek to control and homogenize our computing environments.

Accounting management speaks to our technology purchasing, our management of capital and expense budgets, our inventory control of technology fixed assets and depreciation of equipment.

All of the components of enterprise management can be cost justified with a solid business case. Each component enables one of several key factors including reduced costs, improved technology investments, lowered head count, lowered maintenance and support costs and solid financial tracking.

Identified projects and activities include the following examples:
- Develop service level agreements for systems availability
- Evaluate and select server and network monitoring tools
- Evaluate and select remote desktop management software
- Establish target capital budget plans for next three years

## 2.    Technology projects

The architecture statements are used to select the appropriate technology projects. There are three chapters in this book that are particularly important in technology selection and technology project execution. They are as follows:
- Chapter 10 - Simplified project management for all projects
- Chapter 13 - Package evaluation and selection for component software package selection projects
- Chapter 14 - Vendor selection and management for selecting technology partners during and after the sales

Additionally, the package evaluation and selection chapter should be used to select hardware and infrastructure components. The requirements and criteria will differ but the use of the approach is critical. It emphasizes developing detailed requirements before you start. Also critical are other factors like surveying the market place for solutions, keeping the vendor at the appropriate distance, managing the process tightly, establishing solid selection criteria and conducting customer visits. All of these tips and techniques translate well to the infrastructure selection process as well.

# D. Architecture and Personnel

The primary IT staffing challenge here is to find the appropriate mix of strategic and tactical skill sets. The SMB needs to hire an architecture expert or more preferable needs to outsource the development of this strategy to a third party service provider. Remember infrastructure is a common challenge and the solutions will be fairly standard with only specific exceptions provided by clients or other business partners. Architecture skill sets at the appropriate level of experience are very difficult to find. Most engineers are tactical by nature. They do not recognize the value of developing an architecture strategy and developing infrastructure against that strategy. At the same time the SMB needs to execute the tactics in the form of projects and activities. This requires a tactical execution skill set and these tactical skill sets are much easier to find. Good engineers who understand the technology and can execute these solutions should be readily available. In summary the SMB, should consider outsourcing the creation of the architecture vision and allowing the internal employees (engineers) to execute it.

## Organization and Service

> ### WISDOM to work by:
>
> 1. *Organize your way to IT success.*
>    *Organize around process, not technology.*
> 2. *Organize with a service focus.*
>    *The business does not care how it gets done or who does it as long as it gets done. Make sure it does.*
> 3. *Embrace the plan, build, run approach!*
>    *It works every time.*
> 4. *Provide clarity.*
>    *Define roles and responsibilities through a department charter.*

## A. Organization and Service Strategy

As defined in *IT is about the Strategy*, the third strategy that the SMB will need to embrace is the business process strategy. The focus of this strategy is to define the IT and business processes, align them, and improve upon them thereby improving the overall performance of IT and the SMB. Please refer to Appendix 7-1 for a pictorial view of this strategy.

The purpose of the organization and service component of the strategy is to organize IT with a process and service approach. This strategy will require IT management to make critical observations about the existing organization structure. In most cases the organization structure will show a lack of suitability for addressing and managing the major IT processes. The overriding strategy is the need to reorganize and realign around the identified IT processes. The strategic direction is the process based organization structure as depicted in Appendix 8-1.

## B. Organization and Service Tactics

Strategy becomes execution by changing both the organization structure and the focus of the organization. The focus needs to be one of process and service not technology. I am certain that IT at this point in time is a technology based organization focused around the various technologies. IT has a server group, a network group, a telecom group and so on. Each technology group owns all of the processes surrounding their technologies. That is the problem.

The technology based organization is built around technology skill sets. In it one group is responsible for each technology. This structure works until the maintenance and support load gets so large that day-to-day support will begin to drastically suffer. When given a choice engineers will choose to do what they enjoy and not what the business needs. Engineers will work on new project after new project and stop picking up the phone once that new project is done. Questions, problems and support sink to the bottom of the "To Do" list. Is it any wonder that the organization is seen as non-responsive? Who wants to do support? The result is that nine out of ten of the IT interactions (read opportunities) to support the business go unresolved. This is critically wrong! This situation reveals the need to organize around process by creating distinct IT groups responsible for core processes like user interactions and user communications. That is why service desks were invented. The process of satisfying the user needs goes directly to the service desk. These and other organizational hindrances and obstructions can be resolved by a process and service based organization structure.

# C. Organization and Service Tactics Execution

## 1. Introduction

The best organization structure will not make a weak IT organization successful and the worst organization structure will not keep a strong one from being so. Why then should an SMB change the IT organization structure? It is simple. The right structure makes it much easier for the IT organization to be successful. It does away with all the thrashing about and the roles and responsibility confusion that normally reigns. It removes the frustrations and barriers that good employees encounter each day in dealing with the business and the user community. Sure, good IT departments will find a way to work around the wrong organization structure and make it somehow work. Why put them through it? Why tie their hands? There is a solid workable organization structure that will assist your IT department in daily work and make life easier for them. It will also result in vastly improved service to the business and a solid reputation for responsiveness as well. The real question should be why the IT organization structure should not change. There is no good response to that.

## 2. The process based organization

The process based organization is the answer to the question of how IT should organize to best support the identified IT processes. Please refer again to Appendix 8-1 for a process based organization structure. Referencing each of the major overriding processes listed there we have the following:
- **Plan** - planning, budgeting, project management, process management
- **Build**
    ○ Infrastructure construction
    ○ Software applications (back office and customer facing) construction
- **Run** - systems administration, help desk level one support, computer operations, second level and field support.

Please refer to Appendix 9-1 for a process view of these responsibilities. The next step is to dissect these broad process categories into smaller categorizations. Hold a single group responsible for each process.

This structure will allow IT to define and document how they will deal with users, provide services, arbitrate priorities, communicate, manage projects, meet service level agreements, recruit the proper talent, build a knowledge base and implement technologies. IT management can now develop IT process responsibilities using the new model. The process based organization works. I have implemented it several times and it always solves a number of basic problems. It allows for process owner-ship, improves performance and provides distinct career paths. I will expound on this during the execution discussion.

### 3. Process planning

Before this exercise can begin IT management must plan the entire organization realignment exercise through to the end. Recognize that IT management is attempting to retool the entire IT department to provide clear roles and responsibilities with a focus on process. IT management must pull the management team together and work through all of the details and gain total acceptance. Even one naysayer can pull down and derail the entire effort. The department will have the most trouble with the IT technical management who still dabble in programming or technology solutions. These managers often resist change. If the business and IT management plans and executes properly they will succeed. It is critical to first recognize and acknowledge that IT cannot continue to function under a technology based organization structure.

I also strongly recommend a strategic exercise to build a department charter docu-ment for each of the six groups. The charter is a foundational directional document that defines what each department is all about. I find it best generated by a one day offsite meeting with the sole purpose of producing the charter. Please refer to Appendix 8-2 for an example of an entire department charter. The beauty of this approach is that it allows the department to start with a broad strategy and drive it down to a tactical level of detail. The charter can define specific roles and responsibilities as well as specific projects and deliverables. Include as many of the following sections as possible in the document:
- Guiding principles
- Mission
- Objectives
- Operating plan with projects
- Core processes
- Core processes mapped to functional responsibilities
- Work flow
- Roles and responsibilities
- Job descriptions
- Performance objectives
- Projects
- Activities

## 4.  Process responsibilities

The new organization structure will be process driven. Please refer to Appendix 9-1 for a spreadsheet of process responsibilities in a process driven IT organization. These process responsibilities are detailed below.

### a.  Plan

The planning function is performed by the planning and project management department. This group is responsible for the strategy and the long range plans for the entire IT department. They set up standards and guidelines for planning and own the policies, procedures and standards. They execute and manage all projects as well as assist the business in training on simple repeatable project management processes. Process responsibilities include the following:
- Project identification
- Project compilation
- Project estimation (size and scope)
- Project management
- Project portfolio management
- Capital budgeting
- Project planning

### b.  Build

There are two distinct build groups. One builds the underlying infrastructure. The other builds or assembles the back office and customer facing software and application systems that run on it.

**Architecture Engineering**

This group provides cost effective technology solutions and third tier technology support. They are a consulting resource as well as a research and development resource. They build the infrastructure based on business requirements to support existing and future applications. They are proactive not reactive and strive to do it right the first time. Process responsibilities include the following:
- Develop infrastructure technology strategy
- Define and implement technology solutions
- Provide technology research and development
- Provide consulting services to the business (particularly sales)
- Provide infrastructure project management
- Provide third tier technology support

**Software Engineering**

This group is a service driven organization that acquires, constructs, and enhances the software and application technology solutions for the business. This includes both back office and customer facing applications. This group

acquires or builds the appropriate software solutions through the use of appropriate methodologies. They must use published standards in the area of coding, testing, selection, installation, documentation and user training. They are responsible for the following processes:
- Provide software acquisition
- Provide software construction
- Provide software enhancements
- Provide software project management
- Provide third tier software support
- Conduct software research and development

## c. Run

The run group is really three distinct groups responsible for the day-to-day activities and support for the IT organization.

### Computer Operations

This run group focuses on running the production processes and managing the computer components on a daily basis. Their mission is to schedule, run and monitor all aspects of the production computing environment. Some of these vary from business to business. This includes everything that the build groups build. Once the infrastructure and applications are installed, responsibility for these technologies are transferred to the computer operations group. They will insure all resources are directed toward the timely and accurate completion of all production tasks. This includes scheduling, availability, performance, documentation, procedures, results, quality assurance and process management. Process responsibilities include the following:
- Run installed infrastructure components
- Run installed application software components
- Manage any inputs and outputs
- Delivery of any produced products or services

### Help Desk Tier One Support

This run group owns business user communication and tier one technology break/fix. It is a service driven organization that is basically the voice of IT. They provide primary service and support to the users of technology. This includes anything that the build groups build and anything that the run groups run. Once the infrastructure and applications are installed, responsibility for all communications and break/fix activities are transferred to this group. They must insure that all technologies are serviced and supported properly. Their primary mission is to properly manage user expectations and user relationships. Process responsibilities include the following:
- Maintain and manage user communication
- Manage technology break/fix
- Solve user problems where possible

- Coordinate problem resolution with other groups
- Coordinate the application of resources to problems
- Manage IT communication where applicable with customers

### Systems Administration

This run group is responsible for system maintenance and system monitoring for the operating systems, layered products and infrastructure. They should also make system usage recommendations and control system administration. This includes partition usage and controls as well as job priorities and controls. This group is also responsible for systems security, maintenance and support agreements and contracts, infrastructure vendor relationships, infrastructure vendor management and assisting in vendor negotiations.

This group is responsible for maintaining and monitoring system performance including but not limited to daily performance monitoring, performance recommendations, and hardware upgrades such as storage allocation and usage. One very important responsibility also includes all components of disaster recovery including the data and system backup plan, system and data backup execution and execution of the Disaster Recovery Plan.

## D. Organization and Process Personnel

I recommend IT leadership conduct a tactical exercise where existing IT personnel are evaluated and judged against specific performance criteria. Please refer to Appendix 8-3 for a sample skill set evaluation work sheet. The challenge here is that many of the skill sets required in the previous organization structure will not map easily into the new one. This organization structure requires specialization, a customer focus and a service vision that most immature IT organizations lack. On a department by department basis fill out the work sheets for every member. Try to map employees into the new organization structure where they can best contribute and have the highest chance of success. In some cases adjustments will have to be made. Some employees will lack appropriate skill sets or have improper attitudes for the new structure.

## Process

> ### WISDOM to work by:
>
> 1. <u>*Process, process, process.*</u> *I can't say it loud enough. It's an over worked phrase and a boring word but build success through a process approach.*
> 2. <u>*Write it down.*</u> *Document your processes and improve them again and again.*

## A. Business Process Strategy

As defined in *IT is about the Strategy*, the third strategy that the SMB will need to embrace is the business process strategy. The focus of this strategy is to define the IT and business processes, align them and improve upon them thereby improving the overall performance of IT and the SMB. This third component of the business process strategy focuses on the actual IT and business processes and business process reengineering. The goal of this strategy is to accomplish the following:

- Identify all of the IT business processes
- Document all of the IT business processes
- Assign ownership for every IT business process
- Review and improve on each process

The overriding strategy is to identify, document and improve the IT processes. This strategy is tightly coupled with the organization/reorganization strategy component and must track tightly with its execution. Please refer to Appendix 7-1 for a pictorial view of this strategy. At this critical juncture in the company history the IT department will not be successful without a process approach.

## B. Business Process Tactics

Strategy becomes execution only when the IT processes are improved upon and made a focus for the department. The focus needs to be on making all work follow a standard process. Improvements can be made to each process by documenting that process and implementing standard tools and techniques in support of the handling of that process. I think the best example I can use to illustrate the point is the use of a standard process for handling business problems with IT technology components. Here is a recommended abbreviated standard process:

- User calls the service desk
- Service desk opens a work ticket
- Service desk assigns the work ticket to a work group
- Work group member accepts work ticket
- Work group member does work on the work ticket.
- Work group member closes ticket
- Work group member calls service desk with resolution
- Service desk calls user with resolution

Now given this basic flow this process can be improved and enhanced. The process can be changed to allow the user to enter a self serve ticket instead of calling the service desk. The service desk can set up a process for off-hour coverage. The service desk can set up a priority level for the ticket and handle different priorities differently. The ticketing system can be set up to automatically email updates. The ways to improve the process are endless but they start with identifying "handling user problems" as a discreet process and focusing on standardizing and improving that process.

## C. Business Process Tactics Execution

As detailed in the book *IT is about the Strategy*, each IT department in the organization will be held responsible for their own identified processes. These will be assigned at a high level by the strategic exercise and expanded upon and refined by the charter exercise. Please refer to the process based organization structure given in Chapter 8 by Appendices 8-1 and 8-2. This is the starting point for defining and documenting all IT processes. I have also taken the liberty of defining many of the major processes and sub-processes as given in Appendix 9-1. Feel free to eliminate or add to these as IT responsibilities grow and change. Using the list of processes and sub-processes, the next step is to document the processes. I have also provided some sample forms that may be used and are included as follows:

- Procedure definition form (9-2)
- Process definition form (9-3)
- Example of an entire process definition - change management (12-1)

Just as I will recommend in common tactics, process improvements must be executed in an iterative fashion. Take a large leap to get a crude process in place and then refine and improve the structure and process methodology a little at a time. Try adding a process step to solve an ongoing problem. Try adding a form to the existing process. Continue to take improvement steps and firm up the processes.

There are several ways to go about executing the process tactical approach and there are now numerous tools available in the market place to assist you. I recommend starting with one of your simpler but critical processes and using the templates I have provided to complete the exercise. This may be done in a vacuum by one of the IT staff members and later reviewed and approved by committee. Alternately, each process can be defined and documented as a group exercise. I have seen both approaches work. The level of structure and formality are not the key factors at the beginning. The key factors are the efforts expended and the understanding that processes are the focus and that ownership is defined.

## D. Business Process Personnel

The type of employee required changes as the strategy changes to a business process strategy. More detail is provided in Chapter 15 (Personnel Administration and Management). Unfortunately many IT individuals lack a process focus and have a difficult time developing an appreciation and affinity for this approach. For many of them it is all about the technology. These are the wrong individuals for this organization and the strategic process approach. Some retooling of the IT resource may become necessary. I have discussed this in detail in the book *IT is about the Strategy*.

# Simplified Project Management

---

**WISDOM to work by:**

1. *Don't make that mistake!*
   *Avoid the three most common project management mistakes that nearly every SMB will make.*
2. *Here it is...one of the most important nuggets in the book.*
   *The real secret to project management in the SMB is to match the project management methodology to the maturity of the organization.*
3. *Use an iterative approach.*
   *There are no quick fixes and no way to jump on a moving train. Start with a rough approach, any approach, and improve it again and again.*
4. *Process, process, process.*
   *This simplified project management methodology is a recipe for project success.*
5. *Embrace the plan, build, run approach!*
   *It works every time.*
6. *Don't build it right the first time.*
   *Consider the crawl-walk-run approach to technology solutions.*

---

## A. Introduction

This chapter and the following six chapters are common tactics that track through the three strategies and should be executed in conjunction with them.

Nothing is more frustrating than experiencing project management at most SMBs. The SMB usually commits one of three classic mistakes and continues to do so to this day. Which one have you committed?

1. The "technology" mistake - This is the mistake of buying an expensive tool like Microsoft Enterprise Project and concluding that project management is now "solved". This usually happens when the reigning management is technology focused and assumes every problem has a technology solution. When the only tool you have is a hammer, every problem looks like a nail.

2.  The "it's simple" mistake - This is the mistake of assuming that smart people can be put in charge of projects and that project management will just happen because smart people are working on it. This usually happens in an immature organization where leadership does not respect the experience of other organizations. They also do not comprehend the complexity of project management or the need for a methodology.

3.  The "it must be world class" mistake - This is the antithesis of the "it's simple" mistake where the SMB goes to the other extreme and makes the mistake of jumping from no methodology to a full blown comprehensive project management methodology. The chosen methodology could be a purchased methodology, an internally designed one or even something quite complex. This usually also happens in an immature organization where leadership does not respect experience and does not understand how to affect change or how to implement process.

**The real secret to project management in the SMB is to match the project management methodology to the maturity of the organization.** I can not say this loud enough. Please read it again. There are so many opportunities for mistakes with project management. On one extreme you have the SMBs that want no part of formal project management because they feel it will slow them down and provide no value. This is a terrible misconception and the fact is that the appropriate simplified project management methodology will both speed up project delivery and greatly improve the chances for project success. The other extreme is the SMB that takes months to define or select a methodology and then tries to implement it in one fell swoop. This, too, is a doomed approach since you cannot go from no methodology to a mature methodology with no stops in between. The fact is that even a simplistic methodology will begin to provide returns on your investment without jumping to an unworkably complex structure. The challenge is to select the appropriate project management methodology and to gain some acceptance and some use of that methodology. The best tool or methodology provides absolutely no value if it is not embraced and used. The worst tool provides some value even if it is just sparingly used. The overriding requirements for any SMB are speed and nimbleness. These must be reconciled with the application of some degree of structure and the ongoing attention to developing a full set of repeatable processes.

Jumping into a full blown project management methodology will be not only fruitless but some times catastrophic. The business ends up fighting against both the methodology and the project itself. I liken this to trying to board a moving train. **I recommend building a project management methodology in an iterative fashion.** I prefer the "crawl/walk/run" approach where the business uses a very simplistic initial approach and then graduates to more formality and more functionality over time. By this I mean the SMB should start with rough informal project steps and add formality and structure a little at a time. For example, I recommend starting with a simple Excel spreadsheet for a project plan and a simple one page Word document for a project definition. That is enough to get the process started.

Using my three business strategies as a framework, I can describe the creation and evolution of the project management methodology as a series of iterative steps.

## B. Simplified Project Management and the Business Layer Strategy

As I recommend above, the project management methodology that will work best when the SMB is using the Business Layer Strategy is necessarily brief and fairly informal. It needs to lay the foundation for project management in a solid way so that the SMB can build on it as the SMB grows. I will outline this methodology as a series of steps that can be followed in order to develop a structured project management approach. Remember, do not get hung up on tools and technologies. The simpler the better here.

I am a proponent of the Franklin Covey methodology which promotes begin with the end in mind. I say that because the SMB should have a rough target methodology defined from the beginning and all work on methodology is done to arrive at that target state. This simplified project management target state is defined in Appendix 10-1. Please review it briefly before continuing. Here are the iterative steps I recommend for the Business Layer Strategy.

### 1. Define a project and commit to managing it

It sounds simplistic and redundant but the first step in simplified project management is to realize the difference between an activity and a project. This can be more complicated than it sounds. I like to define a project as a series of related activities with a common goal or end result. Defining a project can be a point of contention for the business but a rule of thumb is that it is a series of repeatable processes with a desired outcome. The critical step here is the commitment to recognizing and attempting to standardize and manage projects. Activities are just the individual things that are performed in the course of a normal business day and may or may not be part of a larger set of project activities. A project is a series of activities that all contribute to a desired end state. Once agreement is reached on what can be termed a project then a commitment needs to be made by the SMB to project management. If project management continues to be viewed as an obstacle and bureaucratic, then project management will continue to flounder.

### 2. Identify the two broad steps of planning and execution

Full blown structured project management gets some of its reputation for being too cumbersome partially because of the large number of steps that are usually identified and managed. The SMB does not need that level of formality. To begin, the two broad simple steps of "plan" and "execute" will suffice. This level of structure simply states the SMB should attempt to identify the various activities that will take place at a high level and identify the deliverables that will be produced to signify the activity is successfully completed. Some thought will have to be given to project dependencies but it is helpful to start planning in a sequential fashion as if activities occur in a linear mode. This simplistic way of viewing a project gets the process started.

### 3.  Implement Excel spreadsheets as the formal project planning tool

Take the identified activities and create a project plan in the form of an Excel spreadsheet. Please refer to Appendices 10-4 and 10-5 for a recommended format and a simple project plan example. Start simple and expand over time. Identify the activity, the responsible person and the deliverable that must be accomplished to show the activity is complete. Do not skip the deliverable column. If possible, estimate the man hours related to the activity and try to establish start and end dates. That is it. Then use the project plan to conduct the project. Use it to identify the steps you missed, the change in deliverables, the inaccuracy of your estimates and so on. Each subsequent project plan should get better by being more comprehensive and more accurate. It becomes an iterative process of repeated improvements.

### 4.  Define the specific broad types of projects

Using the Business Layer Strategy the SMB should be able to identify three broad types of projects based on the technology layers and then possibly additional types within the three layers.
- Infrastructure projects
  - Outsourcing infrastructure components
  - Major upgrades or enhancements to infrastructure components
- Back Office projects
  - Outsourcing back office components
  - Major upgrades or enhancements to back office components
- Customer facing projects
  - Building customer facing applications
  - Buying customer facing applications

The business could be engaged in other types of projects like opening branch offices or doing acquisitions, so these projects would need defined as well. The goal is to build a preset project plan template for each project type and to refine and improve that template over time. This improves the project management methodology and delivery. Since each of these projects will have different components or steps, it pays to treat them differently and build various project templates for them. Another problem with standard project management methodologies is that they try to use the same format and templates for every project. Customization and simplicity are more important. Please refer to Appendices 10-6, 10-7 and 10-8 for sample templates.

### 5.  Add the first gate between planning and execution

To review, by this time in the evolution of the methodology the SMB has begun to formally recognize and initiate projects, has implemented a crude but effective project planning tool and technique, has identified and defined different types of projects and has begun to build templates for the different types of projects. These are big steps and will go a long way to formalization of a methodology and laying the foundation for future project steps. One additional step that can be taken is to add a formal step between the planning of a project and the execution of the project. This step can be referred to as a gate. It could be as informal as an email distribution or a topic on a meeting agenda. It just states that the project plan is complete, the resources are committed and the time frames are set. It is like the starting gun to a foot race. The SMB has now added a gate between planning and execution and an additional level of structure and formality has now been attained.

### 6. Develop the project list

One last thing that can be accomplished at this stage of the project management methodology evolution is to develop a project list. Please refer to Appendix 1-3 for a sample project list format. It is simply a one page summary of all the active projects so that management at a glance can see what is being done. It has numerous uses including showing how resources are being committed, the target timeframes and the availability of project deliverables. Include on this list the columns for the type of project, owners or sponsors, project name, project due dates and so on. I am always amazed at how few SMBs have something as simple as an up to date project list. This later becomes a project portfolio and larger organizations sometimes dedicate an individual to managing the list. That should emphasize the importance of the project list.

## C. Simplified Project Management and the Business Model Strategy

The SMB is growing in size and complexity and has migrated from the Business Layer to the Business Model Strategy. This transition should also be seen as an opportunity to expand and refine the project management methodology into a more formal structure and to build on the foundation that has been previously built. The recommended formalization steps that should now take place are detailed below.

### 1. Add a Charter/Scope document

Now it is time to resolve some of the problems that will have been encountered with projects where the scope seems to shift and where the outcome and deliverables always seem to miss the mark. This can be accomplished by a definitive charter/scope document. The purpose of this document is to identify what the project is about and establish an understanding and agreement among all project participants regarding scope, purpose, costs, deliverables and timelines. Please refer to Appendices 10-9 and 10-10 for a working template and instructions on how to fill it out and use it. These are the target or end state documents that you should be using by the time the project methodology structure is totally built. Feel free to start with an abbreviated document and add bullet points or paragraphs a few at a time. Start with just six or eight of the elements below and add a bullet element a month. Please do not try to start out with the full blown document as this will be seen as needless structure. Remember our iterative approach and build this document over time. Here are some recommended possible project charter/scope inclusions.

- Purpose
- Background
- Details
- Stakeholders
- Scope
- Goals/Objectives
- Deliverables
- Boundaries
- Constraints
- Dependencies
- Estimates and Resources
- Costs and ROI
- Benefits
- Assumptions
- Milestone Plan
- Organization of participants

I am always impressed at how little agreement truly exists on the scope of any project. The charter/scope document will broker these disagreements and go a long way to improving project delivery by providing clarity and understanding.

**2.   Add a communication plan**

The purpose of a communication plan is to document and structure all project communications among project participants. Projects may take a few days or a few months (by the way, any project that exceeds ninety days should be immediately suspect, more on this later). It is necessary to keep all stakeholders informed about project progress and more importantly project problems. The tendency is to have ad hoc communications throughout. This is a bad project habit. Structured communications force a rigidity and structure that can contribute to project success. Please refer to Appendices 10-11 and 10-12 for a sample communication plan and instructions. To create the plan, do the following:
- Identify what messages need to be sent (progress, problem, decision needed)
- Identify the audience (project team, stakeholders, management)
- Select a frequency (weekly, as needed, monthly)
- Assign responsibility for putting out the message
- Define how the message will be sent (email, meeting, report)
- Define the intent of the message (progress, problem, phase completion).

If there is one step that seems to bring a project together it is the communication plan. Please also review the appropriate chapters on project reporting and incorporate these in the communication plan. Project reporting needs to follow a standard structure and focus solely on exceptions. Project reporting tends to become cumbersome because so much time can be spent on projects that are on schedule and meeting deadlines. There is no need to report on a project that is on schedule. Focus instead on the projects with problems. Make project reporting focus on just the exceptions. Then consideration can be given to remedies to get the project back on track. A communication plan will assist with this approach.

### 3.   Add a testing plan

Testing is a key component of any project. Having a test plan is another step to formalization that improves project success. Most SMBs take testing very lightly. They tend to put things into production and fix problems on the fly. This should be avoided at all times. Any production problem comes with a real cost to the business. Testing, as with the project management methodology and as with any other approach, should be implemented in an iterative fashion. Begin by doing some commonsense testing focusing on what is changing in the production environment. Expand from there. Add levels of testing for things like interfaces. Add testing against requirements. Introduce enhanced processes like user acceptance testing. The more formality that can be introduced over time, the less amount of down time will be experienced after installation. Things break when they are changed. Please refer to Appendices 10-13, 10-14 and 10-15 for test plan instructions, test plan example and testing goals. In lieu of something formal and for earlier stages, a verbal walk through of how the developer or engineer intends to test the project requirements is always an adventure. The goal here is to get the project participant to plan testing and make it an integral part of the project. Testing can address many levels of the project. For new software applications, a true test environment should be maintained and the business user needs to do acceptance testing against the project deliverables. A good guideline is to have three environments if at all possible. These would be development, testing and production. For infrastructure and back office applications, the IT project participant needs to work with the vendor to assure adequate testing is accomplished. Vendor participation is the key.

### 4.   Replace the two broad steps of planning and execution with a Plan-Build-Run methodology

It is now time to abandon the broad and somewhat nebulous planning and execution phases for a three phased approach. I have had great success with a plan-build-run approach to project management. I have developed several tools and techniques for explaining this methodology to project teams and getting it embraced. Try this. Project management is as easy as one, two, three. There is one summary phrase called PBR (plan, build, run). There are two pass through gates. There is one moving from planning to building and one moving from building to running. There are three project phases called plan, build and run. Something as simple as having a catchphrase for your project management methodology reinforces the message. I have had employees quote this approach to me years after working with me. It is necessary to build some structure into the methodology to serve as the gates. The gate can be as simple as signature signoff on the charter/scope document and project plan or as complex as a structured user review and acceptance meeting. Start informally and add structure. Please refer to Appendix 10-16 for a pictorial representation of this project approach. Feel free to distribute liberally throughout the SMB.

## 5.   Sharpen the deliverables

The methodology by this time should includes the three phases and the activities and deliverables for each phase. To again quote Stephen Covey, it is time to sharpen the saw. That is to say the SMB must take time our occasionally to do maintenance on the tools that are being used. It is now appropriate to examine the deliverables in regards to form and content and see if improvements can be made. If templates are not being used or are not finalized, now is the time. If the planning documents need refinement or improvement, now is the time. If the deliverables are poorly constructed or not always delivered it is time to tighten things up. The project deliverables are more than just formalities. They are project milestones and project content that will define both the quality and speed of project delivery. Making them better will improve project perform-ance. A word about milestones in general is timely. Never allow a project to go forward without frequent milestones. A project without milestones is like a ship without a rudder. It is critical to manage the milestones to manage the project. I once had a manager who asserted that he would fire me if I came to him with no time left on the project clock and requested a one or two week project extension. He understood several critical things about project management. He understood that a project should never get in trouble at the end of the timeline but somewhere in the beginning or the middle. He understood that I would not have managed to the milestones or the project deadline would not be in jeopardy. He understood that the one or two weeks would probably not be enough to finish a poorly managed project.  The net result was clear to him. Without detailed milestones and meeting those milestones a project would not be completed on time. The project would be a failure.

## 6.   Improve the project reporting

Included in the book, *IT is about the Strategy*, are some project reporting techniques and tool kits. There is also a summary and examples of this methodology in Chapter 6. Project reporting is critical to the success of a project and to the organization as a whole. Large amounts of time, energy and money are always being expended against projects in SMBs. Having the best tools and techniques for monitoring those expenditures is critical to the health of the organization. Please refer to Appendices 6-4, 6-5 and 6-6.

# D. Simplified Project Management and the Business Process Strategy

The SMB has grown to a size where a formal structured but still simplified project management methodology is a must. If the business has worked on the methodology relentlessly during the two previous strategy executions, the work to be done now is simply the icing on the cake. In this strategy phase we finalize the methodology, publish it widely to the organization, sharply define all activities and deliverables, complete all templates, shore up all of the project tools and move beyond project management being a discreet activity to project management being the core process for getting things done.

### 1.  Review the project against the strategy

No matter how vigilant an SMB monitors project activity, a non-strategic project or a project that flies in the face of the strategy is still often initiated. The SMB needs to assure that every project that gets initiated fits with the strategy being implemented. Pressure will come from Finance and Accounting to modify those back office applications. Pressure will come from Operations to build that on-the-fly Access database. These and other like projects will surface. They must be delicately squashed to assure that the projects aligned with the strategy are the only ones that take place.

### 2.  Consider a crawl-walk-run approach to technology

One of the primary challenges with getting projects completed in the SMB is the length of time it usually takes to get a project completed. In most cases the project is critical to the business and the amount of time it takes is legitimate. There is always the push to get it done quicker. One of the approaches I have taken is to foster a crawl-walk-run mode of thinking. Please refer to Appendices 10-2 and 10-3 for a pictorial representation of this approach.

The approach is simply to explore ways to get the requisite functionality sooner without building the ultimate system. The approach was discovered in the area of new products or services where the SMB does not know whether the new product or service is viable and will sell. If not, why go to the expense of building the product or support service? Here the SMB would opt for manual procedures, low initial costs, increased head count and basic tools. As the product or service became viable, over time, these solutions would be replaced by intermediate automation such as "quick and dirty" technologies (Access databases, Excel spreadsheets). Intermediate solutions decrease costs, reduce head count and involve smaller solution tool kits. The ultimate solution or permanent system solutions should be considered when the product or service is deemed viable and needs to become part of the production process. These ultimate solutions should be counted on to reduce overall costs, reduce head count to support, and evoke the enterprise wide tools like VB and SQL and purchased solutions. This, too, is an iterative approach and can be conducted as multiple projects or one project with multiple phases. The goal is to focus on process and build a permanent business system/solution as the product or service matures and proves to be a winner.

### 3.  Formalize documentation requirements

In the early stages of project management in the SMB the business is thrilled to get anything written down at all. As the project management methodology matures it is important that the SMB develop templates. These should be kept in a common source library. All of the deliverables, tools and documentation should follow a standard format. This allows for improvement and enhancement. The business leaders also get accustomed to seeing documents in a set format and can skip right to the sections and information critical to them. Using templates adds much value and clarity to projects. The added benefit is that the project is documented as it is being conducted.

Documentation as a whole does not get left to the end of the project where it is often ignored altogether. It is critical that project documentation is complete and comprehensive and that the project is leaving "foot prints". Over time the SMB does not have to constantly reinvent the wheel for every document. Historically, the core knowledge of the project participants is stored and available for all time.

### 4.  Add a training plan

Often times the success of the technology or software application is based on how well the business users accept and use the new technology. Training is a critical component and is easy to ignore since it seems to add cost to any project. More accurately, training should be viewed as an investment and not as a cost for a project. The better the functionality provided by the technology is used the more it will pay for itself. At this step of the methodology development, it is appropriate to add a training plan. The training plan is a level of formality that assures that those who will benefit most from the training will indeed receive it. Please refer to Appendices 10-17 and 10-18 for a training plan template and explanation. This is another level of structure and formality that will increase your chances for project success.

### 5.  Add an installation plan

An installation plan also adds a formal step to the "go live" portion of any project. The installation plan adds value as a communication device and as a way of assuring a trouble free installation. The intent of the installation plan is to identify and document the steps, sequence and timing of the project installation. It serves to effectively coordinate and execute the project installation. Please refer to the Appendices in 10-19 and 10-20 for samples. The plan resembles a calendar with activities or notations. It allows for a participant to see at a glance what will happen and when it will happen. This is an excellent way for the project participants to review the sequence of events and poke holes in the process at the same time. Any problems caught before installation will ultimately save the SMB real dollars.

### 6.  Add a gate between build and run steps

Just like the gate between "plan and build" there should be a gate between the "build and run" phases of projects. This gate goes hand in hand with the installation plan. It should include formal sign-off by the business that they have completed whatever testing they are responsible for and that the installation plan is both acceptable and will not cause service interruptions. This gate is an important milestone because it signals the end of all testing and the fact that the project is ready to install. This gate should be included in the communication plan as well. This is important additional functionality required to build a solid project management methodology.

## 7.   Add a post project installation review

Another step that will improve the project management methodology is to institutionalize the process improvement surrounding the methodology. The easiest way to do this is to add a post project installation review step. This is a simple informal briefing session after project completion that allows for a little comic relief and a discussion of lessons learned. Please refer to the Appendices in 10-21 for both a template and instructions. This review also forces an examination of the three critical components of project management and project execution.
- Time to deliver
- Budget performance
- Functionality delivered

The goal is to improve the project delivery and execution through this simple project tool that is easily added to the project methodology. Failure to review will doom the SMB to repeating the same mistakes over and over again. You cannot fix the problems until you identify and address them.

## 8.   Publish and advertise the methodology

One thing I have learned from working in IT all of my adult life is that sales and marketing is what it is all about. An IT department that does not market itself and its tools and techniques will not be a successful one. Project management affects the entire corporation. The resulting methodology needs to be understood and embraced by all. I have been successful in creating meaningful marketing campaigns around the more visible principles of the project management methodology. These principles include plan-build-run, crawl-walk-run or as-easy-as-1-2-3. I have found it useful to promote the methodology in all aspects of corporate communications and corporate culture. I have found it useful to conduct open meetings and brown bag luncheons to explain the concepts and extol the virtues. I have made the tools and templates readily available to all. Marketing is a difficult lesson for IT to learn, but the project management methodology is a great place to start. Sell it!

## 9.   Review all document templates and deliverables and seek to improve the  process over time

Most SMBs would do well to establish some form of a project management office with project methodology ownership. It does not have to be overly formal. This makes someone responsible for assuring that the methodology is followed and that the templates, tools, and techniques are dusted off every once in awhile and looked at with a critical eye. It is important to constantly tinker with and improve project management. Even pruning it is not necessarily a bad thing as long as quality does not suffer. The methodology needs to be a living, breathing thing that is used in every project effort. Take great pains to keep it as simple, straight forward, yet as comprehensive as the culture allows.

# E. Summary

There is no need to buy MS Enterprise Project or any other such tool until the SMB becomes moderately large. Simplified project management is about the process. Project management does not add bureaucracy or red tape to a project. It adds structure and value. That is all. Project management increases the chances for project success. It allows the employees to see project management as a set of repeatable processes that can be learned and improved upon. No SMB should squander the opportunity to do project management right.

## Simplified Problem Management

> ### WISDOM to work by:
>
> 1. <u>You can not manage what you do not measure.</u>
>    *Problem management requires measurements.*
> 2. <u>Manage problems or they manage you.</u>
>    *Structured problem management is critical.*
> 3. <u>IT is a service organization.</u>
>    *Every interaction between IT and the business is an opportunity to serve.*
> 4. <u>There is no one size that fits all.</u>
>    *As with project management match the problem management solution to the maturity of the organization.*
> 5. <u>Don't build it right the first time.</u>
>    *Consider the crawl-walk-run approach to developing problem management.*
> 6. <u>Begin with the end in mind.</u>
>    *Define your target state for problem management and work to get there.*
> 7. <u>Use an iterative approach.</u>
>    *There are no quick fixes and no way to jump on a moving train. Start with a rough approach and improve it again and again.*
> 8. <u>Learn something.</u>
>    *Use problem management to learn what is not working within your IT organization and fix it.*

## A. Introduction

Most larger organizations separate problem and incident management. Most SMBs do not. This differentiation, while important is not relevant to many SMBs until they have reached a certain size. I have combined them for the sake of this chapter as I feel most SMBs consider them one and the same.

This tactic goes to the heart of the saying about management and measurement. You can not manage what you do not measure. Problem management involves addressing the service and support issues existing between IT and the business. The stated goal is improving service and support. The true measure of any IT organization is how they service the business. Every interaction between IT and the business is an opportunity to serve. The reputation and success of the IT organization is built on service. The most effective and efficient way to monitor, manage and improve upon that service is through problem management. I recommend an iterative process for building this capability.

Again simply buying a solution or appointing someone a guardian of the process does not solve the problem.

As with project management there is a primary need to match problem management to the maturity of the organization. The truth is that neither the tool nor the person responsible solves problem management. The process is the key. The challenge is to select the problem management methodology and to gain acceptance and use of that methodology. The best tool or methodology provides absolutely no value if it is not embraced and used. The worst tool provides some value even if it is just sparingly used.

Most IT departments want no part of formal problem management. Unjustifiably, they feel that it will add time and expense to providing service and support and that the business will not suffer the formality. This may be partially true in smaller SMBs but does not negate the need. It becomes less true as the SMB grows and matures. The trick is to select the appropriate methodology at the appropriate time and get it implemented. In the early stages of the life of the business the methodology needs to be built in an iterative fashion. Jumping into a full blown methodology will be fruitless. I recommend starting with a well defined manual process and adding formality and structure a little at a time. Over time add steps, tools, formality and measurements. Build the process in an iterative fashion and buy an appropriate software solution. Do not build one from scratch. Using my three business strategies as a format, I can describe the creation and evolution of the problem management methodology as a series of iterative steps.

## B. Simplified Problem Management and the Business Layer Strategy

### 1. Start with the crawl-walk-run approach

Please refer to the section on project management and the Appendices 10-2 and 10-3 where this approach is discussed.

### 2. Define the "as is" existing manual process

Start by understanding the nature of the service and support issues and find out where they originate. Most likely there are informal modes of communication. Business users and business leaders usually have contacts within IT that they call upon when something is broken or when someone has a question. This is usually done through a telephone call or an email. Most of the issues are not urgent but each will be treated as such as long as the informal method of handling the issue is allowed. A good first step is to meet with the IT staff to document their business contacts and the nature of the calls. It will be difficult to break some of the informal bonds. You will be forced to break the habits of both the users and the IT staff. Users like to feel special and do not understand the need for the process. They also will not like the delay inherent in a new process for addressing non-urgent issues. The IT staff member may derive a lot of job satisfaction from solving these issues. It will be necessary to educate the IT staff on the reasons for the problem approach and the cost justification for doing it. This is cultural change and should not be underestimated.

3.  **Define the "to be" target state**

Begin with the end in mind. Take the pains to lay out an ideal process. Agree to begin the actual work process somewhere and build upon it. You will never get it right the first time. It will take refinement. Please refer to Appendix 11-1 for a sample ideal process that may well be adopted. The "to be" state in the business layer strategy is no where near this complex and is necessarily a crude one. Work toward this goal within this strategy. It is important that all problems at this early stage and going forward are first, formally identified and second, registered in a work ticket system as a problem work ticket. Try this as a beginning "to be" state.
  - User calls the service desk
  - Service desk opens a work ticket
  - Service desk assigns the work ticket to a work group
  - Work group member accepts work ticket
  - Work group member performs work on the work ticket
  - Work group member closes ticket
  - Work group member calls service desk with resolution
  - Service desk calls user with resolution

4.  **Start with a simple electronic form**

Do not rush out to buy a software ticketing system. Get the process right first. Start with a simple electronic form that can be attached to an email and kept is some sort of folder or filing system. There are a myriad of choices for electronic forms. The Forms feature in Outlook is fine and even a Word document will work. You just need something that is in a standard format that can be searched and categorized. The catchphrase here is: The simpler the better.

5.  **Work on an early classification system and multiple processes**

All work needs to be classified from a priority perspective since all work should not be addressed the minute it is identified or requested. Some problems and work requests must take priority over others. Start with a simple urgent/non-urgent classification system that can be expanded over time. Resolve to work on all urgent tickets immediately and the non-urgent tickets as time allows. Have one work flow for urgent and one for non-urgent. Attempt to prioritize the tickets within the two classifications by some set of factors. These factors might include impact on revenue, impact on the greatest number of users, impact on specific clients or some other classification. There needs to be a solid rationale for putting first things first. Define the processes in detail for each classification and publish this to the business. The business needs to know and understand how work gets done.

6.  **Make some one responsible**

It will be difficult in smaller SMBs to cost justify and hire an employee who just handles work tickets and problems. It may be necessary at first to just make an existing employee the traffic cop for tickets. This employee has two primary responsibilities. The first is to enter the work tickets or to assure that work tickets get entered for all work. The second is to dole out the work tickets to the support groups and to follow up on the tickets to make sure all problems get addressed. This will be a difficult part time task for a department administrative person or an entry level IT person but it must be done. Without this structure and methodology the IT support will not improve. Making someone, often anyone, responsible is a positive step forward.

7.  **Find a way to document and act on what you are learning**

On a regular basis, weekly or every other week, hold a ticket review meeting or luncheon. The goal will be to review the problems for a given time period and see what you can learn from them. The employee responsible for the work tickets will need to perform some preparatory work by compiling and categorizing the work tickets. The mandate is to identify two to three actionable items from each meeting that will both improve IT customer service and eliminate some volume of recurring problems. Actionable items may include replacing a bad piece of hardware, providing training on a product or system, standardizing a component on the desktop or even removing a capability that is being abused. The important thing is to use the ticket data to make service improvements.

8.  **Develop a rudimentary service flow**

As with any process approach, documentation is critical. Using MS Visio or a similar charting tool, define and document the service flow. The problem management service flow needs to be tightly defined and administered. Follow the flow religiously to improve the chances for success. Over time add to the service flow as you refine and improve your internal processes. This flow is the building block for the next two strategy steps.

## C. Simplified Problem Management and the Business Model Strategy

1.  **Continue the crawl-walk-run approach**

The SMB should now be "walking" with the problem management process and picking up momentum.

2.  **Select a tool and automate**

a.  **Figure out what was learned from the manual process**

The SMB is now outgrowing the manual electronic forms approach and will benefit from having an automated tool. Take the time to document what was learned from the manual process in terms of process, procedures and handling. These will become key requirements in the software selection process. Review the way problem tickets have been classified and routed. Determine the type and level of detail information required to make the process work. Lastly, make sure that your service flow is as solid and error free as possible. Handling the service flow will become a tool requirement as well.

### b. Build requirements and reporting needs

Any problem ticketing system or tool should provide a work ticket data repository, a basic work flow tool and some rudimentary reporting capabilities. Not all tools are created equal. Develop solid requirements and go through a normal software package evaluation and selection process. Please refer to Chapter 13 for a recommended approach. The better job you do of requirements the better the package will work for you.

### c. Select a simple frills free application

There are numerous options for work ticket or helpdesk software applications. The SMB does not have to spend a lot of money for an appropriate solution. There are freeware and shareware options. There are some very powerful and low end products that are well worth the expenditure. I have had great success with Track-It but there are many other choices as well. The key factor, as with any software, is to assure the package will handle the defined process and the identified requirements.

### d. Implement the application

Selecting, buying and installing a problem management package should go very quickly. There is not all that much to do. Simply compare requirements to the product capability. Make sure the package is mature and that the vendor is going to be around for awhile. When implementing the package it may be worth the effort to load past ticket history into the new system. This is a judgment call that must be made. If the problem history appears to have value it may be worth the effort. Do not be afraid to start fresh.

## 3. Add a full time resource

It is now appropriate to add a fulltime employee dedicated to problem ticket handling and the resulting service delivery. During implementation of the business layer strategy, this role will have grown until it has become a challenge for a single employee to handle on a part time basis. The ideal candidate for this role will be an IT knowledgeable individual with a working knowledge of IT terminology. The candidate also needs great administrative and task management skills. In addition, solid communication skills and customer service experience are a must. This is a key role and should not be staffed lightly. Strong business knowledge and an in-depth understanding of how the SMB works are also highly desirable.

### 4.  Structure ticket handling for learning

One of the biggest challenges will be to structure both the ticket handling process and the application data capture to provide the right information. This may not happen right away. It may take a series of adjustments. In addition to handling the immediate problem and providing prompt service to the business, the other goal in the problem management process is to learn. This learning should encompass broad trends and issues as well as specific recurring problems and weaknesses. By this I mean the SMB must start with a solid idea about what needs to be learned and then structure the process, the ticket, the data gathering and the data handling to assure that the proper information is captured. For example, perhaps IT suspects that the desk top is the primary inhibitor to stabilizing the infrastructure. In order to prove this theory, make sure that the "desktop" is captured as the primary ticket category. Make sure that the various and proper sub-categories like "operating system" or "layered software" are captured as well. Based on the number of tickets and the cost to the business of lost productivity, IT can make a business case for actions like pushing out common images, tightening down the desktop controls and disallowing employees from bringing in software from home. The tickets can support and justify the specific measures that need taken.

### 5.  Develop service level agreements based on ticket classification

More formality is now appropriate. Develop a service level agreement approach to handling problem tickets. Develop an expanded ticket classification system. Establish minimum times to start working on an issue. Establish ticket update guidelines to keep everyone in the loop and up to date on progress.

First, expand the simple urgent/non-urgent approach to now include something like the following classifications:
- Urgent
- High
- Medium
- Standard

Establish a service level agreement that the ticket will be worked within a specific time frame. No one can reasonably commit to fixing or resolving a ticket in a specific time frame. You can, however, agree to address it by beginning work on it within a specific time frame. For example, try committing to the following:
- Urgent - will begin work immediately
- High - will begin work in two to four hours
- Medium - will begin work within one to three days
- Standard - will begin work within one week

This time commitment requires more frequent ticket entries. The employee must formally accept responsibility for the ticket within the appropriate time frame in order to track service levels. Then, to improve the communications on ticket progress with the business, the employee must add ticket updates on an established schedule.

- Urgent - update the ticket with progress once hourly
- High - update the ticket with progress every two hours
- Medium - update the ticket with progress every day
- Standard - update the ticket with progress every week

The ticket is naturally closed when the issue is resolved. The ticket updates can be used to track elapsed time to resolve the ticket and whether you are meeting or missing the service level agreements.

### 6. Include service measurements in IT score cards

A major component of any IT score card becomes the performance against the service level agreements. By the way, any vendors performing outsourced services need to be managed in much the same way. Please refer to Chapter 14 on vendor relationship management for a suggested approach. The IT score card should be a self imposed way to objectively measure IT performance. The performance against service level agreements should account for between twenty five percent and fifty percent of the department's performance measures.

## D. Simplified Problem Management and the Business Process Strategy

### 1. Continue the crawl-walk-run approach

The SMB should now be "running" with the problem management process and seeing vastly improved customer service.

### 2. Hire dedicated helpdesk/service desk employees

As the SMB moves through the strategies, the staffing requirements for problem management have gone from a part time resource to a dedicated fulltime resource. Now it requires several fulltime resources. The growth of the problem management process now requires a formal service desk to manage it. This is an evolutionary process. It is time to hire dedicated career service desk employees. They may be experienced employees who are dedicated to the craft or career IT employees using the service desk experience as a stepping stone into a second level support or engineering position. My experience is that the strength of IT can be measured by the strength of the service desk. They become the communication link with the business and the voice of IT. Invest in the service desk to ensure success.

### 3. Develop an enhanced service flow

By now the service flow needs to be exhaustively defined. You should have sections on problem ticket escalation to include the following.
- First level support - The Service Desk should be handling as many calls and tickets

as possible and focusing on speed to answer and first call resolution.

- Second level support - Dedicated support technicians in all technology areas should be committed to problem resolution. The goal should be to handle every ticket that the service desk cannot handle and avoid sending tickets on to the engineering groups.
- Third level support - Dedicated engineers should handle only the most complex and troubling tickets that the first two levels cannot handle.

The service flow needs to include off-hour coverage and work ticket escalation procedures. The business user should know the process and know what to expect. The business user should also have an escalation path should the issue not be resolved to their satisfaction. The service flow needs to include rotating on call coverage with monitored path ways. The process should now be ironclad and error free.

### 4. Begin an "IT as a service organization" marketing campaign

IT management is notoriously bad at marketing their services and contributions to the business. The service desk presents a powerful opportunity to market IT as a service organization. I recommend sending repeated email and other communications to the business touting creation of the service desk, details on how it works and the benefits to the organization. Internally IT management needs to prove how problem solving is more cost effective using the service desk approach. This can be easily accomplished by showing the cost to solve an issue at the service desk on a first call basis measured against the cost of sending the issue to a high powered highly compensated engineer. This marketing effort should be basically a marketing campaign and I have seen IT leadership tap the marketing expertise within the business. What better way to enhance the department image then to enlist the support of the marketing department?

### 5. Move up to the next generation of ticket management application

It now becomes appropriate and often necessary to move on to the next generation of work ticket and problem management application. This move may not be required but it should at least be considered. The work ticket system now becomes an enterprise wide resource. Business users will need access to the system and taught how to use it. Some of the smaller applications used during the previous strategy may not scale effectively. The SMB needs to go through the same structured approach as was used to select the first tool and used to purchase all applications. Please see Chapter 13 for that methodology. Many of the enterprise solutions include interesting add-on components that can support processes like purchasing or change management. These should be considered.

### 6. Link problem management and change management

Whether you accomplish this manually or through the application tool a critical next step is to link the problem management process to the change management process. In

IT departments where an enterprise wide tool is used it is easy to channel all requests for changes and enhancements through the ticketing system. In those cases the relevant information about the ticket, and subsequently about the required change to the production environment, is in your ticketing system. It becomes easy to take the next step and link to the change management process. This provides a systemic way to like problem resolution with required changes. Please refer to Chapter 12 for a simple straightforward and effective approach to change management.

7.  **Link problem management into the organization structure**

Please refer to Chapter 8 on organization structure and the service organization. Problem management is a crucial component of organizing the IT department with a service approach. The department goal will be to resolve as many problems as possible at the service desk. Then the goal becomes resolving as many problems as possible at the second support level. Avoid using third level support engineers if at all possible. As far as service desk personnel, there needs to be a career path for the service desk associates to move up through second level support and eventually into the engineering disciplines. They become better employees because they understand the business, the user community and how technology is used. The tactics of problem management are an integral part of the organization and service tactics and these two process components need to support each other.

8.  **Use ticket statistics to drive day-to-day priorities**

As previously discussed, IT needs to hold periodic and frequent work ticket problem reviews. These reviews need to focus on the types and volumes of tickets. The goal is to find actionable items to reduce the work ticket volume and improve IT service to the business. This can drive the day-to-day priorities for the various groups. There are numerous examples of what might be found. One of the biggest time wasters for the service desk will likely be user access and passwords. By analyzing the number and nature of these work tickets, the IT department can come up with tactics and solutions to clean up and automate the user administration and password administration components. For software applications it may be as simple as identifying the trouble spots within applications and working with in house staff or vendors to clean up the code or the processing. For infrastructure there may be performance or response time issues. The ticket history can assist in problem resolution by isolating time of day and tasks being performed. This allows the infrastructure support team to focus their efforts on resolution. The work ticket system will be a gold mine of information. Service can be vastly improved by paying close attention to this data.

9.  **Use ticket statistics to drive projects**

As with day-to-day priorities, the work ticket reviews will also identify larger projects that need to be done. These may be infrastructure or applications. The work tickets will reveal opportunities for improving work efficiencies and reducing costs. I cannot emphasize enough the importance of mining the work ticket data to improve both the performance and reputation of IT.

## E. Summary

The approach described in this chapter can make the difference between a successful IT department and a failure. It can make the difference between IT leadership keeping their jobs and being forced to move on. The approach is a common sense battle tested iterative approach that works. It has deep ramifications for employee roles and responsibilities. It does require organizational changes to be successful. Execution of these tactics may vary based on the maturity, challenges and demands of any particular SMB. It is safe to conclude, however, that any SMB that fails to focus on the problem management process will fail.

## Simplified Change Management

> ### WISDOM to work by:
>
> 1. <u>*Manage change or it will manage you.*</u>
>    *Ignore structured change management at great risk*
> 2. <u>*There is no one size that fits all.*</u>
>    *As with project and problem management match the change management solution to the maturity of the organization.*
> 3. <u>*Don't build it right the first time.*</u>
>    *Consider the crawl-walk-run approach to developing change management.*
> 4. <u>*Begin with the end in mind.*</u>
>    *Define your target state for change management and work to get there.*
> 5. <u>*Use an iterative approach.*</u>
>    *There are no quick fixes and no way to jump on a moving train. Start with a rough approach, any approach, and improve it again and again.*
> 6. <u>*Process, process, process.*</u>
>    *This simplified change management methodology is a recipe for stability and availability.*
> 7. <u>*Production is king.*</u>
>    *Build a wall around your production computing systems to protect the business.*
> 8. <u>*Give them a voice.*</u>
>    *Get the business involved in change management.*
> 9. <u>*Learn something.*</u>
>    *Use the change management experience to learn what is not working and fix it.*

## A. Introduction

The secret to change management in the SMB is to match the change methodology to the maturity of the organization. Many organizations ignore change management entirely or take a casual ad hoc approach. Most SMBs want no part of formal change management. These are dangerous precedents to set. Change management is a process and one that should not be ignored. The process is the key. The challenge is to select the appropriate change management methodology and to gain acceptance and use of that methodology. The best tool or methodology provides absolutely no value if it is not embraced and used. The worst tool provides some value even if it is just sparingly used. Below is the "to be" process as we again begin with the end in mind.

1. **What is the process?**

    The change management process is a series of written procedures that must be followed to make a change to the production computing environment. It requires that a technician submit a change request to a change committee before a technician can implement a change. The change committee must approve the change before it can be implemented. The technician must develop for the change committee certain critical information before the change request can be submitted. This information includes the following:
    - Description of change
    - Completion success criteria
    - Business impact
    - Technology impact
    - Risk analysis
    - Pre-work description
    - Contingency plans

    The change committee can reject or reschedule a change.

2. **What is the goal?**

    The goal is to provide a stable and reliable production computing environment. The change management process was developed to accomplish the following:
    - Develop the concept of a production computing environment
    - Define the production computing environment
    - Install boundaries around the production computing environment
    - Control and manage change to the production computing environment
    - Provide a high availability production computing environment

3. **What are the features and benefits?**

    The primary features and benefits of this process include the following:
    - Reduce technology downtime
    - Reduce the episodes of erratic and irregular behavior of technology
    - High availability technology
    - Reliable technology
    - Predictable technology
    - Reduce service desk work tickets
    - Reduce emergency changes
    - Eliminate the installation of untested or poorly tested changes

    As with project management, jumping into a full blown change management methodology will be fruitless. I recommend starting with rough informal steps and adding formality and structure a little at a time. For example, I recommend starting with a simple one page word document to register the change. There is no review and no examination. Over time, add steps for change review and approval, publishing change schedules, conducting post change reviews and so on. Build the change tools in an iterative fashion. Using my three business strategies as a format, I will describe the creation and evolution of the change management methodology as a series of iterative steps.

# B. Change Management and the Business Layer Strategy

As I recommend above, the change management methodology that will work best when the SMB is using the Business Layer Strategy is necessarily brief and fairly informal. It needs to lay the foundation for change management in a solid way so that the SMB can build on it as it grows. I will outline the methodology as a series of steps that should be followed in order to develop a structured change management approach. Remember to not get hung up on tools and technologies. The simpler the better here.

I am a proponent of the Franklin Covey methodology which promotes to begin with the end in mind. I say that because the SMB should have a target methodology defined from the beginning and all work on methodology is done to arrive at that target state. This target state, as defined in Appendix 12-1, is a sample entire change management process in one document. Please review it briefly before continuing. Here are the iterative steps I recommend for the Business Layer Strategy.

## 1. Identify and list the production computing systems

The concept of the production computing environment is not a fine line definition but a distinct way to identify the systems that the SMB depends upon in order to do business. It necessarily includes the infrastructure, back office and customer facing systems. The list is the basis for all change management activities. Any changes to any of these systems must go through the change control process. Production computing systems are the heart blood of the organization. The goal needs to be to have one hundred percent system availability for all of these systems. The SMB needs to develop a protective attitude about production computing systems, and in order to do so, must recognize them.

## 2. Draw an imaginary boundary around the production computing systems

I recommend that the IT leadership draw an imaginary boundary around all production computing systems and send the message that these are not to be tampered with. It might be worth the time, energy and trouble to freeze the production computing environment for a set period of time as you begin down the change management path. This would set the tone for the effort and reinforce the concept of the production computing systems. In many SMBs there are no restraints on access and no restrictions on modifications. I have seen system administrators make changes to production systems in the middle of the day with disastrous results. My favorite phrases from the systems groups are "This won't affect anything else." closely followed by "I didn't think this would affect anything else!" as the system is crashing down around our knees. The message here is that production is golden. Any and all changes to production, no matter how small, will be managed and monitored.

### 3. Define an initial change management form

The purpose of the initial change management form is to add formality to change. The content of the form is not as critical as the fact that a form must be filled out. For those of you from the 1970s, this is what Marshall McLuhan meant when he said that the medium is the message. The form is what is important. It reinforces the concept of a boundary around production and the need to manage change. I have attached a form and instructions for filling it out as Appendix 12-2. Take the most critical and easy to fill out components from this master form and create a simple initial change form.

### 4. Publish a change calendar

The next step is to create a change calendar is some shared space where both IT and the business can view scheduled changes to the production environment. The business users will find it convenient to schedule their work around these upgrades and changes. They can also have a heightened awareness for anomalies and be on the lookout for unanticipated changes in the presentation layer or in basic functionality. When software applications change, the IT systems staff can monitor for changes in disk usage, CPU usage, batch production run times or system response times. The IT application groups can monitor application performance more closely when there are changes to core infrastructure. In all cases, merely communicating change throughout the organization makes trouble shooting and problem resolution much clearer and eliminates much of the confusion that can arise. Everyone knows that you look at what has changed when you are trying to identify the source of a new problem. Use the corporate intranet or some other tool like Sharepoint to make the change calendar available to everyone.

### 5. Make communication a major objective

If nothing else is accomplished in change management during execution of the business layer strategy but improved communication, then you have succeeded. This communication should consist of the concepts that there is a production computing environment, that the environment must be protected, and that all change will be registered on a change form and communicated throughout the organization. This is a great start and probably requires a cultural shift. Future steps can easily be added to control change, monitor change, and prevent service interruptions by poorly planned and executed changes.

### 6. Begin to address back-out plans

One additional step that may be attempted during the business layer strategy is the addition of back-out plans. Back-out plans contain the steps that the change engineer will take when something does not go as planned during the change installation. My experience with infrastructure engineering is that they know how to do a specific upgrade or enhancement but will not plan the activities in any detail. They go into the change window without proper planning and figure things out on the fly. They are usually successful anyway due to technical experience and technical competence. Sometimes though the lack of planning does result in a failure to accomplish the change. More often the engineer may not accomplish the task in the dedicated time frame. Without proper planning, engineers may use gut feeling to estimate the time needed and often times miscalculate. The engineer gets into a change exercise and finds it cannot be completed before the system is scheduled to be made available again. Without back-out plans the engineer just keeps slogging through the work until it is done. By forcing the engineer to document and discuss back-out plans the engineer is forced to consider their tactical approach to the upgrade. They are forced to abort the upgrade or change when a certain critical time factor is reached. This time limit forces rigidity on the process and requires presenting the system back to the users at a prescribed time. This allows the change committee to avoid negative impacts on business productivity.

## C. Change Management and the Business Model Strategy

As the business grows and changes, it moves from the business layer strategy to the business model strategy. The change management process must also keep pace. Remember the crawl-walk-run approach used for the simplified project management and simplified problem management processes. We should be "walking" with change management by this time. Here are the additional formalization steps and structure that are recommended for this strategy.

### 1. Appoint a change administrator

As with problem management someone needs to be held responsible for change administration. Start out with an administrative or clerical resource and slowly migrate this to the service desk personnel. Work begins as an administrative chore to keep track of the changes and keep the change calendar updated. Over time the change administrator becomes responsible for tracking and managing the entire change management process and scheduling the change committee meetings.

### 2. Create a change control committee

Creating a change control committee is another important step in the evolution of change management. The change control committee will review all change management forms and will be responsible for the approval or rejection of submitted change requests. The forms will need to be reviewed prior to a regularly scheduled meeting. The IT committee should include representation from the infrastructure and engineering groups, the application software group, the service desk, systems administration and senior IT leadership. The chairperson needs to be the most senior IT leader available who can preside over the meetings of the change control committee. The chairperson will have ultimate authority over requested changes in both normal and emergency situations. The committee becomes the vehicle for managing change within the IT organization.

### 3.  Introduce a review and approval step

The change committee now has control over the change process. They must review and approve all changes. The purpose of the review is to evoke discussion about the change and to create a change dialogue. The application changes need discussed in depth. Discuss such topics as testing procedures, magnitude of the change, the impact on the database and the potential impact on production performance. All potential production impacts should be explored and discussed. The infrastructure changes also require review and approval. All interested parties must be informed and discussion will center on back-out procedures and the possible impacts or production outages. These reviews should be expanded to include a detailed plan from the engineers describing exactly what will be done and in what sequence. The first few of these reviews will be a real treat for the organization.

### 4.  Hold a change management meeting

Hold a change management meeting once a week at the same place and time. Do it early in the week on Monday if possible. Stage the changes into production such that unanticipated results can be quickly attributed to a single change. Avoid changing multiple interleaved technologies at the same time and you will be able to avoid creating an unsolvable problem for yourself. I always recommend changing only one thing at one time if at all possible. Have regularly scheduled days for the different types of changes if possible. Please refer to Appendix 12-3 for a change management schedule that can easily be customized for your use. For example, change all back office applications on a Monday night and all networking components on Wednesdays. Try to avoid application software changes on Fridays since it may be hard to reach support personnel on a weekend. The goal here is moderation in change. Control change so that unanticipated problems are kept to a minimum and are easily corrected. Trouble shooting becomes more manageable and limited in scope. You will need an emergency change management process as well. This is discussed below.

### 5.  Improve the change management form

By this time you will have outgrown the initial change management form and you will need to improve it. The additional details required have already been discussed above. Add the items to the form that support the enhanced procedures that you have put into place. Insist on the back-out plan, a fairly detailed explanation of the engineer's plan, the testing that was done by the application group or the vendor and the possible impacts on the production process. Please refer again to Appendix 12-2. The approach, again, is for iterative change. Improving this form is but one component of continual process improvement.

## D. Change Management and the Business Process Strategy

The business process strategy is implemented when the organization grows to a size and complexity that former business processes no longer work. By this time the organization is usually ripe with inefficiencies. The change process now needs to be formally documented and distributed. It needs to become part of the organization's foundation and basically institutionalized. We should be "running" with change management by this time.

## 1. Document and publicize the change management process

Please refer to Appendix 12-1 for the entire change management process defined in one document. Feel free to use this process as is or modify it to suit your particular organizational needs. The purpose here is to document the change management process and distribute it to the entire organization. It needs to become a foundational document for the IT department. The IT department needs to gain some excellent publicity from it. Include it in any company or departmental publications or newsletters. Try to find ways to publicize the lack of service outages because the process works so well. This is a powerful process. It exhibits elements of sophistication and maturity such that it should become a focal point, not only within IT, but throughout the SMB.

## 2. Create an emergency change process

One of the weaknesses of any change management process will be the business imperative for immediate change. Do not allow this need to derail the core change management process. Please do not confuse production fixes with emergency changes. Production fixes just need to happen. No change management process needs to be invoked. Paper work documenting the fix needs to be prepared. The emergency change is reserved for those production changes that are driven by the business or by a client. These changes cannot wait until the next committee meeting or scheduled implementation time. This emergency change management process is given as part of Appendix 12-1. An emergency change must be approved by the change committee chairperson or another IT leader high enough in the organization to make that decision. This would normally include managers of infrastructure, back office and customer facing applications for their own particular areas of expertise. An emergency change still requires a form but it is reviewed and approved by a committee of one. It can be put into the production environment immediately. Please do not allow an emergency change to go into production and create availability or service issues. The same amount of care, attention and testing must go into an emergency change. Do not forget to publicize the emergency change so that IT and the business can be aware of the impact and any possible ramifications.

## 3. Solicit business participation

A novel but effective twist to change management is to include the affected department management of the various operational and business departments in the change management process. This can be accomplished by inviting them to the change committee meeting whenever some component of their support infrastructure or applications is being changed. You can grant them rights of approval, rejection or rescheduling. This involvement is a tremendous team building vehicle. One difficulty may be getting a time commitment from the business leader. If they will commit to participation you can avoid scheduling changes at the more risky times for the business. For example, if month end processing is critical to the back office then changes to back office applications or infrastructure should not be changed within a designated month end window. The business users I have seen involved find this participation valuable. They also greatly appreciate the ability to participate in the decision making process.

### 4.  Implement a post change review step

For what I like to call icing on the cake, nothing beats a post change review step. This can be part of the normal change management committee meeting, scheduled as a separate event, or as part of a normal weekly management meeting. The necessary information is included as part of the change form. The focus will be on those exceptions which are the unsuccessful changes. These should not be finger pointing sessions or sessions to assess blame. These are opportunities to improve the process. The opportunity may include the need to improve documentation, improve communication between groups, more rigid testing procedures, or more formalized change planning. You will learn more from one aborted change than from ten successful ones. You will be paying the price with a service outage.

### 5.  Link change management to problem management

As the process matures, and as recommended in the simplified problem management process, strive to link the problem management process to the change management process. If IT is using work tickets to track problems, projects and activities, then it is an easy and natural extension to allow the work ticket system to generate a change management request when the ticket is marked completed. This can be done automatically by any solid work ticket system. The results of the change management approval and installation processes can be captured back in the work ticket system. This gives a complete view of the work from beginning to end.

### 6.  Use change management as a learning process

For the change management process or any other process, an ongoing exercise should be to look at the process from beginning to end and make improvements to it. Complete process documentation is important. All forms and templates need to be firmly defined. The best way I know to improve overall IT performance is through process improvement. This is especially true for change management. The post change review is one good way to integrate an ongoing learning process. There needs to be other institutionalized ways as well. These might include the need for more formality in planning, testing and implementation. The lessons learned from the process need to be leveraged.

# E.  Summary

Pardon the cliché, but manage change or it will manage you. The IT department will benefit more from this common tactic than from any other except possibly project management. I have instituted change management in several companies. It always leads to technology stability and reliability. Those SMBs that take change management lightly or refuse to manage change with a structured process approach will forever suffer from service disruptions and service outages. Unfortunately the SMB cannot always trust the judgment of the individual IT department members when it comes to production environment changes. Nothing reflects so poorly on IT as service outages and service interruptions.

## Package Evaluation and Selection

**WISDOM to work by:**

1. *Process, process, process!*
   This package evaluation and selection process is a winner.
2. *Wait, wait don't call.*
   Don't just pick up the phone and call a vendor. Stick to the selection process. It works.
3. *Don't fall for the "it worked there" approach.*
   Don't let employee experiences from other companies taint your package selection process.
4. *Don't make that mistake.*
   Avoid making the two major package selection mistakes. Don't ignore solution scope and don't ignore requirements.
5. *Manage your vendors or they will manage you.*
   You must exercise strict control over the package evaluation and selection process.
6. *Make the numbers work for you.*
   Develop selection criteria and a numerical scoring system.

## A. Introduction

In my experience, this is the area that most SMBs fail miserably time after time after time. The most common mistake is jumping to a solution. Under the guise of research, many SMBs jump right to the telephone and call a vendor. That is basically asking them to sell you their solution. I have never seen a vendor refuse to sell the SMB anything so once that first call is made, all process goes out the window. My advice would be to simply stop. Don't pick up the phone! Buying the wrong software application is a critical and costly mistake. It can be avoided! Contained within this chapter are some very simple but effective tools and techniques for doing package evaluation and selection. This chapter alone is worth the cost of this book. Despite the misgivings of any SMB, buying a package does not have to be a long drawn out bureaucratic process. Structure and methodology does slow the process down...not much, but in a good way. A solid process can save an incredible amount of lost time and money. The SMB needs to slow down, spend some quality time and get it right.

Another common mistake in many SMBs is to buy a package based on the recommendation of a single employee. In this case, one employee with previous package experience or exposure drives the selection process. The SMB buys the back office package that someone on the accounting or finance team has used at some other company. The SMB buys some customer facing application because a member of the sales or marketing team knows of a competitor who uses it. This approach seldom works. Each business is different. Each business has gone about solving their technology and business problems in different ways. What works for other companies or at other companies in back office or customer facing applications may not necessarily work at your company. Each SMB should strive to standardize and homogenize the back office application software components. This standardization will be limited, however, by other factors. These include the pre-existing suite of tools, the existing infrastructure and the required interfaces. These factors play a major role in the selection process.

## B. The Process

Here is the recommended process for package evaluation and selection. I have included a full set of package evaluation and selection templates and some examples as Appendices 13-1, 13-2, 13-3 and 13-4. Ignore any of these steps and you increase the risk for failure.

- Define business and technical requirements
- Scope the initiative
- Prepare a package evaluation summary in the form of a request for information (RFI)
- Conduct an initial search and identify all potential candidate solutions
- Conduct initial research (buy reports)
- Eliminate all but the top four to six candidates
- Send out the RFI
- Evaluate the RFI responses
- Narrow the candidate solutions to three to four
- Schedule and conduct vendor product presentations
- Encourage written vendor questions and deliver responses
- Conduct vendor client visits and demonstrations
- Develop final selection criteria
- Map selection criteria to vendors and solutions
- Make selection
- Conduct contract negotiations
- Purchase
- Install

### 1. Define business and technical requirements

This is the step that I generally see skipped. It is the most important step in the entire process. What is the SMB trying to accomplish? If you don't know where you are going, then any road will do. If you don't document and agree upon your business and technical requirements, then on the surface any package will work for you. But it won't! You might satisfy some of the high level requirements but the package solution will surely miss the mark. An excellent way to document these requirements is through an RFI (request for information) or an RFP (request for proposal). A project charter and scope document may be substituted in a smaller project. The goal of any of these documents is to define what the vendors will need to know to understand your challenges, to provide a template for your business and technical requirements and to define how you are going to meet them.

## 2.   Define scope

The scoping exercise is critical to the entire selection process. The SMB can solve a specific business challenge or a whole series of challenges with a given solution. By this statement I mean that the selection process can simply focus on a single problem area or on several problem areas simultaneously. For example, the business may attempt to fix the problems with paying sales commissions. Conversely, sales commissions are a part of most back office application suites and can be included in a larger more comprehensive back office solution. The SMB can buy a single sales commission point solution or look at a broader array of solutions to solve interrelated problems as well.

Vendors do not share a cohesive view of how any particular SMB works. Instead, they have developed their own view and have built and tailored their solutions to meet that view. If the SMB does not share or closely align with that view, the solutions offered by the vendor may be less than applicable. The scoping exercise puts bounds on what solution sets will be considered and what the SMB wishes to accomplish. Please refer to Chapter 3, Section C where I discuss the scoping exercise in great detail.

## 3.   Prepare a package evaluation summary in the form of an RFI

Remember that the purpose of the RFI is to both summarize the package evaluation effort and to solicit feedback and information from potential vendors about their solutions. As with any recommend process in this book, try to keep the document as brief yet comprehensive as possible. Try selecting the most critical components from the list below. Please refer to Appendix 13-2 for a workable template.
   - Company overview (include basic revenue and market information)
   - Project overview
   - Project background and details
   - Project scope
   - Project purpose
   - Project objectives
   - Project benefits
   - Project requirements
   - Business requirements
   - Technical requirements
   - System interfaces
   - The request for information or proposal itself
   - Purpose of the request
   - Response and evaluation schedule

- Evaluation criteria
- Evaluation process
- Response instructions
- Confidentiality
- Disclaimers and disclosures

A couple of comments about the RFI are warranted. The point here is that you have taken control of the project and the process while denying that control to a vendor. You have also answered many if not all of the questions that the vendors are going to ask. You have done it once all in one place. This act alone saves an incredible amount of project time and speeds up the selection process. Last, and most critically, you have defined what you are going to accomplish.

## 4. Conduct an initial search and identify all potential candidate solutions

There are numerous compiled lists of solutions available for any back office suite or of tools for building customer facing ones. Most IT and business publications run these lists periodically. They are basically a pick list of the available package solutions and vendors. Importantly, they are usually segmented by company or market size so you do not waste time and energy on Fortune 500 appropriate solutions. If you are looking for back office accounting applications try the publications targeted for the accounting or finance groups. If you are looking for generic back office tools like fax servers, try the office management publications for office or building services. It may take a little effort.  You do ensure that you are not leaving out a key potential solution. The goal is to start the process with the known available universe of solutions for your particular business problem. There are numerous publications and websites targeted at IT professionals that build and maintain these lists. They are the natural starting point for the package selection exercise.

It is always important at this juncture to include any recommendations from internal employees. To be a candidate these should be included on the appropriate resource list and fit roughly within the initial screening parameters. This assures the input and participation of the business in the process.

## 5. Conduct initial research (buy reports)

This is another critical step that is often ignored. It includes reading periodicals, researching potential solutions and buying product comparisons. Product comparisons show functions and features of all products in an application space but do not make package recommendations. The SMB must still match their specific requirements to the strengths and weaknesses of the package solutions to select the most appropriate ones. These reports do make the job much easier to accomplish. One of the hidden responsibilities of any IT organization should be research on package solutions. One member of the team needs to take responsibility for knowing what products play in the relevant market spaces and what the competition is doing in regards to software applications solutions. Obviously the internet is the place to start. Research should be done in a structured and repetitive manner.

### 6.  Eliminate all but the top four to six candidates

Use your initial research to narrow the field of potential solutions to a manageable number. You can not thoroughly research and fully comprehend all of the available solutions. Focus on the most appropriate ones. Your initial research should consist of matching your business and technical requirements to the strengths and weaknesses of the solutions and selecting the ones that appear to be the most closely attuned. This underscores the importance of clear and concise business requirements. It also allows you to use your strategic drivers as a way to assure the packages are consistent with your strategy. Please reread the sections on strategic drivers and apply these to your selection process.

### 7.  Send out the RFI

Now send out the RFI to the top four to six candidates. Just an aside here, I prefer an RFI to an RFP since an RFP usually brings the process right away down to pricing. While pricing is important and must be addressed, you are more concerned at this juncture about functionality and fit. When you distribute the RFI, be sure to provide rigid guidelines for both delivery of the written responses and how the vendors can ask questions. I recommend a brief period later in this process where vendors can submit written questions. The SMB answers all questions in written form and copies the questions and responses to all vendors. This eliminates the one on one selling that all vendors strive for and keeps them from wasting your time trying to establish a sales relationship. If the SMB does not go the RFI route, then all research must be done in sort of a vacuum. This is much more difficult to do. I recommend the RFI approach.

### 8.  Evaluate the RFI responses

I find it valuable to have a small committee appointed to evaluate the vendor responses. This approach usually instigates some good discussions and allows for a more critical evaluation process. One critical component of the RFI should be not only to ask the vendors whether they can handle a specific requirement, but to also ask how it is done. This is the telling factor. If the response is that the requirement is handled by the application as part of the core functionality, then the requirement is met. If the response is some sort of modification, change or work around then the requirement is not going to be met. The RFI response should give the SMB a "feel" for how the application is constructed and how data is kept and organized. A quick comparison of the RFI responses should enable the SMB to eliminate several from the competition. Again the SMB is driving the process and the time lines.

Do not be surprised if one or more of the vendors fails to respond to the RFI. They may feel they do not want to expend the effort to reply or do not want to participate in a sales process that they cannot control. I weed out these vendors immediately and I do not take telephone calls from them. I see it as them trying to subvert the process. Expect less than a one hundred percent response, but rest assured that those vendors who do respond are going to be better to work with over time.

9.   **Narrow the candidate solutions to three to four or less**

The previous exercise should allow the SMB to now pick the best vendors from the larger group. This part of the evaluation and selection process has both elements of an art and of a science. In addition to evaluating how well the solution meets the business and technical requirements, the RFI responses will give the evaluators an overall "feel" for the products. Once you are immersed in the selection process, the evaluation allows for a ranking based on both business and technical requirements as well as how the vendor handled the RFI. Do not be surprised if several of the application options appear to be a fit. Once again your business is not unique. Back office applications all do basically the same job. The challenge to the SMB is to pick the one that meets the most requirements and allows the SMB to avoid custom add-ons and custom development. It is important now to limit the candidate solution set to three to four vendors or less. Each vendor who stays in contention will require a large time commitment. Each one that stays in contention increases the energy that must be expended to give them a healthy look.

10.  **Schedule and conduct vendor product presentations**

Contact each remaining vendor and explain to them that you are allowing them to make a one time fixed length presentation. Schedule the presentations as closely together as possible but not more than one in a single day. Select a comfortable duration like three to four hours. Have a hard stop when the time limit has been met. Again, the business must continue to control the vendors and the vendor interactions. The agenda for the presentation needs to be prepared by the SMB and should be the same for all vendors. I recommend something like the following:
   - Participant introductions
   - Company introductions
   - Review of the entire selection process
   - RFI review and clarification
   - Review of the candidate application in detail
   - Review of the navigation and flow of the system
   - Review of the functionality of the system
   - Review of the data storage and data structure
   - Review of system reporting
   - Review of interfaces
   - Review of any other linked or connected applications
   - Discussion of installed base and current customers
   - Discussion of markets served and market focus
   - Policy on written questions and responses
   - Close

Here is where SMBs often get off track by being wowed by a sales person or otherwise becoming enamored with a given product before the selection criteria is applied. Take your time and follow the process. Vendors with strong sales capabilities will try to move in and take over the selection process. It is critical that the SMB does not allow this to happen. The goal of the presentation is to focus on how the vendor will address the requirements and on their experience with similar companies and similar projects.

## 11. Encourage written vendor questions and deliver responses

Now that you have met the sales teams for the various candidate solutions it becomes even more critical to maintain control of the process. To keep the vendors busy and not calling you for an update every other day, set up a question and response process. Notify all vendors via email that you are soliciting questions. The window for questions should be a preset prescribed timeframe. I recommend one week. Ask them to submit all of their questions in writing. Discourage them from contacting you in any other way. This allows you time to digest the presentations and work on your selection criteria. Take all questions submitted by the deadline. Provide written responses to all questions from all vendors to each vendor. This keeps the playing field level and keeps you from answering the same question over and over again later in the process. Late questions are left unanswered and all other queries are denied. This allows you to continue to control both the communications and the selection process.

## 12. Conduct vendor client visits and demonstrations

Nothing is more telling than seeing an application in full blown production. It is appropriate now to ask the vendor to set up a visit with one of their customers. The visit should be structured such that the product is viewed in a real time production environment. This will allow you to see the flow of the system as well as the general look and feel. The key is to select a customer who is using the software the way you intend to use it. For example, if the product is a call center product, the SMB should make sure it is used for the same functionality. If the SMB call center is an inbound center and the vendor's customer focuses on outbound calling, then the visit has less value. Pressure the vendor to provide several options and do the visit selection yourself if at all possible. The vendor will be trying to select a client who is thrilled with their application whether the usage is similar to yours or not. Vendors are selling products. Your goals are different. You are trying to gather information. Since the next step is finalizing your selection criteria the pre-visit work should involve preparing a series of questions. These questions, when answered during the customer visit, will support your effort to provide detailed selection criteria.

## 13. Develop final selection criteria

The first criteria for package selection will naturally be meeting requirements. All candidate solutions at this point should clearly meet the basic business and technical requirements as given in the RFI or they should be eliminated. Usually several vendors will be able to meet the requirements at this juncture. The next step is to assure that you select the best solution from this list. You accomplish this by developing additional selection criteria to which each solution and vendor will be subjected.

Here is where all of the other factors about the vendor and the potential solution come into play. All solutions and all vendors are not created equal. The purpose of this step is to establish the critical criteria that will be applied to narrow the field to one. Some examples are as follows:

- Cost
- Service (cost plus terms)
- The viability of the vendor in the market place
- The healthiness of the company
- The company's reputation
- Other products offered
- Contract details
- Conduct during evaluation process (tells a lot)
- Ease of doing business

### 14. Map selection criteria to vendors and solutions

The work is done and the selection can begin. Some criteria are more important than others and these can be weighted. Please refer to Appendix 13-4 for a sample of how this matrix should look. Develop this one page matrix with the vendors scored against the criteria to make your selection. One or two vendors will "pop out" at the top. If one or more vendors are equal or very close in the scoring, you can use a little discretion and apply the art portion of the process. By that I mean that some of the softer factors may be considered, like how comfortable you are with the vendor.

### 15. Make selection

Pick your vendor and notify all vendors of their ranking. Let each vendor know that the process is not totally complete but that you are going into contract negotiations with a selected vendor. This is another time when a vendor may start to hard sell you. You must find a way to close off that dialogue. Expect some blue light specials and some one time pricing. You must communicate again that the process will be followed and that you will only reopen the relationship should the contract negotiation process falter or fail.

### 16. Conduct contract negotiations

You have selected the best vendor. It is time to go into contract negotiations and work on pricing and other issues like support and maintenance. Unless the IT leadership has a skilled and experienced contract negotiator, they will need both financial and legal assistance in these negotiations. There are numerous issues that need considered and negotiated. Many SMBs without the proper background or experience find themselves signing boiler-plate contracts yielding few concessions and little wiggle room. The vendor wants to sell the SMB a product or service, so the SMB should maintain control of the negotiations. Never to go into negotiations on a deal you cannot walk away from.

**17. Purchase**

Contract negotiations are about pricing, terms and timeframes. Make your expectations known. Let the vendor know your timeframes and expectations and expect compliance with them. There is no need for a long delay between contract signing and the completion of the installation project.

**18. Install**

Make sure that you are following the standard simplified project management methodology as given in Chapter 10. The focus on the project now becomes planning, communication and testing.

## C. Summary

This simple, but effective, methodology will enable the SMB to focus on the important factors in application software and vendor selection. It forces attention to the two most critical factors of scope and requirements. It will allow the SMB to drive and manage the process and go at a rapid but respectable speed. It takes the vendor's salespeople out of the equation and does not allow the SMB to be sold on a less than perfect solution. It takes the needs of the SMB, the requirements and provides a structured way for those needs to be met.

I do now wish to be disrespectful of vendors and salespeople. I have excellent relationships with all of my vendors and there is usually mutual trust and respect. I was trying to point out in this chapter that the vendors and salespeople are trying to sell products. It is up to the customer to make sure that what they are buying is right for the SMB. This is not a decision that should be left to any vendor.

## Vendor Selection and Management

> ## WISDOM to work by:
>
> 1. <u>*Manage your vendors or they will manage you.*</u>
>    *Take control of the vendor relationship. After all, you are writing the checks.*
> 2. <u>*Process, process, process.*</u>
>    *There is a solid process for vendor selection and management. Don't leave it to chance.*
> 3. <u>*Tell them what you need.*</u>
>    *Define your vendor expectations.*
> 4. <u>*Set the boundaries.*</u>
>    *Don't let that professional relationship with your vendors blur into a personal one.*
> 5. <u>*Reciprocate.*</u>
>    *Let the vendors tell you what they expect.*

## A. Introduction

Vendor selection and vendor relationships are a difficult thing to discuss. All IT groups have a group of vendors that they work with on a regular basis. It is necessary and unavoidable. In many cases for proprietary products there are few or no choices, so the vendor is dictated by the product choice. In other areas there are so many vendor choices that it seems difficult if not impossible to choose one. The goal of this chapter is to offer some commonsense approaches for vendor selection and vendor management. This chapter offers guidance on how to cultivate and handle the difficult relationships with vendors. Foremost, remember that this is a vendor relationship based on monetary exchanges and you neither want nor need the vendor to be your friend. It is not a friendly relationship. It is a business relationship that is based on mutual trust and benefit. The vendor takes your money and provides to you in return not only a product or a service but their knowledge and understanding of their segment of the industry. Vendor relationships are the same no matter the size of the organization. They are critical when the business is small and vendors are few. They are even more critical as the business grows and the number of vendors multiplies.

## B. The Process

The following process should be used as a guidebook for vendor selection and management. It is the result of many years of experience and almost any IT management person will benefit from this approach. Remember that you must manage the vendors or they will manage you. Any void you leave in the relationship will be filled by the vendor. You will find yourself reacting to them instead of having them react to you and your needs. These statements are not meant to be critical of vendors. The vendor can be the most valued and trusted resource in their particular technology area. But the goal of any vendor must be to make money and that critical element of any vendor relationship should never be ignored. Vendors like other business partners can be either good or bad for the IT organization. Your challenge and your responsibility is to make it good.

### 1. What you should expect

Go into the vendor relationship with some predefined expectations. Here are some that I recommend:
- Expect market competitive pricing and the best deal that the vendor can provide. You should get these without asking. If you find out this is not the case, then the vendor must go.
- Expect the vendor to go through the proper channels in the IT organization. The vendor should not go over your head to higher IT management or the business leadership. You need to control vendor access to your SMB.
- Expect the vendor to be a business partner with a stake in your success.
- Expect the vendor to educate you on their products and other products in the market place.
- Expect the vendor to serve as a resource for you and your SMB.
- Expect the vendor to keep you apprised of the changes to their product solution set and to their organization. You should not find out news in other ways.
- Expect honesty and trust at all times. You should never find your vendor was not upfront and straightforward with you.
- Expect the vendor to not service you in areas where they are not qualified. You should suspect a vendor who does not involve their business partners and tries to be all things for you.

### 2. Evaluating existing vendor relationships

I have taken several new management positions in my career and have had to start over with a new company and a fresh set of vendor relationships. I always begin by assuming that the existing set of vendors are meeting the needs of the organization and are going to continue to do so. I give them the benefit of the doubt. I then use the first ninety days of the relationship to determine whether the relationship will continue or whether I need to take my business elsewhere. I always advise the vendor pool of my intentions. I take them through my expectations in a face-to-face session. I ask them pointblank if they have been servicing the organization properly. Then I check them out with the business and IT management. I always reserve final judgment for myself. I have personally witnessed some very bad practices and some very poor relationships where both the vendor and the IT team themselves were out of bounds. It may be a good idea to develop the expectations defined above into a requirements spreadsheet and use them for ongoing vendor selection and management. Once I determine that a new vendor or business partner is required I use the following methodology.

## 3.  Vendor selection

Vendor selection is not unlike software application package selection in that you need to follow a similar process. In abbreviated form the following approach has worked for me.
- Research and develop a list of vendors.
- Develop a set of vendor selection criteria using the hints in Section 1 and then customize them for the particular relevant technology.
- Conduct research on the vendors by using industry contacts and local IT and business organizations. Request that the vendor supply you with a reference list of contacts. Check them out.
- Pare the field down to two or three vendors.
- Prepare a brief request for information and distribute to the finalists.
- Analyze the responses and rate and rank the vendors.
- Make your selection based on your selection criteria and on your request for information.

## 4.  Set the boundaries

I strongly recommend that the SMB write a brief policy on what financial interactions can take place between the vendor and the IT relationship manager. In this document, spell out that the vendor will not provide any kind of financial remuneration whatsoever to the IT employees. This should include training visits, golf outings, sporting events, lunches and dinners and any other exchange of promotional items. I know a pen or a cup or a leather folio is not a federal crime but gifts can lead to blurring the relationship between the vendor and the SMB. It is best just not to start down that path. If lunch or dinner is convenient then the vendors need to pay their own way and the IT employee theirs. Believe me, it is easier to cut a vendor loose for poor performance if you are not golfing or luncheon buddies. The IT leadership must be vigilant in keeping the relationship on professional terms, and the exchange of gifts or promotional items muddy the water.

## 5.  Make the terms of the relationship known

It is wise to have a brief session early in the vendor relationship where the terms of the relationship are clearly spelled out and discussed. Once the vendor understands the policies and guidelines it becomes easier to maintain and monitor the relationship. In my experience, a vendor greatly appreciates the discussion of the relationship ground rules as it allows them to avoid a lot of wasted time and energy in presenting these options to the SMB. It will also set the expectation that vendor service is the key to a successful ongoing relationship and may weed out vendors who cannot keep a relationship on a professional level. It is also wise to push this approach down into the organization. Have discussions with the staff members and set the proper expectation for everyone.

6. **What the vendor expects from you**

Keeping the relationship on a professional level also obligates the SMB to a particular level of conduct and behavior as well. It is a two way street and the vendor needs to both understand your business needs and where they stand in your world. Here are some expectations I have discussed with my vendors:
  - Payments are made on time and within the terms and agreements of the contracts and purchases. You are also obligated to work with your own payables department should payments fall in arrears.
  - Keep the vendors informed about your strategic planning exercises and your long term goals and objectives. This allows them to research and be prepared.
  - Keep the vendors informed about projects and short term activities. This will give them a chance to expand their role in your organization where appropriate.
  - Give the vendor visibility but not relationships elsewhere in the organization. Take them on an occasional tour and make introductions to other IT leadership and to business leadership. This solidifies their role in your organization and validates the relationship.
  - Don't be afraid to ask the vendor to do some research, make a presentation or give you advice. The vendor should be used as another information resource. That's what business partners are for.
  - Allow the vendor to bring in and introduce their business partners. You never know when you might need to call upon their talents.
  - Be honest with how the vendor is doing and give them plenty of time to prepare if you are going another direction or substantially altering the relationship.

7. **Conduct periodic evaluation of the vendor relationships**

The goal here is to not let either party get too comfortable. At least annually you need to have a discussion among the IT and business leadership about the state of the vendor pool and any imperatives for change. The vendor relationship should be seen as an extension of the staff and held to the same standards of accountability. I have even seen organizations do performance reviews on vendors but I think that may be going a bit too far. The evaluation needs to be systematic, however, and conducted without fail over time. Vendors should be strong business partners and strong performers. You can not afford a vendor weak link.

## C. Summary

Vendors can make or break the average IT professional. Good vendors or business partners can provide great benefit and value while weak ones can pull you down. Most IT professionals in SMBs have no clue about how to manage and leverage these critical business relationships. They are continually managed by their vendors. In many cases the vendor may take advantage of them. Only as the organization grows and matures do they seem to get some clues that all is not right with their vendors. Read and use this chapter. Take control of the vendor relationships. Manage them like you manage your own employees. Only then will you reap the real benefits of vendor relationships.

## Personnel Administration and Management

> ## WISDOM to work by:
>
> 1. *Help yourself.*
>    Do not rely solely on Human Resources Departments (HR) for personnel administration and management. Take responsibility.
> 2. *Organize your way to IT success.*
>    Organize around process, not technology.
> 3. *Provide clarity.*
>    Define roles and responsibilities through a department charter.
> 4. *Tie it all together.*
>    It fits. Tie the following elements together to allow for proper personnel administration and management.
>    - *Organization structure*
>    - *Department charter*
>    - *Process responsibilities*
>    - *Job titles and job descriptions*
>    - *Pay and pay bands*
>    - *Performance evaluations*
>    - *Performance measurements*
> 5. *This stuff counts.*
>    Employees are judging you on how well you handle personnel administration and management. Get it right.

## A. Introduction

The HR departments in most SMBs are usually small and often ill-equipped to handle the complex personnel administration and salary compensation components of IT. That is not said to disparage the HR departments but to state a fact. Most HR departments in most SMBs are there to keep up with the rank and file of the organization. They are severely challenged working on critical HR components like recruiting and benefits. The IT needs differ from the rest of the organization and require a different approach. The HR department generally does not have time to specialize in IT. In my experience, when this void exists, the IT department needs to take control of the HR functions and structure all components of the personnel side of IT in a constructive way. Even in the SMB where the HR department has some time and attention for IT, I have not met an HR person yet who did not appreciate the work I am going to describe in this chapter.

# B. Personnel Administration Management and the Business Layer Strategy

The primary challenge with personnel management in this strategy will be the difficulty with budget and consequently headcount. The SMB will provide little funding for the IT department. There will be constant pressure for IT employees to multitask and multithread. Any new requests for headcount will be suspect. The organization is by necessity a flat one with no middle management between IT leadership and the department staff. The critical factor here will be to match the existing personnel to the three strategic layers and assure that the requirements of each layer are adequately met. As a reminder the organization structure will be centered on the following.
- Infrastructure support personnel
- Back office support personnel
- Customer facing support personnel

The sections below under the Business Process Strategy in Section D are the end state. Those concepts and tactics need to be kept in mind as the IT department grows. Until then the following approach needs to be taken.

## 1. Infrastructure support personnel

There are no special requirements for IT management with this tactical execution. There are no organizational requirements. The organization structure is flat.

At the individual staff level in infrastructure for managing projects and activities, the business needs a technical relationship manager skill set. An in-depth understanding of the infrastructure technology is a must. Their responsibility will be to manage the vision, direction, vendors, solutions, projects, consultants and relationships. The IT department will need one or more of these technical relationship management employees.  It will probably begin with one employee and add additional employees over time based on functional areas like networking, servers or desktop. The critical responsibilities of this position will be to manage the vendor relationships and the SLAs. Please refer to the skill set evaluation worksheet in Chapter 8 for guidance in filling these positions.

## 2. Back office support personnel

There are no special requirements for IT management with this tactical execution. There are no organizational requirements. The organization structure is flat.

At the individual level in the back office for managing projects and activities, the business needs an applications relationship manager skill set. An in-depth knowledge of applications software and the business is a must. Their responsibility will be to manage the vision, direction, vendors, solutions, projects, consultants and relationships. The IT department will need one or more of these relationship management employees. They should begin with one and add additional employees over time. Natural segregation can occur around specific back office components like finance or office services. The other important skill sets are the ability to manage projects, to do package evaluation and selection and to select and manage vendors. Please refer to the skill set evaluation work sheet in Chapter 8 for guidance in filling these positions.

### 3. Customer facing support personnel

There are no special requirements for IT management with this tactical execution. There are no organizational requirements. The organization structure is flat.

At the individual level for customer facing applications, the business needs a creative technical skill set. Development experience is a must. Their responsibility will be to research, design, develop, install and support customer facing solutions. The skill sets here are mostly tactical. They require an excellent technical understanding and more than a little creativity. The hacker mentality is important but needs to be tempered with market awareness and the ability to evaluate and select software solutions. The other important skill sets are the ability to manage projects, to do package evaluation and selection and to select and manage vendors. Please refer to the skill set evaluation work sheet in Chapter 8 for guidance in filling these positions.

## C. Personnel Administration Management and the Business Model Strategy

Following the crawl-walk-run analogy used in previous chapters, we should now be ready to "walk". The primary challenge with personnel management in this strategy will continue to be the difficulty with headcount. The SMB will have little funding for the IT department. There will be constant pressure for IT employees to multitask and multi-thread. Any new requests for headcount will be suspect. The critical factor here will be to match the personnel to the business model strategy and assure that the requirements of each model are adequately met. The organization structure will transition in this strategy and will be centered on the following:
- Hardware/Platform/Network support personnel
- Software/Database back office support personnel
- Software/Database customer facing support personnel

The sections below under the Business Process Strategy in Section D are the end state. The concepts and tactics need to be kept in mind as the IT department grows. Until then the following approach needs to be taken. The organizational structure of the department becomes one layer deeper with a managerial role required for each of the following strategic areas.

### 1. Hardware/Platform/Network support personnel

The infrastructure person or persons generally becomes a team here. In non-strategic environments, the business would see the evolution of several teams. The IT department would generally have a network team, a server team, a systems administration team, a telecom team and so on. With the strategic approach of using independent external systems integrators, the number of IT employees should be considerably less. While you may have an employee dedicated to each (or several) technology areas you do not need a team of technologists. If one IT employee can handle the vision, direction, vendors, solutions, projects, consultants, and relationships of several technology focus areas, then staffing may be kept even more reasonably low.

The manager of each strategic area will not be a true manager who does nothing but management. The manager will also be a technology worker, a project participant, and have project and support responsibilities. The management role will be one of communication, administration and single point of contact. The strongest member of each team in terms of organization skills, business knowledge and technology understanding will be a logical leadership choice.

The IT manager will need to be a visionary. There are numerous mistakes to be made in terms of infrastructure. Risks include the following:
- Choosing the wrong external integrator
- Letting the integrator run the relationship
- Thinking too small or too large in terms of solutions
- Spending too much or too little
- Not understanding the project impacts on infrastructure
- Not keeping up with the back office and customer facing applications
- Not meeting the SLAs

## 2.   Software/Database support personnel - Back office

The back office application person or persons generally becomes a team here. In non-strategic environments, the business would see the evolution of the software development team or teams. The IT department would generally have a team of systems analysts, programmer analysts, programmers, database administrators, business analysts and so on. With the strategic approach of using independent external systems integrators, the number of IT employees should be considerably less. You do not need a team of development technologists. At this point in time one IT employee probably cannot handle the vision, direction, vendors, solutions, projects, consultants and relationships for this entire technology focus area. It will take several, and possibly one for each business process area like finance/accounting or administrative systems. The organizational structure of the department becomes one layer deeper with a managerial role required for this strategic area. The other important skill sets are the ability to manage projects, to do package evaluation and selection and to select and manage vendors.

The manager of this strategic area will not be a true manager who does nothing but management. The manager will also be a technology worker, a project participant, and have project and support responsibilities. The management role will be one of communication, administration and single point of contact. The strongest member of this team in terms of organization skills, business knowledge and technology understanding will be a logical leadership choice.

The IT manager will need to be a visionary. There are numerous mistakes to be made in terms of back office applications. Risks include the following:
- Choosing the wrong external integrator

- Letting the integrator run the relationship
- Misusing an application
- Falling behind in releases and upgrades
- Failing vendors
- Applications that come to the end of their life cycle
- Applications that do not handle new requirements like Sarbanes-Oxley

### 3.   Software/Database support personnel - Customer facing

The customer facing application person or persons generally becomes a team here. In non-strategic environments, the business would see the evolution of the software development team or teams. The IT department would generally have a team of systems analysts, programmer analysts, programmers, database administrators, business analysts and so on. With the strategic approach of using system components or tool kits and not doing custom development, the number of IT employees should be considerably less. You do not need a team of development technologists. At this point in time one IT employee probably cannot handle the vision, direction, vendors, solutions, projects, consultants and relationships for this entire technology focus area. It will take several, and possibly one for each business process area like work flow, document management or distribution systems. The organizational structure of the department becomes one layer deeper with a managerial role required for this strategic area. The other important skill sets are the ability to manage projects, to do package evaluation and selection and to select and manage vendors.

The manager of this strategic area will not be a true manager who does nothing but management. The manager will also be a technology worker, a project participant and have project and support responsibilities. The management role will be one of communication, administration, and single point of contact. The strongest member of this team in terms of organization skills, business knowledge and technology understanding will be a logical leadership choice.

The IT manager will need to be a visionary. There are numerous mistakes to be made in terms of customer facing applications. Risks include the following:
- Choosing the wrong components or tool kits
- Building unsupportable applications
- Buying the wrong applications
- Letting vendors run relationships
- Misusing or misapplying the components
- Falling behind in releases and upgrades
- Failing vendors
- Applications that come to the end of their life cycle
- Applications that do not handle new requirements like Sarbanes-Oxley

## D. Personnel Administration Management and the Business Process Strategy

Following the crawl-walk-run analogy used in previous chapters we should now be ready to "run". The tactics are more sophisticated and complicated for the business process strategy. They are to structure a tightly knit personnel administration and IT management plan that ties in all of the major components. These include the following:

- Organization structure
- Department charter
- Process responsibilities
- Job titles and job descriptions
- Pay, pay bands, and salary administration
- Performance measurements
- Performance evaluations
- Performance management and accountability

The goal here is to interweave all components of recruiting, organizing, managing, compensating and retaining IT employees into one manageable package.

## 1. Organization structure

Proper personnel administration and management requires having the right organization structure, a process focus and emphasis on doing the right things for the organization. I encourage you to reread the recommended approach to properly organize the IT department in Chapter 8. The proper organization structure allows for clearly spelled out process expectations and clearly defined roles and responsibilities. The goal is to organize around process and not technology.

Allow me to also sneak in my personal pet peeve here about the usage of the terms IT and IS. I know that the accepted name for the technology department is IT and not IS. That bothers me. I think the name IT or Information Technology is what we do and not who we are. I much prefer IS or Information Services because that is who we are. We are a service organization. I have caved into this labeling pattern. I chose not to fight the battle with the name of my books. I thought it best to address it with the content. My preference is to emphasize what we do and the fact that we are a service organization. My organization department title recommendations are as follows:

| Old | New |
|---|---|
| Corporate IT Management | Corporate IS Management |
| Network Support | IS Delivery |
| Field Support | IS Delivery |
| Systems | IS Delivery |
| Telecom | IS Infrastructure Construction |
| Networks | IS Infrastructure Construction |
| Applications Development | IS Software Construction |
| Computer Operations | IS Delivery |

## 2. Department charter

Begin by conducting the strategic exercise in Chapter 8 and build a department charter document for each of the six recommended IT groups. Hold a one day offsite meeting with the sole purpose of producing the charter document. Please refer to Appendix 8-2 for a sample charter. The beauty of this approach is that it allows the department to start with a broad strategy and drive it down to a granular level of tactical detail. This detail includes specific roles and responsibilities as well as specific projects and deliverables. The tactics are derived from the strategy and the two are tightly linked. The following components should be included in the document:

- Guiding principles
- Mission
- Objectives
- Operating Plan with projects
- Core processes
- Core processes mapped to functional responsibilities
- Work flow
- Roles and responsibilities
- Job descriptions
- Performance objectives
- Projects
- Activities

## 3. Process responsibilities

The organization structure and the department charter will allow clear delineation of process responsibilities. This is the broad delineation within the department of who does what. Everything about personnel administration and management builds from these process responsibilities.

## 4. Job titles and job descriptions

The next step after nailing down the organization structure and process responsibilities is to create job titles and write job descriptions. Nothing frustrates me more than an IT organization that abuses job titles. They use them as rewards or as ways to keep their IT staff intact. The use of titles should be a tactic that fits with the strategy and that has rationale and meaning. The title and job description further delineate the process responsibility by bringing it down to the individual level. Now individuals own processes.

I also recommend that you not allow yourself to be encumbered by traditional job titles. Start with a fresh perspective and allow the job title and job description to reflect the service and process philosophy of the new IT structure. For example, I prefer titles like the following:

| <u>Old</u> | <u>New</u> |
|---|---|
| Helpdesk Analyst | Service Desk Analyst |
| Programmer/Analyst | Software Support Analyst |
| Applications Manager | Manager of Back Office Software Support |
| Network Administrator | Technology Support Analyst |
| Telecom Engineer | Infrastructure Engineer |
| Network Engineer | Infrastructure Engineer |

The job titles now emphasize what the organization structure was devised to do. The focus is service. The job descriptions should be written to focus on the service elements of the job instead of the technology elements of the job. I have attached a couple of examples as Appendix 15-1. Note the use of job descriptions like the one below for the manager of the service desk.

**Requisite Skills:**
  **Technical** - Must understand and show proficiency with the underlying technology.
  **Communication** - Must have excellent communication skills, verbal and written, and solid presentation skills.
  **Leadership** - Must be able to lead people toward a common goal and develop a team approach.
  **Management** - Must be able to manage numerous level one support processes simultaneously without deterioration of service delivery.
  **Mentoring** - Must mentor and enrich the professional lives of employees. Must deal with all employees showing dignity and respect.
  **Projects** - Must adopt and understand standard project management methodology and define and document repeatable processes.
  **Service** - Must have a customer service mentality for both internal and external customers.

**Performance Measurements:**
  **Administration** - Performance measurements will include development and communication of the level one support process vision, leadership and team building, mentoring and employee development, understanding and projection of a service mentality.
  **Projects** - Performance measurements include technical appropriateness of service solutions, delivery of projects on time/within budget/and with full functionality, adherence to project management methodology, adherence to documentation and procedures standards.
  **Process** - Performance measurements will include ability to standardize, document, and develop means for institutionalizing repeatable processes and instilling a process approach within the team.

**Allocation of Time:**
| | |
|---|---|
| Construction: | 70% |
| Service/Support: | 10% |
| Project Management: | 20% |

### 5.  Pay, pay bands and salary administration

Nothing is more frustrating for IT midlevel management than salary administration. I know because I have been there. Many SMBs lack structured pay bands. Many practice haphazard and inconsistent salary administration. Many create inequities and rifts within the organization. Salary administration can be simple. Pay should always be a reflection of the value of the employee to the organization based on the job performance and the length of service. Pay should reward the behaviors you seek to encourage. In our example this means performance on process responsibilities. Show me just the salaries of any IT organization and I will tell you how well the organization is being run. These inequities result in employees being paid far more or far less than they are worth. This is a fairly common state in most SMBs. This shows that IT management is in a constant reactive mode and has taken no time to work on a fair and equitable pay and salary administration policy.

The goal of salary administration should be to allow IT employees not to have to think about compensation and benefits on a daily basis. They should be able to take comfort in the fact that they are being treated fairly and are being paid at market rates. They need to know they cannot improve their lot by jumping to another job.

The process begins by a thorough examination of salary surveys. These are readily available through numerous IT consulting placement vendors and on the internet. These surveys are regionalized and have numerous job descriptions. It does take a little effort to create a solid pay structure with meaningful pay bands but it is well worth the effort. The pay bands should be a list of titles and a minimum, midpoint and maximum salary based on region of the country (Midwest, East Coast, and West Coast). Then map your IT titles into the pay band structure based on job descriptions. You should be able to map very closely. Map your employees into the pay band structure and see where you stand. The requisite next step and the really hard part is to make one time salary adjustments for those who fall outside of the pay bands. You are now ready to start using the pay band structure to manage future compensation including pay raises and promotions. It can be quite simple and straightforward.

## 6.   Performance measurements

Starting with the strategic exercise described above we can use all of the work to date to create tactics. We have broad process responsibilities, narrower roles and responsibilities and individual job descriptions. Tactics in this case are the specific activities and projects for each group. We can now identify expectations for each group and each individual in terms of tangible deliverables. This will allow us to begin to measure performance. You now have the clearest picture possible of where you are trying to go and what you are trying to do. These become the performance objectives against which you need to create performance measurements and do performance management. I have included an entire chapter on measurements and performance as Chapter 16. Please refer to that chapter.

## 7.   Performance evaluations

At the individual level, performance evaluations should be conducted against the expectations derived from the assigned activities and projects. Performance should be reflective of the deliverables. Please refer to Chapter 16 for sample recommended performance evaluation forms. The performance evaluation should be based on the individual roles and responsibilities, the job description and the individual activities and projects. These must all link seamlessly together for performance evaluations to make sense.

8.  **Performance management and accountability**

The last exercise is an effort to link the personal goals and objectives of every employee to the performance measurements of the organization. I discuss this approach in my book on strategy but a synopsis here is relevant. While IT management is measuring the employee, the employee needs to be evaluating their position and their future. This is facilitated by two things. The first is a weekly one on one session between employee and manager. The second is an agenda for the first, an accountability manual. The goal of the meeting and the manual are to allow the employee to take control of their career and be accountable for it. The accountability manual has three major sections:
- Expectations
- Performance
- Training and enrichment

The topics to discuss from a management perspective include the following:
- Performance on tasks shown as quality of work
- Performance on deadlines shown on quantity of work
- Adherence to policies, procedures, and standards
- Attendance and punctuality
- Customer service focus
- Planning and organizing
- Other observations

The topics to discuss from the employee's perspective include the following:
- Feelings about the work
- Feelings about the company
- Benefits and compensation
- Training
- The future including career and job growth

Each session should be concluded with notes from both the manager and the associate to continually document status and progress.

# E. Summary

Personnel administration and management is critical from the time the SMB first opens the doors until it is deep into the Business Process Strategy. These tactics should not be ignored. They are carefully crafted tactics that will enable execution of your strategy. IT management is constantly sending messages to the staff. The best message that can be sent is that what is important to the staff is important to management. Proper personnel administration and management is a key component in running the right kind of IT organization. The IT management can get it right if it embraces the right management tactics.

The approach of using the proper organization structure, a department charter and a process perspective is not magic, but good common sense. These tactics can be used to drill down into the organization and create the correct job titles, job descriptions, pay bands, performance measurements, activities and projects. This approach debunks the haphazard approach seen in so many SMBs. The results are a tight knit and seamless approach to interweaving all of the components of personnel administration and management into one cohesive solution.

## Measurements and Performance

## A. Introduction

Everything about the following tactics must fit cohesively together.
* Organizing the IT resource to focus on service
* Personnel administration and management
* Building measurements to monitor performance

If the SMB can make this happen, the IT department can be gloriously successful. This is an opportunity to tie the strategy to the tactics and the tactics to the individual in an insightful trilogy. Below are some very simple measurements that can be designed and installed to assure that the tactics are working.

## B. Measurements and Performance

There are some simple ways to build performance measurements into performance evaluations. By now you have decided what is important to the SMB and to IT. You simply have to devise a way to make sure you are getting the desired results. You started with the strategy. You drove the strategy down into tactics. You drove the tactics to the behavior and performance of the individual. The measurements go in the reverse. You start at the bottom and come back up. Measurements start at the individual level. They build back up through the team layer. The team layer builds up through the department performance.

1.  **Individual measurements**

    a.  **Roles and responsibilities**

         During the charter session that I recommend in Chapter 8, the SMB developed roles and responsibilities for each position within IT. These roles and responsibilities begin with the team (infrastructure, service desk) mission. They must be broken down to a more granular level to apply to the individuals. The roles and responsibilities are the source documents used to prepare the job descriptions. The roles and responsibilities are the actionable items that make the job description come alive. What I am recommending here is to leverage a poorly used and misaligned form like the job description. Make it come to life through the application of the results of the charter exercise in the form of roles and responsibilities. I have attached a couple of roles and responsibilities as Appendix 16-1.

    b.  **Job descriptions**

         Job descriptions are not just words on paper. The IT department misses out on a real opportunity if they are not taken seriously. A job description is the starting point for establishing employee expectations. It needs to clearly spell out the work that is to be performed and the attitude that needs to be adopted. I have attached a couple of job descriptions as Appendix 15-1. Please note that they reinforce the message of IT as a service organization. They make the position a full featured position with an emphasis on doing the right things. I recommend that IT management develop their own job descriptions. Start with the templates I have provided and conduct a job description meeting. Jointly develop and approve all descriptions. Make it a cohesive exercise.

    c.  **Review forms**

         Now structure the personnel review forms to tie into the job descriptions derived from the roles and responsibilities. Nothing is more of a joke in most organizations than a performance review form. This is especially true in an SMB where the IT employees have a broad range of technical and administrative responsibilities. Usually the form does not cover what is actually being asked of the employee. The personnel review form needs to track directly back through the performance chain including job descriptions and roles and responsibilities. The evolution from the roles and responsibilities to the job description to the review form needs to be a tightly controlled journey that binds the entire process together. Please refer to Appendix 16-2 for a very workable performance review form.

### d. Constructing performance measurements

Now comes the fun part. The IT leadership must find a way to turn those performance expectations into performance measurements. The reason that the performance measurements are so important is that they provide an opportunity to reinforce the proper behavior and attitude. They can also provide an internal gauge of performance that can be shared outside of IT. Nothing speaks so well to solid performance and solid management as internally administered quality and performance measurements. Below are examples of what can and should be measured in the various areas of IT. The important thing is to start out measuring what is easy to capture and move to more complicated measurements over time.

- **Project managers** - Projects should only be considered successful when they are delivered on time, within budget and with the requisite functionality. Assign a numeric value (thirty three percent for each for instance) to each of these factors and conduct a post project review to measure performance. Project delivery dates are easy to track. You either met the date or you didn't. The project budget should be a combination of capital expenditures and man hours expended. Always allow for a small deviation like five to ten percent. Functionality can be assessed by a review of the project requirements. Measure each project in this way.

- **Relationship managers for back office and customer facing software applications** - Performance can be measured by project performance on new projects and by meeting SLAs for existing system maintenance and support. For new projects the same measurements that are used for project management may be used. Just add the factor of impact on production. Any negative impact on production systems should carry a heavy performance penalty. Try using a factor of twenty five percent for each of the four factors. For existing system maintenance and support, use the SLAs for which the relationship manager holds the vendor responsible. These are the ones that the relationship manager must manage. These are the system availability and responsiveness measurements that are discussed earlier in this book. The SMB should already have these in place. The combination of these two broad activities can comprise the score.

- **Service desk associates** - The goals of administering the service desk and managing work tickets can be expressed and measured in several ways. Perhaps you want to emphasize closing as many tickets as possible by the service desk. This is the most cost effective way to handle a work ticket. You can do this by measuring tickets closed by the service desk as a percentage of total tickets opened. Perhaps having a service desk agent answer a call instead of allowing it to go to voicemail is more important. The goal here is to get the user community familiar with the service desk to encourage them to call. You should then measure the percentage of calls answered against the total number of calls. The emphasis may change over time depending on the larger goals that are established. You must simply devise ways to measure what you are trying to manage.

-   **Field and desktop support** - The important first step for any SMB is to make sure all work goes through work tickets. Most business users just want immediate service and do not want to support the work ticket system. This is especially true of desktop issues. The dictate of using work tickets assures that the work on the desktop can be documented and sub-sequently evaluated. Again, monitoring the number of work tickets opened and closed for the desktop will be a good start. Desktop work tickets can be prioritized. The urgent and high tickets can be monitored for the length of time it took to get them resolved. Every lost minute on the desktop is lost productivity to the business. It might be possible to assign an hourly dollar value to lost productivity and manage such that desktop support attempts to keep this number below a given level.

-   **Second level support** - Performance for these support groups can be quantified by simply examining the SLAs and the issues that are escalated to them from the service desk. The SMB should have developed and monitored SLAs for all infrastructure and software applications as a way to manage vendors and vendor relationships. These measurements can also be used to evaluate the relationship manager. Issue resolution can be measured based on the severity of the ticket or for the number of tickets opened and closed. Lost or downtime is lost productivity and lost dollars. The measurements should reflect real dollars to the SMB where possible.

## 2. Team measurements

### a. Individual measurements are only the beginning

The baseline is set when you have developed the individual measurements for each and every staff member. The approach here like many others is iterative in nature. Maybe the first quarter is spent defining and refining the performance measurements. Maybe the second is spent determining what level of perform-ance should be expected and what the measurement really reflects. Then the goal should be to improve performance measurably by improving on the factors being measured. Then you need to raise the bar month after month or quarter after quarter.

### b. Team measurements

The performance of the teams as a whole and the management of that team are a reflection of the sum of the individual measurements. Simply compile the performance statistics of the individual players to see how the team is performing. I believe a team concept is important for an effective IT organization. When I use the word team, I am referring to the service desk team, the field support team or the desktop support team. When one employee is failing, this reflects poorly on the entire team. Poor performance also reflects poorly on the team manager. The manager must deal with the issue by either seeking performance improvements within the team or by replacing team members. This is an effective way to manage.

## 3.  Department measurements

The IT department as a whole is measured by the performance of the individual teams that comprise it. The IT leadership is also measured by the performance of the teams. There are numerous ways to roll these team measurements up to a summary level. I prefer and recommend a department scorecard. There are many software tools available to create performance dashboards and department scorecards. I will assume here that the SMB budget does not allow for such a purchase. If the budget does allow for a purchase, then a package evaluation and selection process should take place.

### a.  Department scorecards

Please refer to Appendix 16-3 for a sample department scorecard. As you can see the example is not very sophisticated or complex. While it limits itself to a few simple measurements, the scorecard includes each functional area or team. The scorecard should focus on the IT support provided and on the activities and projects that are critical to the business, not to IT itself. One of the best results IT can look to achieve is to get feedback from the business on the scorecard. The scorecard sends the message to the business. IT not only wants to be measured regarding performance but that it solicits input and feedback on what and how it should be measured. Constructing these measurements does not require an all out fulltime effort. Many SMB IT managers balk at this because they feel the time commitment is too large. Start with simple measures and build more complex and meaningful ones over time. If the work is done on the other processes and methodologies the scorecard becomes an easy next step. Post the scorecard physically and electronically for all to review. The scorecard needs to be a visible performance measurement.

## 4.  What you don't do

Here is one last cautionary word for the IT department and the IT leadership team. IT performance will be judged not only by what they do but also by what they don't do. By that I mean that IT may be severely punished for taking a narrow view of their job and not figuring out without being told exactly what job performance entails. In one position, I was penalized by not knowing all about all of the software application options available in my industry. In another, I did not bring a new call center technology into discussion while one of our competitors was adopting that key technology. My SMB management did not tell me to do these things. I was just expected to keep track of certain industry and technology developments. It was understood (maybe not by me) and expected. The recommendation is to know not only your management job, but to put no limits on your own personal responsibility or on those of your department members. When gauging your performance, the SMB business management will not. Know your industry and keep track of technology developments. Read the industry magazines and network with others in your industry. Try to include market and technology research as part of your roles and responsibilities. Try to include creatively applying technology to business problems and allow for a certain amount of technology experimenting. Attempt to manage yourself and the department from the perspective of the CEO or other senior leader. IT performance is difficult enough and you will be judged sometimes by what you fail to do.

## C. Summary

I have only skimmed the surface here on measurements and performance. There are numerous other industry sources available that go into greater detail. I included this discussion for several reasons. It is inherent in tactics execution. It is critical to IT success. Development and use of these performance measurements must be done. The IT department will never excel without measurements. One additional benefit is that employees do expect and enjoy being measured. They will respect your efforts in these areas and there will be measurable results in both improved employee satisfaction and reduced employee turn over. Remember that you can not manage what you do not measure.

## In CONCLUSION

If you take nothing else from this book, please consider the following statements. Strategy is critical. Cohesive tactics without a strategy means only that whatever you are doing, you may be doing it right. You may still be doing the wrong things. Cohesive tactics to support the strategies are absolutely essential. You do not have to spend money (which is seldom ever available in the SMB) to execute these tactics. Start small and build. Use the iterative approach. Remember the crawl/walk/run approach. Remember the plan/build/run approach. There are simplified but sound approaches for the key tactics. They work. You will suffer greatly from a lack of methodology. Structure and process are not bureaucratic. Structure and process do not slow you down. Structure and process speed things up, improve quality and assure success. Manage change or it will manage you. Manage your package evaluation and selection process or it will manage you. Manage your vendors or they will manage you. Strategy drives tactics. Tactics drive the individual.

## Common Tactics

# Appendix I-1

## IT Tactics Blueprint

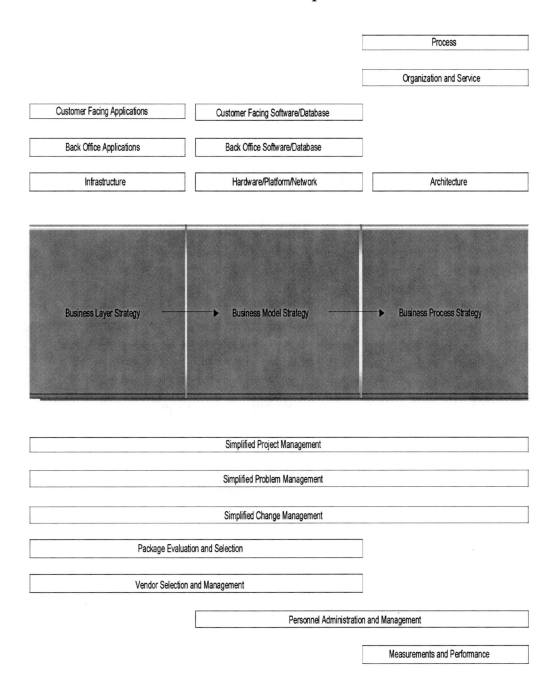

## Appendix 1-1

**Business Layer Strategy Pictorial**

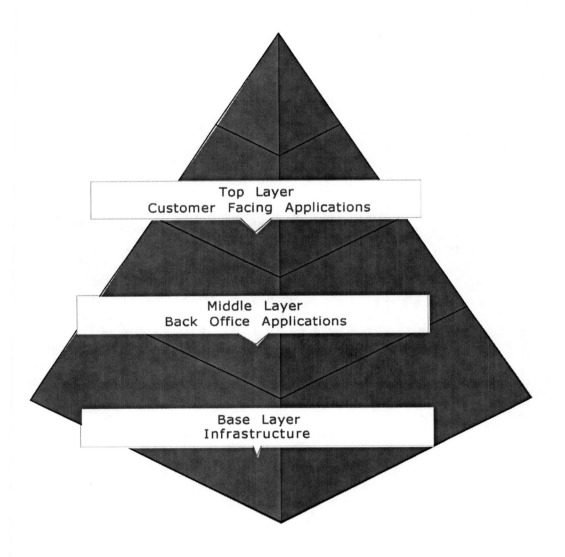

# Appendix 1-2

## Business Layer Strategy Report - Infrastructure (1 of 3)

**Business Layer Strategy Report**                    **Infrastructure**

| Functionality | Components | Specific Devices (Provide names and device numbers) |
|---|---|---|
| Wide area network | Hubs | |
| | Routers | |
| | Connectivity / Circuits | |
| | Servers | |
| | Firewalls | |
| Local area network | Hubs | |
| | Routers | |
| | Servers | |
| | Connectivity / Circuits | |
| Internet | Servers | |
| | Connectivity / Circuits | |
| | Firewalls | |
| Intranet | Servers | |
| | Applications | |
| Servers | Enterprise | |
| | Department | |
| | Print | |
| | Domain | |
| | FAX | |
| | Document | |
| | Exchange | |
| | Storage | |
| | Connectivity | |
| Desk top | PCs | |
| | Dumb terminals | |
| | Network appliances | |
| | Printers | |
| | Faxes | |
| | Copiers | |
| | Scanners | |
| | Connectivity | |
| Telephony | PBX | |
| | Switchboards | |
| | Telephones | |
| Other Devices | Scanners | |
| | Printers | |
| | Copiers | |
| | Faxes | |

# Appendix 1-2

## Business Layer Strategy Report - Back Office Layer (2 of 3)

**Business Layer Strategy Report**        **Back Office Layer**

| Functionality | Package | Status |
|---|---|---|
| Accounts Payable | Macola | Running on internal servers, need to move to outsource. |
| Billing | Macola | Running on internal servers, need to move to outsource. |
| Accounts Receivables | Macola | Running on internal servers, need to move to outsource. |
| Collections | N/A | Functionality outsourced. |
| Fixed Assets | Macola | Running on internal servers, need to move to outsource. |
| Commissions | Macola | Running on internal servers, need to move to outsource. |
| Payroll | ADP | Service provided. |
| Benefits | ADP | Service provided. |
| Human Resources | ADP | Functionality outsourced. |
| Performance Tracking | ADP | Functionality outsourced. |
| Word Processing | MS Word | Running on internal servers, need to move to outsource. |
| Faxing | Quick Fax | Running on internal servers, need to move to outsource. |
| E-mail | MS Exchange | Running on internal servers, need to move to outsource. |
| Purchasing (internal) | Macola | Running on internal servers, need to move to outsource. |
| Inventory Control | Macola | Running on internal servers, need to move to outsource. |
| Distribution | Macola | Running on internal servers, need to move to outsource. |
| CRM for Sales | Sales Logic | Running as ASP, acceptable. |
| Shipping | UPS | Running as ASP, acceptable. |
| Rate Shopping for Shipping | Rate Shopper | Running as ASP, acceptable. |

# Appendix 1-2

## Business Layer Strategy Report - Customer Facing Layer (3 of 3)

| Functionality / Process | Application Name | Package or Home Grown | Status |
|---|---|---|---|
| Marketing efforts | Market Track | Home grown system | Need to replace |
| Sales reporting | Sales Track | Purchased Package | Running on internal servers, need to move to outsource. |
| Sales tracking | Sales Track | Purchased Package | Running on internal servers, need to move to outsource. |
| Call center inbound calls | Avaya | Purchased Package | Running on internal servers, need to move to outsource. |
| Call center outbound calls | Davox – Predictive Dialer | Purchased Package | Running on internal servers, need to move to outsource. |
| Accept new client | Order Processing | Home grown system | Need to replace |
| Accept orders paper | Order Processing | Home grown system | Need to replace |
| Accept orders phone | Order Processing | Home grown system | Need to replace |
| Accept orders web | Order Processing | Home grown system | Need to replace |
| New order processing | Order Processing | Home grown system | Need to replace |
| Document handling | OnBase | Purchased Package | Running on internal servers, need to move to outsource. |
| Document repository | OnBase | Purchased Package | Running on internal servers, need to move to outsource. |
| Sales reorders | Order Processing | Home grown system | Need to replace |
| Sales cross selling | Order Processing | Home grown system | Need to replace |
| Construct product | Manufacturing | Home grown system | Need to replace |
| Package product | Manufacturing | Home grown system | Need to replace |

# Appendix 1-3

## Recommended Project List Format

| Identified and Active Projects<br>Project | Layer | Project # | Date<br>Activated | Status | Target<br>Date |
|---|---|---|---|---|---|
| Enterprise System Enhancements | Back Office | 2006-0001 | 03/24/06 | Active | 7/1/2006 |
| Design and develop generic order capture process | Customer Facing | 2006-0002 | 04/01/06 | Identified | |
| Evaluate and select shipping software | Back Office | 2006-0003 | 04/01/06 | Active | |
| MS Exchange Server & associated e-mail problems | Back Office | 2006-0004 | 05/01/06 | Active | |
| Local & LD vendor telephony analysis | Infrastructure | 2006-0005 | 04/15/06 | Active | |
| Small call center project | Customer Facing | 2006-0006 | 03/24/06 | Active | |
| Network directional project | Infrastructure | 2006-0007 | 04/01/06 | Active | |
| Basic CRM capability for sales | Back Office | 2006-0008 | 05/07/06 | Active | |
| Warehouse Management System Enhancements | Customer Facing | 2006-0009 | 03/24/06 | Identified | |
| Web order capture, inventory, & order inquiry project | Customer Facing | 2006-0010 | 05/31/06 | Identified | |
| Evaluate FAX Server to replace Easylink | Back Office | 2006-0011 | 04/15/06 | Identified | |
| Transition Sales Reporting to Production Status | Customer Facing | 2006-0012 | 03/24/06 | Identified | |
| Release sales support documents & solici more support activities | Customer Facing | 2006-0013 | 04/15/06 | Active | |
| e-Synergy analysis and recommendations | Back Office | 2006-0014 | 05/01/06 | Active | |
| Third Party Logistics (3PL) software for reverse logistics project | Customer Facing | 2006-0015 | 05/24/06 | Active | |
| Move computer room and all server components to outsource vendor | Infrastructure | 2006-0016 | 6/1/2006 | Identified | |

# Appendix 1-4

## Sample Cost Benefit Analysis (1 of 2)
### Commission Calculation Software

### Sample Cost Benefit Analysis

### Commission  Calculation  Software

### 1    Document  Purpose

The purpose of this document is to provide a business case and cost justification (ROI) for:
In general, packaged commission calculation software.
In particular, the Commission Calculation software that interfaces directly with existing vendor software.

### 2    Project  Background

Commission calculation and processing is inefficient, cumbersome, time consuming, and does not provide the requisite information in an accurate and timely manner.  Royalty calculation is also beginning to be an issue.

### 3    Project  Details

We recommend the purchase and installation of the Commission Calculation software to support the commission requirements and the royalty calculation requirements as they have been defined.

### 4    Project  Stakeholders

| Name | Vested  Interest |
|---|---|
| Sales Management | Properly incenting and compensating sales personnel. |
| Sales | Accurate and timely performance statistics. |
| Accounting | Reduced time and effort to produce commission payments and royalty payments on a monthly basis. |

### 5    Business  Case

The business case for commission software and for the Commission Calculation software is as follows:

**Commission Software** – Please reference the attached documents (Commission Requirements and Sales Issues Lists) for more details which document both the problems and requirements of commission calculation software.  The solution we recommend both solves the problems specified by Sales management and meets the requirements that they set forth.  It also allows for the automation of royalty calculations which is now beginning to be an issue for Accounting.

**Commission Calculation** – The commission module in vendor's software will not provide the requisite commission splits or the requisite calculations.  Commission Calculation marketed by a separate vendor and is the sole vendor for add-on software for commission calculations.  During demonstrations and discussions with vendor employees we were able to determine that Commission Calculation can be configured and extended to handle nearly all of our commission requirements.

# Appendix 1-4

## Sample Cost Benefit Analysis (2 of 2)
### Commission Calculation Software

**6    Project Goals**

| Priority | Description |
|---|---|
| 1 | Replace manual effort in Accounting required for monthly calculation of commissions. |
| 2 | Handle current and near-term future commission splits. |
| 3 | Improve timeliness of commission information. |
| 4 | Enable tighter management of the sales team's performance. |
| 5 | Enable management to remedy performance problems sooner. |
| 6 | Handle current and future royalty calculations. |

**7    Estimate and Resources**

Cost Estimates (see attached quote):
Capital:
Software:      $7,400
Hardware:    None.
Expense:      None
Manpower / Time:  None

IT Resources:      Time to understand the product.    Time to train users.

**8    Project Cost and ROI**

ROI Estimates:

| Factors | Current | Savings | Benefit (Annual) |
|---|---|---|---|
| **Manpower Savings** | | | |
| Eliminate manual monthly commission calculations by Accounting | 8 hours per month @ $40 per hour | $320 | $3,840 |
| Eliminate manual monthly royalty calculations by Accounting | 4 hours per month @ $40 per hour | $160 | $1,920 |
| | | | |

Data Source:

Finance Department

Additional Analysis:

| Factors | Current | After Project Install | Savings | Benefit (Annual) |
|---|---|---|---|---|
| | | | | |

Data Source:

Summary:

| Cost | | | Benefits | ROI |
|---|---|---|---|---|
| **Capital** | **Labor** | **Total** | | |
| $7,400 | | $7,400 | $5,760 | 1 year and 3 months |

# Appendix 1-5

## Sample Vendor SLA Scorecard

| Service Level Agreement | Application | Yearly Goal | Q1 Goal | Month 1 measurement | Hrs. Sched | Hrs. Avail | Score |
|---|---|---|---|---|---|---|---|
| Systems Availability | | | | | | | |
| | Back Office Package 1 | 99.999% | 99.999% | What percentage of time was the software application available during scheduled published hours? | 272 | 267 | 0.982 |
| | Back Office Package 2 | 99.999% | 99.999% | | 272 | 265 | 0.974 |
| | Back Office Package 3 | 99.999% | 99.999% | | 272 | 266 | 0.978 |
| | Back Office Package 4 | 99.999% | 99.999% | | 272 | 263 | 0.967 |
| | Back Office Package 5 | 99.999% | 99.999% | | 272 | 272 | 1.000 |
| | Back Office Package 6 | 99.999% | 99.999% | | 272 | 272 | 1.000 |
| | Server 1 | 99.999% | 99.999% | What percentage of time was the server available during scheduled published hours? | 272 | 270 | 0.993 |
| | LAN | 99.999% | 99.999% | What percentage of time was the server reachable through the local area network? | 272 | 268 | 0.985 |
| | WAN | 99.999% | 99.999% | What percentage of time was the server reachable through the wide area network? | 272 | 244 | 0.897 |
| | Nightly batch processing | 99.999% | 99.999% | What percentage of the time did the nightly processing finish on time? | 31 | 30 | 0.968 |
| | Server 2 | 99.999% | 99.999% | What percentage of time was the server available during scheduled published hours? | 272 | 270 | 0.993 |
| | Server 3 | 99.999% | 99.999% | What percentage of time was the server available during scheduled published hours? | 272 | 271 | 0.996 |
| | Web site | 99.999% | 99.999% | What percentage of the time was the web site available and functioning? | 672 | 640 | 0.952 |
| | PBX - Telephony | 99.999% | 99.999% | What percentage of the time was the PBX available and functioning? | 672 | 670 | 0.997 |
| | Composite Score | | | All systems and technology availability | | | 0.907 |

## Appendix 4-1

### Business Model Strategy Pictorial

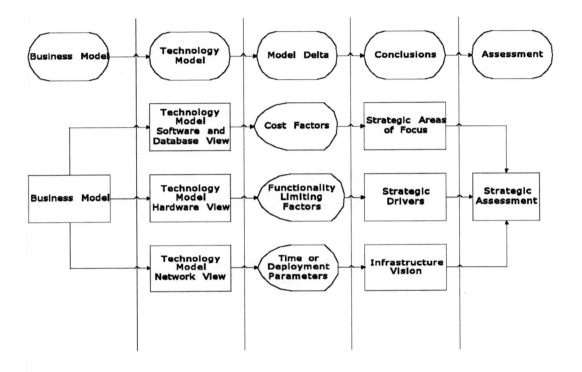

# Appendix 4-2

## Technology Model-Hardware/Platform View

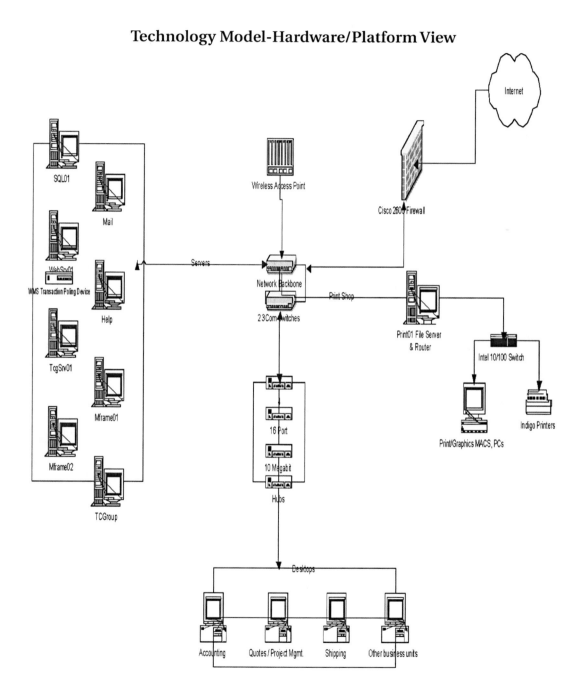

# Appendix 4-3

## Technology Model-Network View

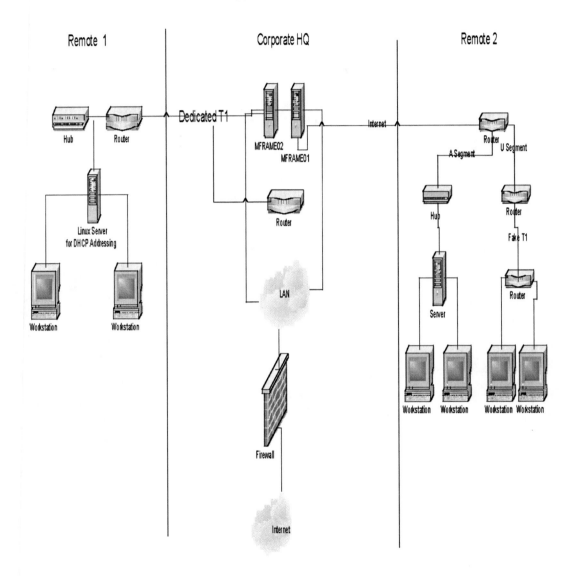

## Appendix 4-4

# The Service Pyramid

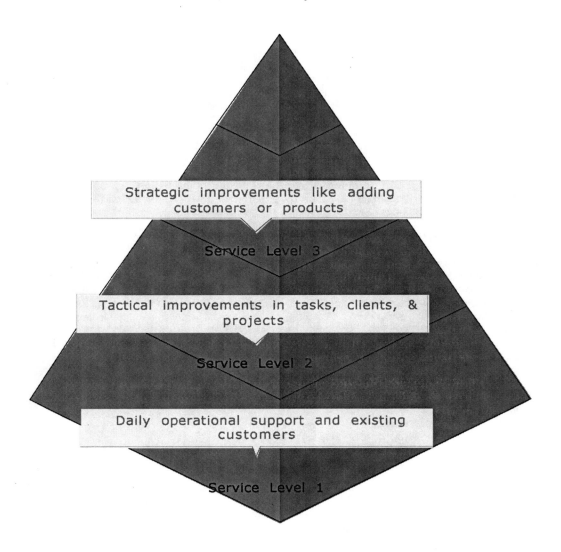

# Appendix 4-5

## The Service Statement (1 of 2)
### Information Services

Please join me in welcoming in a new era in IS (Information Services). Notice I said IS or Information Services and not IT or Information Technology. While this may seem like a subtle difference, it is **the** critical difference in focus that will allow us to succeed in this new era. Information Services is who we are while Information Technology is what we do. A technology organization focuses on technology; a service organization focuses on service. As you will see our new IS organization has a new structure and a fresh approach. Our new mantra is "service is king".

The focus of the IS organization will be on you, our customers, and providing you the best cost to performance ratio for spending your technology dollars. With this new approach in place we have been able to make a few critical observations. Currently we have the wrong organization structure, we lack a strategy and vision, we are not doing the right things and the things we are doing we are not always doing right. Some good examples that support these observations include:

- No time reporting – we don't know how we are spending our time so we don't know what it costs to deliver our services.
- Poor project management – we don't manage projects well so we can't control performance on deadlines or control our costs.
- No strategic plans for technology – we are surely spending too much and not investing in the right things.
- Poor use of the help desk and work tickets – we can't control performance, manage our associates, isolate and eliminate nagging problems, understand where we are succeeding or failing, or know what it costs to provide support.
- In summary, we don't know what we should spend on IS, we don't know what our staffing levels should be, we can't measure how we are performing, and we can't mange our associates.

Our new organization structure is only the first step in resolving these shortcomings. In order to be a breakout service organization we must also do the following things:

- Organize properly.
- Have a clear and concise strategy and direction.
- Do the right things.
- Do things right.

In action, this means we must:
- <u>Organize properly:</u>
  - Organize around process. We will define and document our processes.
    - Our new organization structure is heavy in the service delivery area.
    - Within the service areas we will define every service process and seek to improve on them.
  - Use a planning/construction/delivery approach.
    - Segregate the associates from a technology approach to a process approach. For example there will be no "server group". Server construction associates in the infrastructure construction group will build out new technology and server support associates in the delivery group will provide daily support of the servers.
    - Focus on specific processes allowing for establishing repeatable activities that can be measured and improved upon.

# Appendix 4-5

## The Service Statement (2 of 2)

- o   Focus on service delivery.

- <u>Have a clear strategy and direction</u> (Initiatives are underway to define strategic technology directions and strategic drivers for the all services that we offer.):
  - o   Define the services that IT will offer.  Example – Voice services and data services.  Develop a set of services that vary in functionality and cost.  Offer these services to the business when they are selling new business.  This will allow them to select the most cost-effective solution for any particular client.
  - o   Define and develop the best and most cost effective way to offer these services.  Standardize and either centralize or regionalize.
  - o   Provide the proper level of support for these services.

- <u>Do the right things</u>:
  - o   Based on the value to the business.  We will have a business not a technology focus.  We are here to service the business.
  - o   Based on the return on investment.  We will do only what the business deems to be right.  We will align ourselves tightly with the business.
  - o   Based on the revenue lift or the expense reduction.  No technology for technology sake.

- <u>Do things right</u>:
  - o   Communicate, communicate, communicate:
    - ▪   Our vision, our structure, and our commitments.
    - ▪   Our projects, our progress, and our performance.
    - ▪   Our tools, our techniques and our measurements.
  - o   With a service focus. Focus on you, our customers.
  - o   Using basic project management principles.
  - o   Measure everything that we do (from time reporting to systems availability, you can't manage what you can't measure).
  - o   Understand our costs and the value we provide to the business.

The changes we are implementing take time. They cannot be accomplished over night.  We can't stop what we are currently doing as we try to implement change.  Our management team calls it "changing the tires on a moving bus".  We do have a strong sense of urgency and a "round-the-clock mentality". We are working feverishly to lay the foundation for our future improvements.  There will be confusion and challenges as we move our team from one type of organization to another.  We are confident this is the right thing to do and that we will ultimately provide a breakout IS organization.  We encourage discussions and dialogues with every business leader. The IS management team will do whatever it takes to earn your trust and patience as we move forward.

# Appendix 4-6

## System Availability Messages - Spotlight Approach (1 of 2)

| # | Message | Audience | Frequency | Responsibility | Vehicle | Intent |
|---|---------|----------|-----------|----------------|---------|--------|
| 1 | Nightly Batch Processing Successful | Entire Company | Daily M-F | Computer Operations | Green Light Symbol on the Intranet Home Page | All things normal |
| 2 | Nightly Batch Processing Did Not Complete Successfully | Entire Company | Daily M-F Prior to 8:00 AM | Computer Operations | Yellow Light Symbol on the Intranet Home Page | Report a problem and focus on resolution. |
|   |   | Management | Daily M-F Prior to 8:00 AM or when a problem occurs | Computer Operations | Morning Incident Report w/1 hour updates to management via email | Report a problem and focus on resolution. |
| 3 | Nightly Batch Processing Did Not Complete Successfully - Problem Resolved | Entire Company | Daily M-F within 1 hours of resolution | Computer Operations | Green Light Symbol on the Intranet Home Page | All things normal |
|   |   | Management | Daily M-F within 1 hours of resolution | Computer Operations | Incident report filed on shared drive within 24 hours of resolution | All things normal |

Batch

# Appendix 4-6

## System Availability Messages - Spotlight Approach (2 of 2)

Systems

| | | | | | | |
|---|---|---|---|---|---|---|
| 4 | All Systems Available | Entire Company | Daily M-F | Computer Operations | Green Light Symbol on the Intranet Home Page | All things normal |
| 5 | Daily Production System not Available | Entire Company | Daily M-F Prior to 8:00 AM | Computer Operations | Yellow Light Symbol on the Intranet Home Page | Report a problem and focus on resolution. |
| | | Management | Daily M-F Prior to 8:00 AM or when a problem occurs | Computer Operations | Morning Incident Report w/1 hour updates to management via email | Report a problem and focus on resolution. |
| 6 | Daily Production System not Available - Problem Resolved | Entire Company | Daily M-F within 1 hours of resolution | Computer Operations | Green Light Symbol on the Intranet Home Page | All things normal |
| | | Management | Daily M-F within 1 hours of resolution | Computer Operations | Incident report filed on shared drive within 24 hours of resolution | All things normal |
| 7 | Problem with Batch Processing or Systems Availability that exceed one day | Management | Daily M-F when a problem exceeds one day | Director of IT | Incident Report via e-mail message each hour | Daily status report and daily impact statement |

## Appendix 5-1

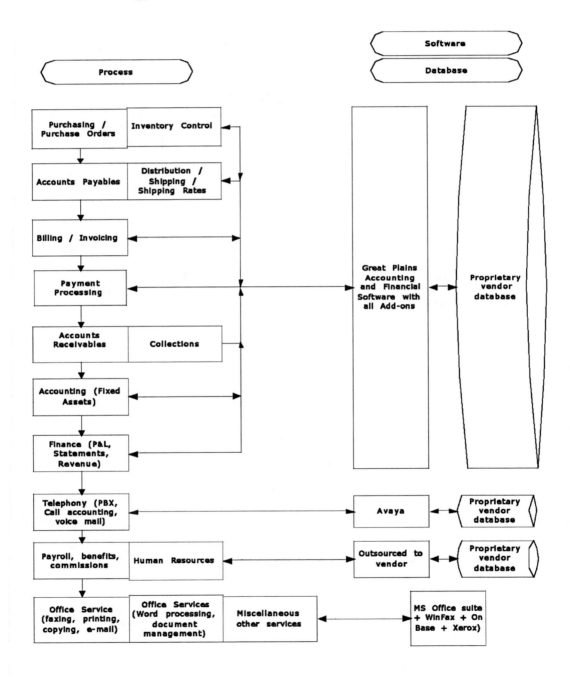

### Technology Model - Back Office Software/Database View

# Appendix 5-2

## Post Mortem Release/Upgrade Summary Report

### 1    Document Purpose

The primary purpose of this document is to document the success and failures of a completed release or upgrade of software applications. The goal is to learn something from every effort and seek to improve over time. This form can also be used to confirm and document project successes.

### 2    Type of Effort

Enter the type of project here. Options back office or customer facing. Sub types include enhancement, upgrade or release.

### 3    Performance against time frames

Start text here. Discuss performance against published time frames for individual milestones and for the deadline as a whole. Use this information to improve scheduling for future efforts.

### 4    Performance against budget

Start text here. Discuss budget performance including cost overruns and validity of cost estimates. Use this information to improve budgeting for future efforts.

### 5    Performance against functionality and requirements

Start text here. Develop a checklist of functionality and requirements and whether these specific measurements were satisfied or not. Pay particular attention to the test plan here and summarize whether the release or upgrade was sufficiently tested. Use this information to improve the planning and testing exercises for future efforts.

### 6    Failures – what can be improved

Start text here. Develop a series of declarative statements detailing where the project failed. This is not an exercise intended to assess blame but to collectively learn from project mistakes. Discuss ways to mitigate these failures and associated risks on future efforts.

### 7    Successes – what is working properly

Start text here. Discuss and celebrate the successes. Document specific milestones that were met. Review the cost/benefit analysis and the value of the effort to the company. Acknowledge exemplary performance.

# Appendix 6-1

## Technology Model - Customer Facing Software/Database View

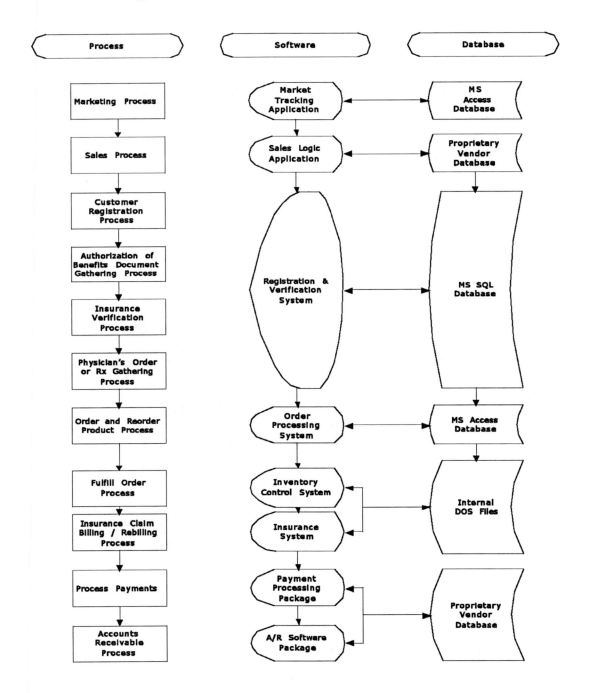

# Appendix 6-2

## Customer Facing - Strategic View

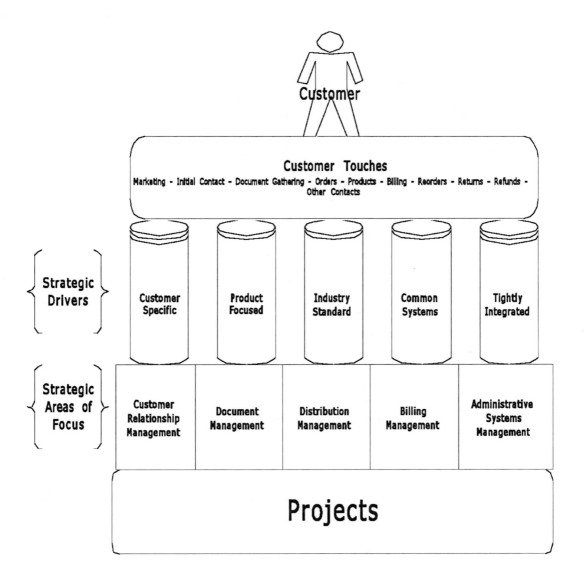

# Appendix 6-3

## Sample Strategic Drivers

Strategic drivers are the guidelines and principles that guide technology selection. These need applied to the strategic areas of focus to guide the selection process.

### a.    Customer Specific

Due to our company focus on customer service our technology and systems will be flexible enough to enable customization based on the specific needs of our customers. We cannot afford to take a mass production approach because our customers require different solutions based on their particular circumstances. It is expensive to acquire and maintain customers, so we must guard them carefully. Our competitors are customizing. In order to be competitive we must also customize.

### b.    Product Focused

Since a wide array of products are required to successfully compete in the marketplace our technology and systems will be full featured enough to support specific demands of the various product groups. There are distinct groups of customers in our customer community with needs that are different enough to require different product groupings. We must build or buy systems that have a broad range of features and that are not single feature specific. We must build or buy flexible solutions that have a wider range of features than we currently provide or support. We need to focus not only on the current products provided but possible related products as well.

### c.    Industry Standards

As an IS organization our technology and selected systems will adhere to industry standards with regards to underlying component technologies and open interfaces. We know we are growing at a rapid rate and that we will face larger integration issues down the road. We must be careful not to select point or one off solutions that solve narrow specific problems but do not fit into a long range strategy. We will be cognizant of the need to tie all of our technology and systems together at a later date and that all technology and systems will be required to interact and share information and data. Only through following industry standards can we assure that our decisions today keep our options open for tomorrow.

### d.    Tightly Integrated

We cannot afford the problems created by disparate systems so our technology and systems will be made to seamlessly integrate among the various selected components. We have a small computer operations capability, and we do not have full production monitoring on all shifts. We cannot afford system outages due to integration problems. We do not have the staff to constantly chase and resolve system related integration problems, so we must tightly integrate all systems from the start.

### e.    Common Systems

We cannot afford to support a wide range of solutions, so our technology and systems will be limited to the smallest number of possible solutions with limited duplication of solution sets. The small budget and limited manpower dictate that we narrow the number of deployed solutions. We must look to add functionality and depth of scope to the solutions already deployed and not add like solutions to the mix. This may entail some lost functionality, but the support required rises exponentially with the number of solutions deployed.

# Appendix 6-4

## Project Capacity and Planning

| Resource | Title | Specialty | Support | Projects | Administrative | Total | January Development Hours | February Development Hours | March Development Hours | Q1 Development Hours |
|----------|-------|-----------|---------|----------|----------------|-------|---------------------------|----------------------------|-------------------------|----------------------|
| | | | | | | | 176 | 160 | 176 | 512 |
| Employee 1 | Infrastructure Support Manager | Infrastructure | 60% | 30% | 10% | 100% | 53 | 48 | 53 | 154 |
| Employee 2 | Infrastructure Support Rep. | Infrastructure | 60% | 30% | 10% | 100% | 53 | 48 | 53 | 154 |
| Employee 3 | Back Office Support Manager | Back Office | 70% | 20% | 10% | 100% | 35 | 32 | 35 | 102 |
| Employee 4 | Back Office Support Rep. | Back Office | 70% | 20% | 10% | 100% | 35 | 32 | 35 | 102 |
| Employee 5 | Customer Facing Support Manager | Customer Facing | 40% | 45% | 15% | 100% | 79 | 72 | 79 | 230 |
| Employee 6 | Customer Facing Support Rep. | Customer Facing | 40% | 45% | 15% | 100% | 79 | 72 | 79 | 230 |
| Employee 7 | Customer Facing Support Rep. | Customer Facing | 40% | 45% | 15% | 100% | 79 | 72 | 79 | 230 |
| Employee 8 | Customer Facing Support Rep. | Customer Facing | 40% | 45% | 15% | 100% | 79 | 72 | 79 | 230 |
| Employee 9 | Customer Facing Support Rep. | Customer Facing | 40% | 45% | 15% | 100% | 79 | 72 | 79 | 230 |
| **Available development man hours:** | | | | | | | 572 | 520 | 572 | 1664 |

Percentages supported by time reporting in the 3 general categories.
Man hours based on available man hours per work days in a month.

# Appendix 6-5

## Capacity Analysis and Project Reporting

| Application Resources | Available Q1 Development Hrs | Total Hours Allocated | Project 1 | Project 2 | Project 3 | Project 4 | Project 5 | Project 6 | Project 7 | Project 8 |
|---|---|---|---|---|---|---|---|---|---|---|
| Employee 1 | 154 | 154 | 100 | | | 54 | | | | |
| Employee 2 | 154 | 154 | | 50 | 50 | | 54 | | | |
| Employee 3 | 102 | 102 | | | | | | 102 | | |
| Employee 4 | 102 | 102 | | | | | | | 102 | |
| Employee 5 | 230 | 230 | 200 | | | | | | | 30 |
| Employee 6 | 230 | 230 | 200 | | | | | | | 30 |
| Employee 7 | 230 | 230 | | 100 | 100 | 30 | | | | |
| Employee 8 | 230 | 230 | | 100 | 100 | 30 | | | | |
| Employee 9 | 230 | 230 | | | | | 230 | | | |
| **Team Total** | 1,662 | 1,662 | 500 | 250 | 250 | 114 | 284 | 102 | 102 | 60 |

# Appendix 6-6

## Milestone Reporting

| Infrastructure Q2 | | | | | | |
|---|---|---|---|---|---|---|
| Project # | Owners | Project/Milestone | Status | Resources | Hours | Due Date |
| Project 1 | Norm Doug | **Enterprise Security Audit** | Initiation | Doug | 40 | |
| | | Complete project initiation doc | | | | |
| | | Identify resource | | | | |
| | | Obtain funding | | | | |
| | | Schedule audit | | | | |
| | | Conduct audit | | | | |
| | | Report results | | | | |
| | | Define action plan | | | | |
| Project 2 | Rich Ray | **Enterprise Backup Tactical** | Active | Ray | 12 | 6/1/2006 |
| | | Identify solution | Complete | | | |
| | | Obtain funding approval | Complete | | | 3/10/2006 |
| | | Order Equipment | On Schedule | | | 3/14/2006 |
| | | Install and Test | Pending | | | 4/30/2006 |
| | | Turn over to Support Services | Pending | | | 5/30/2006 |
| Project 3 | Norm Rich | **Systems Assessment** | Active | Rich | 40 | 6/1/2006 |
| | | Identify resource | Complete | | | 4/1/2006 |
| | | Obtain funding | Complete | | | 4/28/2006 |
| | | Schedule audit | Complete | | | 4/30/2006 |
| | | Conduct audit | On Schedule | | | 5/21/2006 |
| | | Report results | Pending | | | 5/31/2006 |
| | | Define action plan | Pending | | | 6/30/2006 |
| Project 4 | Bob Ted | **Intranet Development / Deployment** | Active | Ted | 10 | |
| | | Obtain funding | | | | |
| | | Schedule with vendor | | | | |
| | | Develop site | | | | |
| | | Install and Test | | | | |
| | | Turn over to business | | | | |
| Project 5 | Bill Ted | **HRIS Replacement** | Active | Bill | 10 | |
| | | Define IS requirements | | | | |
| | | Engineer solution | | | | |
| | | Obtain funding (kiosks) | | | | |
| | | Order equipment (kiosks) | | | | |
| | | Install and Test | | | | |
| | | Turn over to Support Services | | | | |
| Project 6 | Al Leo | **Enterprise Data Center Assessment** | Active | Doug | 40 | |
| | | Identify resource | Complete | | | 4/1/2006 |
| | | Obtain funding | Complete | | | 4/28/2006 |
| | | Schedule audit | Complete | | | 4/30/2006 |
| | | Conduct audit | On Schedule | | | 5/21/2006 |
| | | Define action plan | Pending | | | 6/30/2006 |

## Appendix 7-1

### Business Process Strategy Pictorial

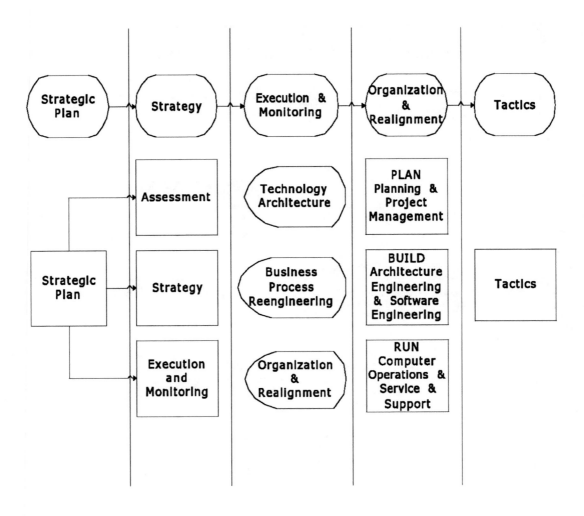

## Appendix 8-1

# Process Based Organization Structure

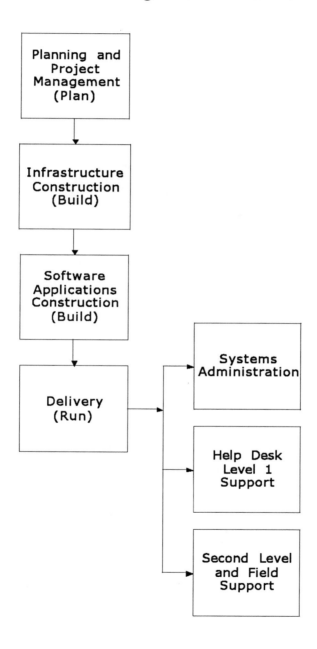

# Appendix 8-2

## Entire Department Charter Document (1 of 8)
### Infrastructure Engineering

### Definitions

| | |
|---|---|
| **Vision:** | What we want to become, where we want to be. |
| **Mission:** | Define why we are here and our purpose within the business which aligns us with the corporate direction. |
| **Objective:** | What we will accomplish to fulfill our mission. |
| **Strategy:** | Overriding strategic focus, the business process strategy. |
| **Priority:** | #1 – What we actively work on.<br>#2 – Scheduled to be worked on as time becomes available.<br>#3 – Work that has no resource or priority assigned. |
| **When:** | Expected date of completion. |

### Infrastructure Engineering Guiding Principles

**We will:**        At all times conduct ourselves in a manner that fosters respect and trust from other groups and our customers.
Continually improve ourselves, our technology, and our Processes.
Take pride in our work.
Celebrate our successes.
And finally, we will always conduct ourselves with the highest degree of professional and ethical behavior.

### Infrastructure Engineering Mission

**Why we exist:**     Infrastructure engineering provides cost effective, technical solutions and tier three support that exceeds our business partner's needs. We are a consulting resource and Research and Development team that keeps ahead of our competition in our industry. Infrastructure engineering builds the technology infrastructure that supports today's requirements and also provides a flexible platform that positions the company for the future. By being proactive, practicing sound project management methodologies, and continually developing the knowledge and expertise of our staff we enable ourselves to do it right the first time.

# Appendix 8-2

## Entire Department Charter Document (2 of 8)

### Infrastructure Engineering Operating Plan 2006/2007

#### 1. Infrastructure:

Implement a scalable, reliable and cost effective backbone that provides connectivity both internally and externally.

| ID | Description | Priority | Lead | When |
|----|-------------|----------|------|------|
| A | Diagram the network | 1 | MT | Q1-06 |
| B | Implement 100 Mb | 2 | RV | Q1-06 |
| C | Implement ISDN | 1 | SK | Q2-06 |
| D | Complete back office implementations | 1 | RV | Q2-06 |
| E | Complete AXP migrations | 1 | MT | Q1-06 |
| F | Implement Ethernet switches | 1 | SK | Q3-06 |
| G | Implement router filters to remove bridged traffic | 1 | RV | Q3-06 |

#### 2. Define Solutions:

Engineer current and future technology that supports the needs of our clients. Infrastructure Engineering will research and design enterprise wide voice, data and video solutions.

| ID | Description | Priority | Lead | When |
|----|-------------|----------|------|------|
| A | Define video tactics | 2 | MT | Q1-06 |
| B | Define data tactics | 1 | RV | Q1-06 |
| C | Define voice tactics | 2 | SK | Q2-06 |
| D | Define network management tactics | 1 | RV | Q2-06 |
| E | Define video standards | 3 | MT | Q1-06 |
| F | Define data standards | 3 | SK | Q3-06 |
| G | Define voice standards | 2 | RV | Q3-06 |
| 1 | Research and design new technologies | | | |
| 2 | Thin client | 2 | RS | Q3-06 |
| 3 | Server design | 1 | PK | Q3-06 |
| 4 | Call centers | 1 | CK | Q4-06 |
| 5 | CTI | 3 | RS | Q4-06 |
| 6 | IVR/VRU | 2 | RV | Q4-06 |
| 7 | Fax solutions | 1 | CK | Q3-06 |
| 8 | Topology | 2 | CK | Q2-06 |

#### 3. Consulting:

To provide consulting services to our business partners.

| ID | Description | Priority | Lead | When |
|----|-------------|----------|------|------|
| A | Predictive dialer class | 2 | MT | Q1-06 |
| B | Networking class | 1 | RV | Q1-06 |
| C | Remote office visits for tech evaluation | 2 | SK | Q2-06 |
| D | P.C. evaluation | 1 | RV | Q2-06 |
| E | Thin client evaluation | 1 | MT | Q1-06 |
| F | R&D on Sharepoint | 1 | SK | Q3-06 |
| G | R&D on Protocol | 1 | RV | Q3-06 |

# Appendix 8-2

## Entire Department Charter Document (3 of 8)

### 4. Project
**Management:** Follow standard project management methodology that will enhance the effectiveness and success of our team.

| ID | Description | Priority | Lead | When |
|----|-------------|----------|------|------|
| A | Refine infrastructure methodology | 1 | MT | Q1-06 |
| B | Improve performance on methodology | 1 | RV | Q1-06 |
| C | Expand change control process | 1 | SK | Q2-06 |
| D | Clarify second to third tier hand off | 1 | RV | Q2-06 |
| E | Rework charter scope document | 1 | MT | Q1-06 |
| F | Evaluate hiring infrastructure project manager | 1 | SK | Q3-06 |
| G | Assure adherence to standards | 1 | RV | Q3-06 |

### 5. Professional
**Development:** Pursue excellence by ongoing education and training.

| ID | Description | Priority | Lead | When |
|----|-------------|----------|------|------|
| A | Enhance cross training | 2 | MT | Q1-06 |
| B | Improve off hour support | 1 | RV | Q1-06 |
| C | Improve on call rotation | 2 | SK | Q2-06 |
| D | Get project management training | 1 | RV | Q2-06 |
| E | 1 off-site 1 day seminar per quarter | 1 | MT | Q1-06 |
| F | Develop 1-on-1 training programs | 1 | SK | Q3-06 |
| G | Encourage higher education | 1 | RV | Q3-06 |

### 6. Implement:
Implement the highest quality and reliable technical solutions for our business partners through testing, documentation and knowledge transfer.

| ID | Description | Priority | Lead | When |
|----|-------------|----------|------|------|
| A | Define testing standards | 2 | MT | Q1-06 |
| B | Define documentation standards | 1 | RV | Q1-06 |
| C | Obtain test equipment | 2 | SK | Q2-06 |
| D | Improve testing lab | 1 | RV | Q2-06 |
| E | Implement black berries across organization | 1 | MT | Q1-06 |
| F | Implement development test server | 1 | SK | Q3-06 |
| G | Implement development development server | 1 | RV | Q3-06 |

### 7. Third Tier
**Support:** Provide third tier mission critical support to maintain maximum infrastructure and software application systems availability.

# Appendix 8-2

## Entire Department Charter Document (4 of 8)

| ID | Description | Priority | Lead | When |
|----|-------------|----------|------|------|
| A | Define roles | 2 | MT | Q1-06 |
| B | Define who to call | 1 | RV | Q1-06 |
| C | Obtain equipment required to support | 2 | SK | Q2-06 |
| D | Resolve existing back log | 1 | RV | Q2-06 |

### Infrastructure Team Core Processes

Technology Infrastructure Tactics – Processes
- Technology needs identification
- Research options
- Define candidates
- Select option
- Install options

Define technology solutions – Processes
- Customer request identified
- Request analyzed
- Solution defined
- Solution implemented
- Request completed

Consulting services – Processes
- Customer request identified
- Request analyzed
- Solution defined
- Solutions presented
- Request completed

Project management – Processes
- Project identification
- Project initiation
- Project development
- Project implementation
- Project closure

Implementation – Processes
- Technology inventory
- Install
- Configure
- Test
- Customer acceptance

Third Tier Support – Processes
- Tier 2 turnover
- Analysis
- Define solution
- Implement solution
- Test
- Close ticket

# Appendix 8-2

## Entire Department Charter Document (5 of 8)

### Core Process Functional Responsibility Matrix

| Process | Tactical | Strategic | Admin. |
|---|---|---|---|
| Infrastructure technology strategy | | * | |
| Define technology solutions | * | * | |
| Consulting services | | | * |
| Project management | | | * |
| Professional development | * | | |
| Implementation | * | | * |
| Third tier support | | | |

### Infrastructure Team Responsibilities

**Infrastructure** - Implement a scalable, reliable and cost effective backbone that provides connectivity both internally and externally:
- Identify voice and data technology requirements that provide the infrastructure that links remote locations into a virtual company and provides for adequate excess growth capacity:
  - LAN/WAN network hardware and software
  - Server hardware and operating systems
  - Transport service and protocols
  - Desktop workstation hardware
  - Network/system integrity and security
  - Voice technologies hardware and systems (PBX, ACD, VRU)
- Identify and implement enterprise management solutions
  - Problem management
  - Change management
  - Network monitoring tools
  - Network management tools
- Research and identify infrastructure to support the business
- Select technologies to meet defined business requirements
- Assist in strategy definition
- Implement strategy
- Develop and issue RFI/RFP documents
- Prepare financial analyses
- Lead product and vendor selection processes.

**Define solutions** – Engineer current and future technology that supports the needs of our clients. Infrastructure engineering will research and design enterprise wide voice, data and video solutions:
- Identify hard and soft technology that solves specific business challenges such as but not limited to the following:
  - Prepackaged applications and utilities
  - Voice related applications and utilities
  - Desktop solutions
  - Client specific EDI requirements

# Appendix 8-2

## Entire Department Charter Document (6 of 8)

- IVR/VRU solutions
- Predictive dialer technologies
- Disaster recovery options
- E-mail and fax solutions
- Distribute technologies
- Remote access methods
* Define scalable, fault tolerant and repeatable solutions that meet existing and future business requirements
* Issue RFI/RFP documents for specific business challenges
* Prepare financial analysis documents for specific business challenges
* Lead product and vendor selection committees.

**Consulting** – To provide expert technical solutions to our business partners:
* Partner with the sales and marketing teams to provide professional consultative advice to our customers and clients
* Set realistic expectations for new business solutions delivery
* Provide training and knowledge transfer for technology deployed
* Present engineering solutions to customers and clients
* Act as a technology liaison among IT, vendors and clients
* Provide input to the development project scope and project planning documents.

**Project Management** – Define and implement work management processes in support of standard project management methodologies that will enhance the effectiveness and success of our team:
* Single point of contact for all new project activities
* Enhance and support project management methodology
* Workload management and scheduling
* Interface with other teams to provide project scope and project plans
* Update and maintain project plans
* Complete capital appropriations documents
* Manage portion of the budget
* Prioritize tactical activities
* Define work flow processes.

**Professional Development** – The Infrastructure team will pursue excellence by ongoing education and training:
* Attain MS certifications
* Attain Cisco certifications
* Attain Network certifications
* Attain PMI certifications
* Cross train
* Knowledge transfer

**Implementation** – Implement the highest quality reliable technical solutions for our business partners including testing, documentation and knowledge transfer:
* Install defined technology solutions
* Define test and acceptance criteria
* Attain customer sign off and acceptance
* Define site documentation standards
* Define turnover and knowledge transfer standards.

# Appendix 8-2

## Entire Department Charter Document (7 of 8)

**Third Tier Support** – provide third tier mission critical support in order to maintain maximum infrastructure and software application systems availability:
- Provide technical guidance and support on escalated work tickets
- Provide 24X7 third tier on call support
- Exceed SLA for third tier support.

## Tactical Operations Role

The Infrastructure team's daily operation focuses efforts on implementation activities. We are responsible for configuring and installing pre-engineered solutions. Emphasis is placed on delivering the highest quality reliable technical solutions for our business partners emphasizing testing, documentation and knowledge transfer. The tactical functions include partnering with the planning and project management teams to deliver supportable turn-key technology solutions to our business partners. The team also provides third tier mission critical ticket support to support maximum technology availability. Team management participates in strategic planning and any technology steering committees. The team contributes to overall excellence by pursuing ongoing education activities and professional development.

## Strategic Role

The infrastructure team focuses efforts on research, design and consulting activities. The team is primarily responsible for guiding all decisions relating to the enterprise information technology needs. The team management partners with business operations leadership to define, document and communicate appropriate technology strategies that meet immediate business and infrastructure requirements and positions the business for future growth. The team management plays a leadership role in the IT strategy development and execution.

## Administrative Role

The infrastructure team function is responsible for providing coordination and leadership regarding technology and infrastructure to the rest of the IT department. They are responsible for participation in all project related activities as well as defining policies, procedures and standards in support of their process responsibilities. Specific members also assist in the capital and expense budget development and management. They provide technical guidance for purchasing, vendor selection and management as well as asset management. There are HR activities that must be supported including performance evaluations, compensation management, staffing decisions and professional development activities.

# Appendix 8-2

## Entire Department Charter Document (8 of 8)

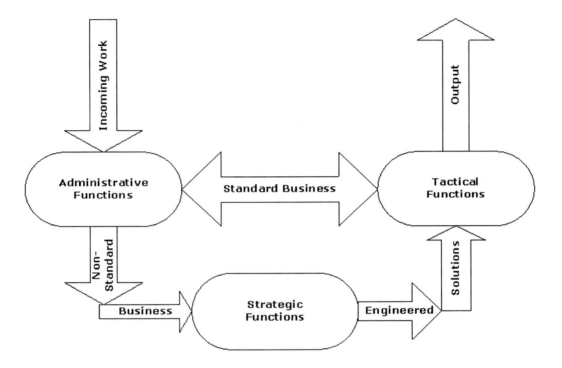

## Appendix 8-3

# Skill Set Evaluation Worksheet

Employee:
Date:

| | Skill set category | | Skill set | Ranking (1-10) |
|---|---|---|---|---|
| 1 | Technical skills | | | |
| | | a | Relevant hardware | |
| | | b | Relevant software | |
| | | c | Other relevant technologies | |
| | | d | Technical concepts and principles | |
| | | e | Underlying technologies | |
| | | f | Assimilates new information | |
| | | g | keeps current on trends | |
| | | h | Stays current on literature | |
| | | i | Assures self-training | |
| | | h | Matches business to technology needs | |
| | | | Technical skills total (sum of a through h) | |
| 2 | Communication skills | | | |
| | | a | Verbal | |
| | | b | Written | |
| | | c | Presentation | |
| | | | Communication skills total (sum of a through c) | |
| 3 | Work habits | | | |
| | | a | Quality of work | |
| | | b | Quantity of work | |
| | | c | Attendance | |
| | | d | Punctuality | |
| | | e | Customer service focus | |
| | | f | Planning | |
| | | g | Organizing | |
| | | | Work habits total (sum of a through g) | |
| 4 | Personal traits | | | |
| | | a | Appearance | |
| | | b | Confidence | |
| | | c | Poise | |
| | | d | Attitude | |
| | | e | Spirit of cooperation | |
| | | f | Critical thinking | |
| | | g | Decision making | |
| | | h | Dependability | |
| | | i | Resourcefulness | |
| | | j | Initiative | |
| | | k | Creativity | |
| | | l | Leadership ability | |
| | | m | Problem solving ability | |
| | | n | Achievement oriented | |
| | | o | Discipline | |
| | | | Personal traits total (sum of a through o) | |
| 5 | Education and training | | | |
| | | a | Formal education | |
| | | b | Adult and follow up education | |
| | | c | Previous experience | |
| | | d | Previous training | |
| | | | Education and training total (sum of a through d) | |
| | Total | | | |

# Appendix 9-1

## Identified IT Processes (1 of 2)

These are the major IT processes in any IT organization.
- **Plan**
- **Build**
- **Run**

These are many of the major sub-processes.
- Plan
  - Planning
  - Budgeting
  - Project management
  - Process management

- Build
  - Infrastructure construction
  - Software applications construction (back office and customer facing)

- Run
  - Systems administration
  - Help Desk tier 1 support
  - Second level and field support

These are many of the major sub-sub-processes.
- Plan
  - Planning
    - Strategic IT planning (Business layer, model or process strategy)
    - Technology architecture (Security, network, data, platform, application, Enterprise management)
    - Business process reengineering
  - Budgeting
    - Capital budgeting
    - Expense budgeting
      - Manage technology expense budget
      - Vendor selection and management process
      - Manage technology acquisition (purchasing)
      - Manage assets
      - Manage maintenance contracts
  - Project management
    - Project management process
    - Project portfolio management
  - Process management
    - Process identification
    - Process documentation
    - Process improvement
    - Work ticket management process

- Build
  - Infrastructure construction
    - Infrastructure definition
    - Infrastructure research and development
    - Infrastructure selection and identification

# Appendix 9-1

## Identified IT Processes (2 of 2)

- Infrastructure configuration
- Infrastructure installation
- Third tier support
- Software applications construction (back office and customer facing)
  - Perform buy or build decision
  - Buy activities
    - Requirements gathering
    - Identifying options
    - Investigating options
    - Developing selection criteria
    - Performing evaluation
    - Selecting solution
    - Testing solution
    - Installing solution
  - Build activities
    - Requirements gathering
    - Application design
    - Application coding
    - Application testing
    - Application installation

- Run
  - Systems Administration
    - Computer Operations
      - Monitor nightly batch processing
      - Manage printing
      - Manage system backups
      - Manage job priorities
      - Manage computing environment
    - Production systems administration
      - Monitor system performance
      - Manage system resources
      - Manage capacity planning
  - Help Desk tier 1 support
    - User communication
    - Handle outbound communications to users
    - Handle inbound communications to users
  - Second level and field support
    - Infrastructure support (break/fix, M.A.C.)
    - Applications support (break/fix, M.A.C.)

# Appendix 9-2

## Procedure Template

**Procedure:**

**Procedure ID:**

**Version:**

Effective Date:

Key Contact:

**Parent Process:**

| Process Name: | Process #: |
|---|---|
|  |  |

**Scope:**

*Functional Participants:*

| Participants: |
|---|
|  |

Procedure Steps:

**Materials Needed:**

 Responsible Party:          Task:

# Appendix 9-3

## Process Template

**Process Name:**
**Process ID:**
**Version:**
**Effective Date:**
**Process Owner:**
## Scope:

**Definition of Process:**

### Inputs:

### Process:

### Outputs:

**Reasons for process:**

|  |
|  |
|  |

### Supporting Documents:

|  |
|  |

**Supporting Procedures:**

| Procedure #: | Procedure Name: |
|---|---|
| 1001 |  |
| 1002 |  |
| 1003 |  |
| 1004 |  |
| 1005 |  |

**Roles:**

<u>Process:</u>

<u>Responsible party:</u>     <u>Process step:</u>

# Appendix 10-1

## Simplified Project Management Methodology Target State

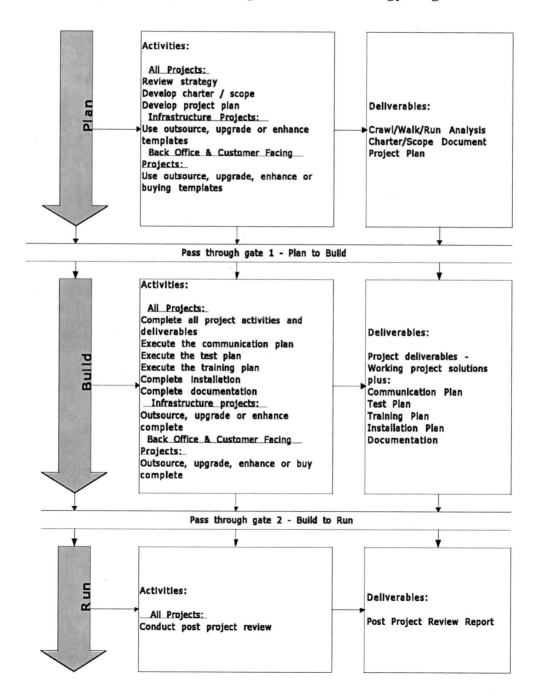

**Plan**

Activities:

All Projects:
Review strategy
Develop charter / scope
Develop project plan
Infrastructure Projects:
Use outsource, upgrade or enhance templates
Back Office & Customer Facing Projects:
Use outsource, upgrade, enhance or buying templates

Deliverables:

Crawl/Walk/Run Analysis
Charter/Scope Document
Project Plan

Pass through gate 1 - Plan to Build

**Build**

Activities:

All Projects:
Complete all project activities and deliverables
Execute the communication plan
Execute the test plan
Execute the training plan
Complete installation
Complete documentation
Infrastructure projects:
Outsource, upgrade or enhance complete
Back Office & Customer Facing Projects:
Outsource, upgrade, enhance or buy complete

Deliverables:

Project deliverables – Working project solutions plus:
Communication Plan
Test Plan
Training Plan
Installation Plan
Documentation

Pass through gate 2 - Build to Run

**Run**

Activities:

All Projects:
Conduct post project review

Deliverables:

Post Project Review Report

# Appendix 10-2

## Crawl/Walk/Run Summary of Approach

| Summary of Approach | | | |
|---|---|---|---|
| | <u>Crawl</u> | <u>Walk</u> | <u>Run</u> |
| **Goal** | Define the business flow. Get the product off the ground. Go through normal start-up activities. Make sure the product or service is viable. | Improve on the manual processes. Automate the most time and person intensive bottlenecks. | Buy a business system. Design and acquire permanent solutions. |
| **Focus** | Manual Processes | Quick and Dirty Technology | Permanent Solutions |
| **Tools** | E-mails, paper, telephone calls. | Access Databases, crude report generators, Excel spreadsheets. | Purchased enterprise production solutions. Visual Basic, SQL relational databases, production processes. |
| **Skill Sets** | Business Analysts. Process experts. Business knowledge. | Small tool kits. Business process improvement skills. Functional level analysis. | Detailed requirements, specifications, software application evaluation and selection, testing, installation. |
| **Business Cost Factors** | Business: Higher increase in FTE costs to support the business. | Business: Moderate increase in FTE cost to support the business. | Business: Low to no increase in FTE cost to support the business. |
| **System Cost Factors** | Systems: Low to no initial system(s) cost. | Systems: Moderate cost to develop initial system(s): Increase IT support costs for systems. | Systems: High cost to develop long term system solution(s). |

# Appendix 10-3

## Sample Crawl/Walk/Run Approach for Document Management

| Engines | Brief engine description: | Crawl Solutions | Walk Solutions | Run Solutions |
|---|---|---|---|---|
| Print Engine with Bar Coding | Printing of documents and bar-coding where appropriate. | **Outsource most.** (Understand volume and costs of printing challenge. Create common area to route and store print jobs, servers and/or storage areas.) | **Outsource some / Print some in-house.** (Select one or more large print jobs. Convert to in-house.) Purchase & install large volume laser printer. | **Print most in-house** (Convert remaining large print jobs and outsource the low volume remainder.). |
| Fax Engine | Faxing of individual documents and mass quantity faxing, both from the desktop and in batch. | **Outsource all** to Mail.com. (Field request from desktop and complete transaction.) | **Outsource high volume** mass fax / **Do low volume** single faxing **in-house**. (Move single fax solution into solution on our desktop) | **In-house faxing for all.** (Purchase & install full solution - single and mass - in-house.) |
| E-Mail (Internet Engine) | Exchange documents through the internet as e-mail attachments or as legal binding documents. | Current Exchange / Outlook functionality. (Document and understand current / future uses) | e-mail forms as attachments that require signatures for recipient to print, sign, and fax back. | **Track style solution.** (Electronic document sharing, electronic signature, satisfies compliance issues.) |
| Imaging Engine (Storage and Retrieval) | Document scanning, imaging, storage, and retrieval. | **Outsource all** - Low volume scan, low volume retrieval. (We get a connection on the desktop to the outsource solution). | **Outsource some** - High volume scan, low volume retrieval. (We move one of the two components in-house, scan or store or retrieve). | **In house solution** - High volume scan, high volume retrieval. (We purchase and install and run an imaging solutions.) |
| Electronic Interfaces | Other electronic file interfaces and transfers of documents. | **Everywhere** with no organization / standard solutions. (Document and understand the current solutions.) | **Single location** with **multiple solutions.** (Move the solutions to a single location.) | **Single location** with **single solution.** (Move the solutions to a single location and standardize the storage, format, counts, and content where possible.) |

# Appendix 10-4

## Project Plan Instructions (1 of 2)

**Overview:**       The intent of the project planning process is to enable a project manager to effectively plan for the execution of a project. The goal of the project plan is to identify the activities required to execute the plan and the deliverables that will signify the successful completion of the activities. The project planning process should be standardized and repeatable. The project planning process should strive for a consistent structure and approach.

**Intent:**          The intent of the project plan is to structure and document all project activities and deliverables as well as estimated timeframes and resources required.

**Inputs:**          Project and business knowledge

**Mechanisms:**      Microsoft Excel and Project Plan Templates

**Outputs:**         Completed Project Plan

**Steps:**           To develop a completed project plan:
1. If this is an infrastructure project review the technology model views of hardware/platform and network.
2. If this is a back office or customer facing application project review the software/database technology model view.
3. Review the IT strategy and the strategic drivers.
4. Conduct the crawl/walk/run analysis and identify the approach.
5. See the "How to create" section below.

### How to create

**Overview:**       Project templates are used to increase standardization and project efficiencies. Select the appropriate template and customize for this particular project.

**Project Name:**    Record the project name in a custom header in the Excel spreadsheet.

**Project Number:**  Record the project number if available in the center of a custom footer in the Excel spreadsheet.

Begin spreadsheet column definitions:

**Step:**            Develop a numbering scheme based on the type of project.

**Procedure
Name:**              Use the project phase as the procedure name. Begin with the

# Appendix 10-4

## Project Plan Instructions (2 of 2)

|  |  |
|---|---|
|  | two steps of planning and execution.  Migrate to the plan/build/run approach.  Select meaningful procedure names for these broad project segments. |
| **Activity:** | List the project activity.  Be as granular as possible.  Try to break down any activity into smaller components if possible.  Broad activities are acceptable early in the project management methodology development.  Break the broader activities into smaller one over time for easier management and tracking. |
| **Planned Start Date:** | Provide the anticipated beginning date for the project activity. |
| **Planned End Date:** | Select the anticipated completion date for the project activity. |
| **Elapsed Time:** | Compare start to end date and compute elapsed time.  Alternately use the anticipated start date and the elapsed time to compute end date. |
| **Man Hours:** | It may be helpful for project planning to develop man hour estimates for each activity.  Strive to improve these estimates over time. |
| **Deliverable:** | Identify the deliverable that will signify that the project activity is successfully completed.  Ask yourself how you will know that the activity has been successfully accomplished. |
| **Actual Start Date:** | Record the actual start date after the project is started. |
| **Actual End Date:** | Record the actual completion date after the project is completed. |
| **Responsibility:** | Assign responsibilities for each and every task. Add to spreadsheet columns here.  Use Microsoft project or other methodologies to add critical components to your project plan.  These columns are the basics and will suffice for most projects in most SMBs. |

# Appendix 10-5

## Project Plan Planning Summary

| Step | Project Type | Activity | Planned Start Date | Planned End Date | Deliverable |
|------|--------------|----------|--------------------|------------------|-------------|
| 1 | Infrastructure | Review the 2 technology model views of hardware/platform and network | | | |
| | | Type of project will be an enhancement, an improvement or an architectural reevaluation | | | Description |
| 1 | Back Office | Review technology model software/database view Type of project will be outsource, replace, upgrade or enhance | | | Description |
| 1 | Customer Facing | Review technology model software/database view Type of project will be outsource, replace, upgrade or enhance | | | Description |
| 2 | All | Review the chosen Strategy | | | |
| 2 | All | Conduct the crawl/walk/run analysis | | | |
| 3 | All | Develop the project Charter / Scope Document | | | Project Charter / Scope Document |
| 4 | All | Develop the Project Plan | | | Project Plan Document |
| 4 | All | Develop the Project Plan | | | Project Plan Document |
| 4.1 | All | Use appropriate template to develop detailed project plan | | | Project Plan Document (from Template) |
| 4.2 | All | List project steps / activities | | | |
| 4.3 | All | Develop broad categories for grouping steps | | | |
| 4.4 | All | Use broad categories to identify milestones | | | Project Milestones |
| 4.5 | All | Estimate times to accomplish activities | | | |
| 4.6 | All | Develop list of deliverables | | | |
| 4.7 | All | Develop milestone time | | | Milestone Delivery |

# Appendix 10-6

## Project Plan Template - Infrastructure Project (1 of 3)

| Step | Procedure Name | Activity | Planned Start Date | Planned End Date | Deliverable | Actual Start Date | Actual End Date |
|---|---|---|---|---|---|---|---|
| 700. 01 | Infrastructure Planning | | | | | | |
| | a. | Accept project assignment. | | | | | |
| | b. | Conduct briefing with business owner. | | | | | |
| | c. | Obtain input and guidance from Tech team. | | | | | |
| | d. | Review strategy where appropriate. | | | | | |
| | e. | Develop project charter / scope document. | | | Project charter / scope document. | | |
| | f. | Obtain sign-off and approval to proceed. | | | | | |
| 700. 02 | Technology Research | | | | | | |
| | a. | List technology alternatives. | | | List of alternative solutions. | | |
| | b. | Develop criteria for evaluation and selection. | | | Technology selection criteria. | | |
| | c. | Research and investigate alternatives. | | | | | |
| | d. | Visit vendor web-sites. | | | | | |
| | e. | Review vendor and industry literature. | | | | | |

# Appendix 10-6

## Project Plan Template - Infrastructure Project (2 of 3)

| | | | | | | | |
|---|---|---|---|---|---|---|---|
| | f. | Host vendor presentations where appropriate. | | | | | |
| | g. | Conduct evaluation. | | | | | |
| | h. | Select appropriate technology solution. | | | Document recommendation. | | |
| 700. 03 | Technology Installation | | | | | | |
| | a. | Work with vendor to quantify order by: selecting appropriate configuration, selecting from vendor options, evaluating features, and providing configuration instructions. | | | Order | | |
| | b. | Prepare site and environment for technology installation. | | | Installation Plan | | |
| | c. | Receive shipment of technology solution and review against configuration and ordering instructions. Do preliminary testing. | | | | | |
| | d. | Schedule technology installation with staff, vendors and project members. | | | Communication plan | | |

# Appendix 10-6

## Project Plan Template - Infrastructure Project (3 of 3)

| | | | | | | | | |
|---|---|---|---|---|---|---|---|---|
| | | e. | Update change management documents to reflect impact of installation on environment and on systems availability and usability. | | | Change Management Documents | | |
| | | f. | Install technology solution at site and configure and install any additional functions or features. | | | | | |
| | | g. | Test technology solution from end to end including both unit and systems testing. | | | | | |
| | | h. | Go live with technology solution by turning up the solution into a production status and make any installation modifications required. | | | | | |
| 700.04 | Post-Project Review | | | | | | | |
| | | a. | Conduct post-mortem meeting. | | | | | |
| | | b. | Modify infrastructure plan template. | | | | | |
| | | c. | Publish report. | | | Post project review report. | | |

# Appendix 10-7

## Project Plan Template - Back Office or Customer Facing Project (1 of 2)

| Step | Procedure Name | Activity | Planned Start Date | Planned End Date | Deliverable | Actual Start Date | Actual End Date |
|------|----------------|----------|--------------------|------------------|-------------|-------------------|-----------------|
| 600. 01 | Requirements | | | | | | |
| | a. | Accept project assignment. | | | | | |
| | b. | Conduct briefing with business owners. | | | | | |
| | c. | Obtain input and guidance from Development team. | | | | | |
| | d. | Review strategy where appropriate. | | | | | |
| | e. | Develop business and technical requirements | | | Project charter / scope document. | | |
| | f. | Develop scope | | | Project charter / scope document. | | |
| | g. | Develop project plan | | | Project plan | | |
| | h. | Obtain sign-off and approval to proceed. | | | | | |
| 600. 02 | Research | | | | | | |
| | a. | Research major publications | | | | | |
| | b. | Research through the internet | | | | | |
| | c. | Research through member affiliations | | | | | |
| | d. | Buy applicable reports | | | | | |
| | e. | Research through company networking | | | | | |
| | f. | Develop initial list of candidate packages / vendors | | | List of potential solutions | | |

# Appendix 10-7

## Project Plan Template - Back Office or Customer Facing Project (2 of 2)

| 600.03 | **Screening** | | | | | | | |
|---|---|---|---|---|---|---|---|---|
| | a. | Prepare RFI | | | Request for Information | | | |
| | b. | Distribute RFI | | | | | | |
| | c. | Continue researching potential solution candidates | | | | | | |
| | d. | Receive and evaluate RFI responses | | | | | | |
| | e. | Complete all research | | | | | | |
| | f. | Limit field to 3 to 4 vendors | | | Reduced list of potential solutions | | | |
| 600.04 | **Selection** | | | | | | | |
| | a. | Interview each vendor in a controlled environment with a set format | | | Vendor presentations | | | |
| | b. | Accept and respond to vendor written questions | | | | | | |
| | c. | Develop selection criteria | | | Vendor selection criteria | | | |
| | d. | Conduct vendor client visits | | | Site visits | | | |
| | e. | Map vendors to requirements and selection criteria | | | Mapping report | | | |
| | f. | Select vendor and solution | | | | | | |
| | g. | Prepare written report | | | Project summary | | | |
| 600.05 | **Contract Negotiations** | | | | | | | |
| | a. | Determine price | | | | | | |
| | b. | Determine support, maintenance, SLAs and other options | | | | | | |
| | c. | Negotiate contract | | | | | | |
| | d. | Sign contract | | | Contract | | | |
| | e. | Establish project for installation | | | New project | | | |

# Appendix 10-8

## Project Plan Template - Infrastructure - Outsource Server (1 of 2)

| Title<br>Preparatory Work | Task | Details | Owner | Day | Date | Elapsed Time | Est. Start | Est. Stop | Done |
|---|---|---|---|---|---|---|---|---|---|
| | Set up icons on PCs | Provide locations & number of PCs | Brad | | 5-Jul | | | | |
| | Set up login Ids and passwords | Into HP Host - 1 day | Tom | | 12-Jul | | | | |
| | Set up and test peripherals | | Tom | | | | | | |
| | | Printers - 30 | Tom | | | | | | |
| | | Dialers - 3 | Justin | | | | | | |
| | | Terminal Servers - 6 | Brad | | | | | | |
| | Establish schedule for support | | Brad | | | | | | |
| | | Tech team | | | | | | | |
| | | Vendor 1 | | | | | | | |
| | | Vendor 2 | | | | | | | |
| | | Field representation at all locations | | | | | | | |
| | Bandwidth need satisfied | | Joe | | | | | | |
| | | VPN between HQ and new Center by 7/12 | | | | | | | |
| | Notify users of password change | | Brad | | | | | | |
| | | Send out e-mail | | | | | | | |
| | | Put printed flyer on screens | | | | | | | |
| | Set up conference bridge | | | | | | | | |
| Installation | | | | Thur | 11-Jul | | 11:59p | | |
| | Shut down System | | Deb | | | | 11:59p | | |

# Appendix 10-8

## Project Plan Template - Infrastructure - Outsource Server (2 of 2)

| | | | | | | | | | |
|---|---|---|---|---|---|---|---|---|---|
| | Assure no updates take place | | Deb | | | | | | |
| | Take backup number 1 | | Deb | Fri. | 12-Jul | 7 hrs. | 12:00m | 7:00am | |
| | Take backup number 2 | | Deb | | | 7 hrs. | | | |
| | Pick up backup | | Bill | | | | | | |
| | Transport backup to Columbus | | Bill | | | 4-5 hrs | 7:00a | 12:00n | |
| | Receive tape in Columbus | | Tom | | | | | | |
| | Restore tape on HP | | Tom | | 14 hours? | 8-10 hrs | 12:00n | 10:00p | |
| | Reorganize file system | Single file system to multiple file system (17). Move files. Scripts written. | Tom | Sat. | 13-Jul | 4-5 hrs | 10:00p | 3:00am | |
| | Development team testing | Joe has detailed testing plan. | Joe / Chris | | | 6 hrs | 3:00am | 9:00am | |
| | Test connectivity to remote centers | | Brad | | | 1-2 hrs | 9:00am | 11:00a | |
| | | Test connectivity | | | | | | | |
| | | Change IP addresses on terminal servers | | | | | | | |
| | | Test icons | | | | | | | |
| | Final shake out | | Tom | Sun. | | | | | |
| | System ready to go live | | Tom | | | | | | |
| | Perform first new backup | | Tom | | | | 5 mins. | | |
| | Run Thursday night processing | | Tom | | | | | | |
| | Run Week-end processing | | Tom | | | | | | |

# Appendix 10-9

## Charter Scope Instructions (1 of 3)

**Overview:**        The purpose of this document is to assist the project manager
in using the project charter / scope document template to
define the project charter and scope components and
consequently the project itself.  This project definition goes a
long way to increase chances for project success.

**Intent:**          The intent of the Project Charter / Scope Document
development exercise is to assist the project manager in
predicting a project's scope, required efforts, timeframes,
milestones, deliverables, and costs.

**Inputs:**          Project and business knowledge

**Mechanisms:**      Microsoft Word and the Charter / Scope Template

**Outputs:**         Completed Project Charter / Scope Document

**Steps:**           To develop a completed project plan:
See the "How to create" section below.

**Controls:**        Key stakeholders should be encouraged to sign off on this
document to signify approval and acceptance of the project as
defined.

### How to create

**Overview:**        Project templates are used to increase standardization and
project efficiencies.  Select the charter / scope template and
customize for this particular project.

**Document
Purpose:**           Provided in the template.  It explains why the document exists.

**Project
Background:**        Be comprehensive.  Include information that will give the
project participant or reader greater context and a better
business understanding of the project charter.  This is a non-
technical description.

**Project
Details:**           Describe the type of project.  Possibilities include infrastructure,
back office or customer facing.  Additional details include
enhancement, replacement, upgrade, outsource or architectural
reevaluation.  List the strategy being executed and make any
additional relevant comments.

# Appendix 10-9

## Charter Scope Instructions (2 of 3)

**Stakeholders:** List by name and title and give their vested interest in the project.

**Project Scope:** Describe what is included and excluded. Remove ambiguity and provide focus. This is a critical component and sets the proper expectation.

**Project Purpose:** Describe the reason for doing the project in business terms.

**Project Goals:** Indicate the goals by providing brief concise statements that established the project direction and binds the project at a high level. Show by priority and give a clear description.

**Project Objectives:** Define the major reasons why the project is being undertaken. The objective should facilitate closure by identifying the deliverable that comes out of each activity.

**Project Deliverables:** List the project deliverables that will be produced throughout the project. Include any tangible results of the activities.

**Affected Systems:** List existing systems affected in any way by this project.

**Project Boundaries:** List what is included and what is not. List the inclusions and exclusions that provide definition and clarity.

**Project Constraints:** Define the project limiting factors which may have an adverse affect on delivery. These should include things like budget, resources, time, and other limiting factors.

**External Dependencies:** What is out of the project manager's control? These are products and services that have to be acquired externally from vendors or business partners or other parts of the SMB. It may also include external events.

**Project Cost And ROI:** First list the costs associated with the project. This is the Investment portion of the ROI (Return on Investment) calculation. Include capital, expense, and manpower expressed in dollars. List the Return on Investment and complete the ROI calculations. The Return includes the anticipated savings, revenue, or benefit derived from the initiative. Reference appendix 1-3 for a simple example.

# Appendix 10-9

## Charter Scope Instructions (3 of 3)

| | |
|---|---|
| **Project Benefits:** | List the non-monetary project benefits that will result from the project. Include benefits to the customer, the SMB, the industry and the community. |
| **Risk Analysis:** | Identify risks the can jeopardize the project. Consider personnel, budget, quality, time and technology. |
| **Assumptions:** | Assumptions are issues that are in a state of uncertainty but for planning purposes need to be viewed as certain. Assumptions can become risks. |
| **Constraints:** | Define the project limiting factors which may have an adverse affect on delivery. These should include things like budget, resources, time, and other limiting factors. |
| **Milestone Plan:** | List the milestone associated with the project plan and the proposed delivery date. Include responsibility where possible. |
| **Project Organization:** | Identify roles and responsibilities of the project participants. At a minimum you need a business sponsor, a steering committee, a project manager and project participants. |
| **Scope Revision Index:** | Use this to track changes to scope. Changes to scope will affect delivery date and functionality. It is wise to track scope changes. |
| **Project Approvals:** | Have key stakeholders approve the charter scope and the project plan. |
| **Project Completion:** | Have key stakeholders approve the project when it is completed. |

# Appendix 10-10

## Charter Scope Template (1 of 4)

### 1    Document  Purpose

The primary purpose of this document is to identify and define the project laying the
foundation for all subsequent work.  The aim is to establish at a high level a common
understanding of the projects scope and to estimate initial timeframes and costs.
The secondary purpose of this document is to identify and document the scope of the
project building on the initial project information to fully define the required effort.
The aim is to establish at a detail level a common understanding of the project costs,
boundaries, timeframes, milestones and deliverables.

### 2    Project  Background

Start text here.

### 3    Project  Details

Start text here.

### 4    Stakeholders

| Name / Title | Vested  Interest |
|---|---|
|  |  |
|  |  |
|  |  |
|  |  |

### 5    Project  Scope

Start text here.

### 6    Project  Purpose

Start text here.

### 7    Project  Goals

| Priority | Description |
|---|---|
|  |  |
|  |  |
|  |  |

# Appendix 10-10

## Charter Scope Template (2 of 4)

### 8    Project Objectives
Start text here.

### 9    Project Deliverables
Start text here.

### 10   Affected Systems
Start text here.

### 11   Project Boundaries

Inclusions:
• Start text here

Exclusions:
• Start text here

### 12   Project Constraints
Start text here.

### 13   External Dependencies
Start text here.

### 14   Project Cost and ROI

Cost Estimates:

Capital:

Expense:

Manpower / Time:

ROI Estimates:

# Appendix 10-10

## Charter Scope Template (3 of 4)

| Factors | Current | Savings | Benefit (Annual) |
|---|---|---|---|
|  |  |  |  |
|  |  |  |  |
|  |  |  |  |

Data Source:

Additional Analysis:

| Factors | Current | After Project Install | Savings | Benefit (Annual) |
|---|---|---|---|---|
|  |  |  |  |  |

Data Source:

Summary:

| Cost | | | Benefits | ROI |
|---|---|---|---|---|
| Capital | Labor | Total | | |
|  |  |  |  |  |

### 15   Project Benefits
Start text here.

### 16   Risk Analysis
Start text here.

### 17   Assumptions
Start text here.

### 18   Constraints
Start text here.

### 19   Milestone Plan

- Start text here:

| | |
|---|---|
| Milestone 1 | Date 1 |
| Milestone 2 | Date 2 |
| Milestone 3 | Date 3 |
| Milestone 4 | Date 4 |
| Milestone 5 | Date 5 |
| Milestone 6 | Date 6 |
| Milestone 7 | Date 7 |
| Milestone 8 | Date 8 |

### 20   Project Organization

# Appendix 10-10

## Charter Scope Template (4 of 4)

### Roles and Responsibilities

➢ Executive Sponsor:

➢ Business Strategy (Program) Manager:

➢ Steering Committee:

➢ Project Sponsors:

➢ IS Project Manager:

### 21  Scope Revision Index

| Version | By | Change | Date |
|---|---|---|---|
| Version 1.0 | | | |
| Version 1.1 | | | |
| Version 1.2 | | | |

### 22  Project Approvals

| Title | Name | Signature | Date |
|---|---|---|---|
| Business Strategy Manager | | | |
| Project Sponsor | | | |
| I/S Project Manager | | | |

### 23  Project Completion

| Title | Name | Signature | Date |
|---|---|---|---|
| Business Strategy Manager | | | |
| Project Sponsor | | | |
| I/S Project Manager | | | |

# Appendix 10-11

## Communications Plan Instructions (1 of 2)

**Overview:**       The intent of this process is to enable the project manager to communicate effectively with all project participants and other stakeholders throughout the build and run phases of a project. The goal is to have an effective communication plan in the form of a repeatable process with consistent output and deliverables.

**Intent:**         The intent of the Communication Plan is to document and structure all project communications to effectively report status and project information and deliver a consistent message to all project participants and stakeholders.

**Inputs:**         Project status

**Mechanisms:**     Microsoft Excel and the Communication Plan Template

**Outputs:**        Completed Communication Plan

**Steps:**          To develop a completed communication plan:
- Schedule a project team meeting
- Publish an agenda
- Hold the meeting
- Identify the number and type of messages that will need delivered
- Identify the audience for the message
- Decide on the frequency of the message
- Assign responsibility for composing and sending the message
- Identify the vehicle to be used to deliver the message
- State the intent and expected response from delivering
- See the "How to create" section below.

### How to create

**Overview:**       Project templates are used to increase standardization and project efficiencies. Select the appropriate template and customize for this particular project.

**Project Name:**   Record the project name in a custom header in the Excel spreadsheet.

**Project Number:** Record the project number if available on the left of a custom footer in the Excel spreadsheet.

Begin spreadsheet column definitions:

**Type of Project:** Record the type of project in the center of a custom footer in the Excel spreadsheet. Options include infrastructure, back office or customer facing. Sub types include outsource,

# Appendix 10-11

## Communications Plan Instructions (2 of 2)

enhance, replace, upgrade, improvement or architectural reevaluation.

**Message:** State the message you wish to convey. Examples include project on schedule, milestone in jeopardy, project in jeopardy, meeting being scheduled, update provided.

**Audience:** List the intended audience for the message in both IT and the business.

**Frequency:** State the frequency with which the communication message will be delivered. Frequencies include:
- Daily
- Weekly
- Monthly
- Monday through Friday
- At specific project milestones

**Responsibility:** Assign responsibility for delivering the message.

**Vehicle:** Define the vehicle or method of delivery. Examples include:
- Email message
- Written report
- Excel spreadsheet
- Verbal

**Intent:** Describe the outcome you wish to reach by disseminating the message. What do you wish to accomplish? Examples include:
- Status reporting
- Solicit feedback
- Modify delivery dates

# Appendix 10-12

## Communications Plan Template

| | 1 | 2 | 3 | 4 | 5 | 6 | 7 |
|---|---|---|---|---|---|---|---|
| Message | | | | | | | |
| Audience | | | | | | | |
| Frequency | | | | | | | |
| Responsibility | | | | | | | |
| Vehicle | | | | | | | |
| Intent | | | | | | | |

# Appendix 10-13

## Test Plan Instructions (1 of 2)

Overview:     The intent of this process is to enable the project manager to identify what testing is required to assure all requirements and deliverables are met and that the project goes as planned. The goal is to assure that there is no down time or adverse effect on the production process or the business.

Intent:       The intent of the Test Plan is to document and structure all project testing and to effectively test all project requirements and deliverables.

Inputs:       Project plan

Mechanisms:   Microsoft Excel and the Test Plan Template

Outputs:      Completed Test Plan

Steps:        To develop a completed test plan:
- Review the project plan
- Review the project requirements
- Determine what level of testing is required:
    o Unit (device or program)
    o Integration (multiple devices or programs)
    o System (an entire business system)
- Determine how testing can best be accomplished
- Determine what signifies a successful test
- Establish time frames
- Establish responsibility
- Determine test plan details
- See the "How to create" section below.

## How to create

Overview:     Select the test plan template and customize for this particular project.

Project Name:   Record the project name in a custom header in the Excel spreadsheet.

Project Number:  Record the project number if available on the left of a custom footer in the Excel spreadsheet.

Begin spreadsheet column definitions:

Type of Project:  Record the type of project in the center of a custom footer in the Excel spreadsheet. Options include infrastructure, back office or customer facing. Sub types include outsource, enhance, replace, upgrade, improvement or architectural reevaluation.

# Appendix 10-13

## Test Plan Instructions (2 of 2)

Step:                    Based on the project number or your own internal numbering
                         scheme develop numbers for each testing step.

Procedure:               Based on your level of testing you will have 1 to 3 levels to
                         test.  Each level can be a separate procedure.  They are unit,
                         integration and system.

Activity:                Identify the individual testing activity within each procedure.
                         This should be a detailed statement of what general
                         functionality will be tested.

Responsibility:          Assign responsibility for the testing activity.

Planned
Start Date:              This is the date when testing of the individual activity must
                         begin in order to meet the testing and implementation
                         deadlines.

Planned
End Date:                This is the date when testing of the individual activity must
                         Be completed in order to meet the testing and implementation
                         deadlines.

Deliverable/
Details:                 Provide what will signify that the testing is successfully
                         completed.

Actual
Start Date:              This is the actual date when testing of the individual activity
                         began.

Actual
End Date:                This is the date when testing of the individual activity was
                         completed.

# Appendix 10-14

## Test Plan Example (1 of 2)

| Step | Procedure Name | Activity | Owner | Start Date | Start Date | Deliverable/Details | Start Date | End Date |
|------|----------------|----------|-------|-----------|-----------|---------------------|-----------|----------|
| 700. 03. 01 | Module Level / Unit Testing | | | | | Module or configuration testing completed | | |
| | a. | Test individual back office components | | | | List here | | |
| | b. | Test all data input screens | | | | List here | | |
| | c. | Test all display screens | | | | List here | | |
| | d. | Test changes high lighted in release notes | | | | List here | | |
| | e. | Review all output reporting | | | | List here | | |
| | f. | Test specific changed functionality | | | | List here | | |
| | g. | Test critical calculations | | | | List here | | |
| 700. 03.02 | Integration Testing | | | | | System design testing including screen navigation and interfaces to other major components or systems | | |
| | a. | Test all screen navigation | | | | List here | | |
| | b. | Test all interfaces to GL | | | | List here | | |
| | c. | Test all interfaces to AR | | | | List here | | |
| | d. | Test all interfaces to Fixed Assets | | | | List here | | |
| | e. | Test interface to commission module | | | | List here | | |
| 700. 03.03 | System Testing | | | | | Compare project requirements in a broad sense to the system/ technology functionality delivered | | |

# Appendix 10-14

## Test Plan Example (2 of 2)

| | | | | | | | | |
|---|---|---|---|---|---|---|---|---|
| | a. | Test against individual project requirements | | | | List here | | |
| | b. | Test against specific functionality requirements | | | | List here | | |
| | c. | Test against specific timing requirements | | | | List here | | |
| | d. | Update change management documents to reflect impact of installation on environment and on systems availability and usability. | | | | List here | | |
| | e. | Install technology solution at site and configure and install any additional functions or features. | | | | List here | | |
| | f. | Test technology solution from end to end including both unit and systems testing. | | | | List here | | |
| | g. | Go live with technology solution by turning up the solution into a production status and make any installation modifications required. | | | | List here | | |
| 700.03.04 | User Acceptance Testing | | | | | Test against understanding and acceptance of users of the system or technology | | |
| | a. | Conduct post-mortem meeting. | | | | | | |
| | b. | Modify infrastructure plan template. | | | | | | |
| | c. | Publish report. | | | | Post project review report. | | |

# Appendix 10-15

## Testing Goals

|  | Infrastructure | Back Office | Customer Facing |
|---|---|---|---|
| **Unit/Module/ Stand-alone** | Test the individual technology component. Assure that the component itself works. | Test the individual software program. Assure that the program itself works. | Test the individual software program. Assure that the program itself works. |
| **System Design/Integration** | Test the individual component plus the larger technology component or system within which it resides. | Test the individual program and all other related programs within the sub-system or set of application components. | Test the individual program and all other related programs within the sub-system or set of application components. |
| **Requirements and Deliverables** | Test the individual component plus the larger technology component or system within which it resides plus the requirements the technology was purchased to satisfy. | Test the individual program plus all other related programs within the sub-system plus the application software system as a whole. | Test the individual program plus all other related programs within the sub-system plus the application software system as a whole. |

# Appendix 10-16

## Plan - Build - Run Pictorial

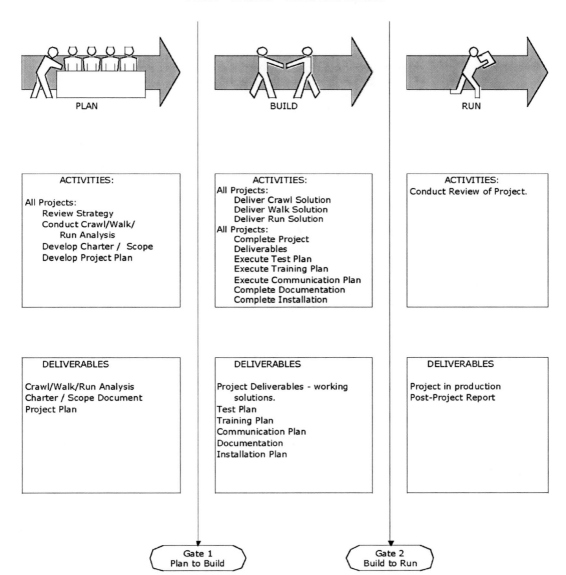

**PLAN**

**ACTIVITIES:**

All Projects:
   Review Strategy
   Conduct Crawl/Walk/
     Run Analysis
   Develop Charter / Scope
   Develop Project Plan

**DELIVERABLES**

Crawl/Walk/Run Analysis
Charter / Scope Document
Project Plan

**BUILD**

**ACTIVITIES:**
All Projects:
   Deliver Crawl Solution
   Deliver Walk Solution
   Deliver Run Solution
All Projects:
   Complete Project
   Deliverables
   Execute Test Plan
   Execute Training Plan
   Execute Communication Plan
   Complete Documentation
   Complete Installation

**DELIVERABLES**

Project Deliverables - working
   solutions.
Test Plan
Training Plan
Communication Plan
Documentation
Installation Plan

**RUN**

**ACTIVITIES:**
Conduct Review of Project.

**DELIVERABLES**

Project in production
Post-Project Report

Gate 1
Plan to Build

Gate 2
Build to Run

# Appendix 10-17

## Training Plan Instructions (1 of 2)

**Overview:**    The intent of this process is to enable the project manager to identify what training is required to assure project implementation goes smoothly and to schedule that training. The goal is to assure that there all training is completed and there are no questions about usage such that all participants understand and use the system properly.

**Intent:**    The intent of the Training Plan is to document and structure all project training and to effectively train all project participants and users.

**Inputs:**    Project plan

**Mechanisms:**    Microsoft Excel and the Training Plan Template

**Outputs:**    Completed Training Plan

**Steps:**    To develop a completed test plan:
- Review the project plan
- Review the project requirements
- Determine what level of training is required
- Determine how training can best be accomplished
- Develop or confirm training content and materials
- Establish time frames
- Establish training responsibilities
- Determine training plan details
- See the "How to create" section below.

### How to create

**Overview:**    Select the training plan template and customize for this particular project.

**Project Name:**    Record the project name in a custom header in the Excel spreadsheet.

**Project Number:**    Record the project number if available on the left of a custom footer in the Excel spreadsheet.

**Type of Project:**    Record the type of project in the center of a custom footer in the Excel spreadsheet. Options include infrastructure, back office or customer facing. Sub types include outsource, enhance, replace, upgrade, improvement or architectural reevaluation.

Begin spreadsheet column definitions:

# Appendix 10-17

## Training Plan Instructions (2 of 2)

**Training For:**    Identify the general group of users that need to be trained.

**Participants:**    Identify the individuals who will need to be trained and will participate in the training.

**Content/
Purpose:**    Identify the type of training that will be required.

**Trainer:**    Identify who will provide the training. Choices include internal staff or external vendors.

**Planned Day:**    Schedule the training on the appropriate day or days.

**Planned
Duration:**    Note the duration in days or hours.

# Appendix 10-18

## Training Plan Example

| Training for: | Participants | Content/Purpose | Trainer | Planned Day | Planned Duration |
|---|---|---|---|---|---|
| Front line system users | | Application/ user training | Vendor | | 3 days |
| | Department 1 | | | | |
| | Department 2 | | | | |
| Supervisors & Managers | | Application management training | Vendor | | 3 days |
| | Payables | | | | |
| | Finance | | | | |
| Senior management / executives | | Application overview and satisfaction of system requirements | Project manager | | 2 hours |
| | VP and above | | | | |
| IT Back Office support | | Systems administration training | Vendor | | 2 days |
| | Back office support personnel | | | | |
| IT Service Desk support | | Application/user training, Application management training, and Systems administration training | Vendor | | 5 days |
| | Service desk personnel | | | | |
| IT Computer Operations Support | | Systems administration training | Vendor | | 2 days |
| | Computer Operations personnel | | | | |

# Appendix 10-19

## Installation Plan Instructions

| | |
|---|---|
| Overview: | The intent of this process is to enable the project manager to plan and execute the installation phase of the project. The goal is to assure that project implementation goes smoothly and according to schedule. |
| Intent: | The intent of the Installation Plan is to document and structure all project installation activities required to bring the project live. |
| Inputs: | Project plan |
| Mechanisms: | Microsoft Excel, Installation Plan Template, calendar, production schedule |
| Outputs: | Completed Installation Plan |
| Steps: | To develop a completed test plan: |

- Review the project plan
- Conduct a meeting with both IT and the business
- Review steps required for project installation
- Provide list of installation activities
- Discuss time frames and production schedules
- Discuss potential business impacts
- Suggest rough schedule and map to calendar
- Refine schedule
- See the "How to create" section below.

### How to create

| | |
|---|---|
| Overview: | Select the installation plan template and customize for this particular project. |
| Project Name: | Record the project name in a custom header in the Excel spreadsheet. |
| Project Number: | Record the project number if available on the left of a custom footer in the Excel spreadsheet. |
| Type of Project: | Record the type of project in the center of a custom footer in the Excel spreadsheet. Options include infrastructure, back office or customer facing. Sub types include outsource, enhance, replace, upgrade, improvement or architectural reevaluation. |

Begin spreadsheet column definitions:

| | |
|---|---|
| Month/Day: | Using a calendar prepare the installation plan to include the specific month/days that installation activities will take place. |
| Installation Activity: | Identify and schedule the installation activities required to install the completed project. Be as specific as possible and go down to the greatest level of detail of activities. This basically maps the installation details down to a specific day. Include times and/or elapsed times if at all possible. |

# Appendix 10-20

## Installation Plan Template

| Sunday | Monday | Tuesday | Wednesday | Thursday | Friday | Saturday |
|---|---|---|---|---|---|---|
| Month/Day | Month/Day | Month/Day | Month/Day | Month/Day | Month/Day | Month/Day |
| Installation Activity | Installation Activity | Installation Activity | Installation Activity | Installation Activity | Installation Activity | Installation Activity |
| Month/Day | Month/Day | Month/Day | Month/Day | Month/Day | Month/Day | Month/Day |
| Installation Activity | Installation Activity | Installation Activity | Installation Activity | Installation Activity | Installation Activity | Installation Activity |
| Month/Day | Month/Day | Month/Day | Month/Day | Month/Day | Month/Day | Month/Day |
| Installation Activity | Installation Activity | Installation Activity | Installation Activity | Installation Activity | Installation Activity | Installation Activity |
| Month/Day | Month/Day | Month/Day | Month/Day | Month/Day | Month/Day | Month/Day |
| Installation Activity | Installation Activity | Installation Activity | Installation Activity | Installation Activity | Installation Activity | Installation Activity |

# Appendix 10-21

## Post Project Installation Document and Template

### 1      Document Purpose

The primary purpose of this document is to document the success and failures of a completed project.  The goal is to learn something from every project and seek project management and project methodology improvements over time.  It can also be used to confirm and celebrate project successes.

### 2      Project  Name

Enter the project name here.

### 3      Project  Number

Enter the project number if applicable here.

### 4      Type  of  Project

Enter the type of project here.  Options include infrastructure, back office and customer facing.  Sub types include outsource, enhance, replace, improvement or architectural reevaluation.

### 5      Project  Performance  against  time  frames

Start text here.  Discuss performance against published time frames for individual milestones and for the project deadline as a whole.  Use this information to improve scheduling for future projects.

### 6      Project  Performance  against  budget

Start text here.  Discuss budget performance including cost overruns and validity of cost estimates.  Use this information to improve budgeting for future projects.

### 7      Project  performance  against  functionality  and  requirements

Start text here.  Develop a checklist of functionality and requirements and whether these specific measurements were satisfied or not.  Use this information to improve the project scoping exercise for future projects.

### 8      Project  failures  –  what  can  be  improved

Start text here.  Develop a series of declarative statements detailing where the project failed.  This is not an exercise intended to assess blame but to collectively learn from project mistakes.  Discuss ways to mitigate these failures and associated risks on future projects

### 9      Project  successes  –  what  is  working  properly

Start text here.   Discuss and celebrate the project successes.  Document specific milestones that were met.   Review the cost/benefit analysis and the value of the project to the company.  Acknowledge exemplary performance.

## Appendix 11-1

### Problem Management Process Target Approach (1 of 4)

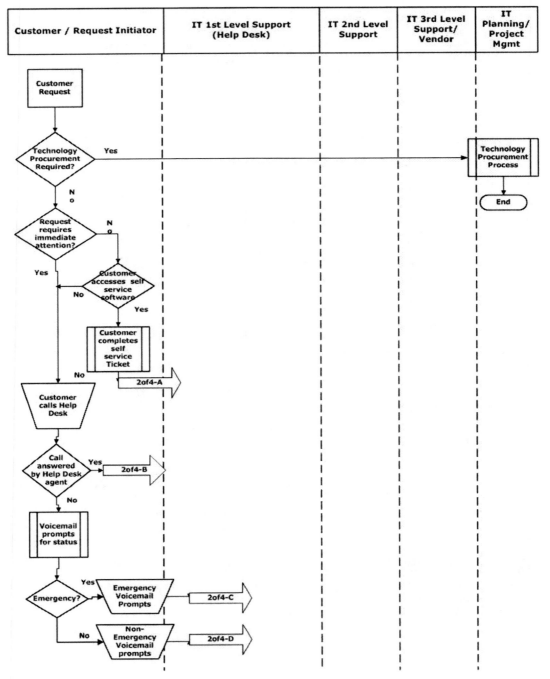

# Appendix 11-1

## Problem Management Process Target Approach (2 of 4)

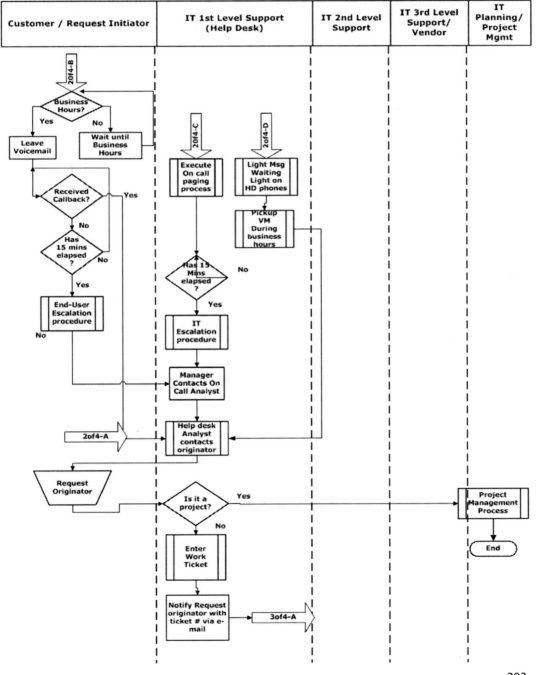

# Appendix 11-1

## Problem Management Process Target Approach (3 of 4)

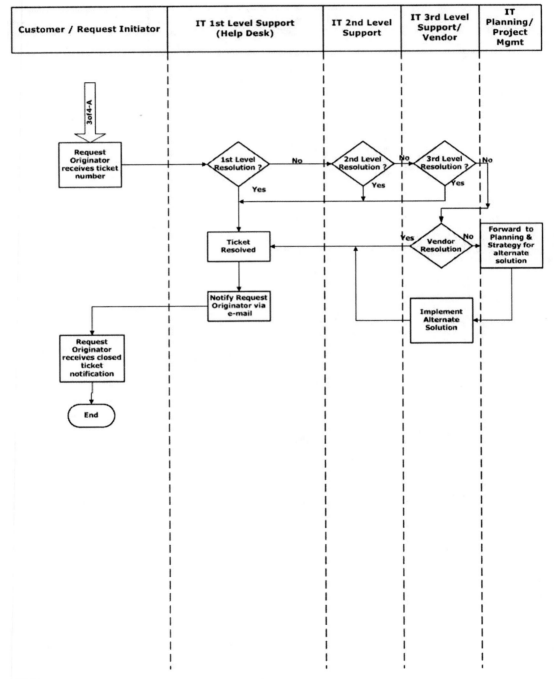

# Appendix 11-1

## Problem Management Process Target Approach (4 of 4)

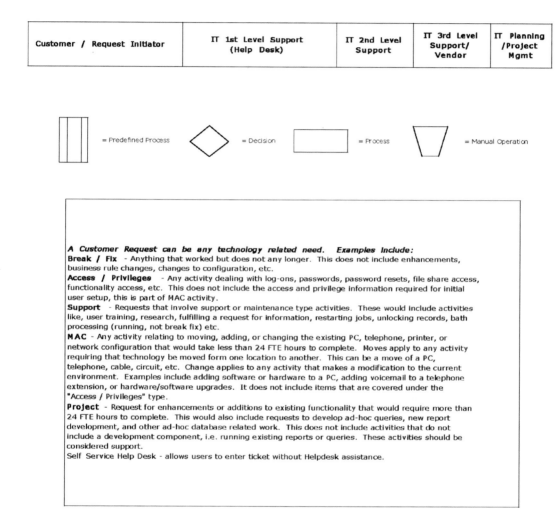

| Customer / Request Initiator | IT 1st Level Support (Help Desk) | IT 2nd Level Support | IT 3rd Level Support/ Vendor | IT Planning /Project Mgmt |
|---|---|---|---|---|

= Predefined Process          = Decision          = Process          = Manual Operation

*A Customer Request can be any technology related need.   Examples include:*
**Break / Fix**  - Anything that worked but does not any longer.  This does not include enhancements, business rule changes, changes to configuration, etc.
**Access / Privileges**  - Any activity dealing with log-ons, passwords, password resets, file share access, functionality access, etc.  This does not include the access and privilege information required for initial user setup, this is part of MAC activity.
**Support**  - Requests that involve support or maintenance type activities.  These would include activities like, user training, research, fulfilling a request for information, restarting jobs, unlocking records, bath processing (running, not break fix) etc.
**MAC** - Any activity relating to moving, adding, or changing the existing PC, telephone, printer, or network configuration that would take less than 24 FTE hours to complete.  Moves apply to any activity requiring that technology be moved form one location to another.  This can be a move of a PC, telephone, cable, circuit, etc.  Change applies to any activity that makes a modification to the current environment.  Examples include adding software or hardware to a PC, adding voicemail to a telephone extension, or hardware/software upgrades.  It does not include items that are covered under the "Access / Privileges" type.
**Project** - Request for enhancements or additions to existing functionality that would require more than 24 FTE hours to complete.  This would also include requests to develop ad-hoc queries, new report development, and other ad-hoc database related work.  This does not include activities that do not include a development component, i.e. running existing reports or queries.  These activities should be considered support.
Self Service Help Desk - allows users to enter ticket without Helpdesk assistance.

## Appendix 12-1

Entire Change Management Document (1 of 16)

Published:

Version:

### Table of Contents

I.   Change Management Process – narrative description

II. Change Management Process – process description

      A. Submit Change Request Form procedure
      B. Review Change Request Form procedure
      C. Communicate Change Event Calendar procedure
      D. Execute Change procedure
      E. Post Change procedure

III. Emergency Change Management Process - description

IV. Change Form (itself)

V. FAQs for the Change Management Process

# Appendix 12-1

## Entire Change Management Document (2 of 16)

### What is the process?

The change management process is a series of written procedures that must be followed to make a change to the production environment.  It requires that a technician submit a change request to a change committee before a technician can implement a change.  The change committee must approve the change before it can be implemented.  The technician must develop for the changed committee certain critical information before the change request can be submitted.  These include:
- Description of change
- Completion success criteria
- Business impact
- Technology impact
- Risk analysis
- Pre-work description
- Contingency plans

The change committee can reject or reschedule a change.

### What is the goal?

The goal is to provide a stable and reliable production environment.  The change management process was developed to:
- Develop the concept of a production environment
- Define the production environment
- Install boundaries around the production environment
- Control and manage change to the production environment
- Provide a high availability production environment.

### What are the features and benefits?

The primary features and benefits of this process include:
- Reduce technology down-time
- Reduce the episodes of erratic and irregular behavior of technology
- High availability technology
- Reliable technology
- Predictable technology
- Reduce service desk work tickets
- Reduce emergency changes
- Eliminate the installation of untested or poorly tested changes

## Appendix 12-1

### Entire Change Management Document (3 of 16)

What is considered production?

| Critical Systems: | Important Systems: | Non-critical: |
|---|---|---|
| System 1 | Account Administration | Call Accounting |
| Clients – Top 20 | CMS | Desktop Hardware |
| Collect | Internet | Desktop Software |
| System 2 | Intranet (Navision, Finance) | File Shares |
| Dialers (any) | Magic | Printers |
| Print | OWA | Printing Services |
| E-mail | RAS | |
| System 3 | RTA | |
| FTP | TCS | |
| System 4 | Time Track | |
| VPN / Network | VOP | |
| Voice Circuits / PBX | Witness | |
| | Voice Mail | |

Who are the change committee?
The change committee are a group of both IT and business associates who have a vested interest in the technology being available. There will be standing change committee members from IT who are responsible for the technology. The selected members of the business will vary by application and technology but will include center managers, super-user groups, and senior leadership.

Want to learn more?
Contact:
Richard Skinner
Strategic IT Associates
4994 Henderson Heights Road
Columbus, Ohio 43220
Office - 614-459-2325
Cell - 614-208-9964
IT is about the Strategy
rskinner@ITisaboutStrategy.com

# Appendix 12-1

## Entire Change Management Document - Process (4 of 16)

| | |
|---|---|
| *Process Name:* | *Change Management Process* |
| *Process ID:* | *101* |
| *Version:* | *04.01.04* |
| **Effective Date:** | April 01, 2004 |
| *Process Owner:* | *VP IT* |

**Scope:**     The purpose of this process is to control change.  It establishes a common methodology that must be used when a technology change is required in the production environment. This process will ensure that changes are communicated within the organization prior to a scheduled event that may directly or indirectly affect production.  The process will establish risk evaluation, accountability, and the ability to measure success.

*Definition of Change:*     ***Changes include any alteration to production hardware, software, or procedures in the data or voice technologies that have a potential to impact our external or internal clients.***

Reasons for Change:

| Reasons for Change Include: |
|---|
| New infrastructure |
| New applications |
| Enhancements to existing infrastructure |
| Enhancements to existing applications |
| Non-emergency Problem resolution |
| Expansions to existing operations |

**Supporting  Documents:**

| Supporting Documents: |
|---|
| I.T. Change Request Form |
| F.A.Q.'s Change Management Process |
| Emergency Change Process |

# Appendix 12-1

## Entire Change Management Document - Process (5 of 16)

**Supporting Procedures:**

| Procedure #: | Procedure Name: |
|---|---|
| 1001 | Submit Change Request form |
| 1002 | Review Change Request forms |
| 1003 | Communicate event calendar |
| 1004 | Execute change |
| 1005 | Review change results |

Roles:

**Change Control Chairperson:**

The Chairperson, VP of Information Technology, will preside over the meetings of the Change Control Committee. The Chairperson will have ultimate authority over requested changes in both normal and emergency situations.

**Change Control Committee:**

The Change Control Committee will be responsible for the approval or rejection of submitted change requests.

**Information Technology:**
Representation should include associates from the Infrastructure Construction, Software Construction, the Service Desk, Systems Administration, Second Level Support, and the VP of Information Technology.

**The business community:**
Representation should include leadership from collection operations selected in the following manner: one manager representing each vertical market segment and selected shared services groups like Analytics.

**Change Requester:**

The Change Requester requests approval for a change by completing and submitting a Change Request Form.

# Appendix 12-1

## Entire Change Management Document - Process (6 of 16)

**Change  Technician:**     The person who performs the change is the
Change Technician.  He/she is responsible
for implementing the activity. This technician
is accountable for the success of the change.
While he/she may assign the change to
another technician for implementation,
he/she is still ultimately responsible. The
Change Requester and Change Technician
can be the same person.

**Change  Administrator:**     A Change Administrator will manage
and distribute calendar and change forms.

| Responsible party: | Process step: |
|---|---|
| Requester | 1. Submit Change Request form. |
| Change Committee | 2. Review Request Forms. |
| Change Administrator | 3. Communicate change event calendar. |
| Change Technician | 4. Execute change. |
| Change Committee | 5. Review change requests. |

# Appendix 12-1

**Entire Change Management Document - Change Request Form (7 of 16)**

| | |
|---|---|
| **Procedure:** | Submit Change Request Form |
| **Procedure ID:** | 1001 |
| **Version:** | 04.01.04 |
| **Effective Date:** | April 01, 2004 |
| *Key Contact:* | *Change Administrator* |

**Parent Processes:**

| Process Name | Process |
|---|---|
| Change Management Process | 101 |
| Emergency Change Management Process | 102 |

**Scope:**          The purpose of this procedure is to control change. It outlines the tasks involved with initiating a technology change.

*Functional Participants:*

| Participant |
|---|
| Change Requester |

## Procedure Steps:

| Materials Needed: | Change Request Form |
|---|---|

| Responsible party | Task |
|---|---|
| Change Requester | 1. Complete the following sections of the IT Change Request Form: Change Scope, Risk Analysis, Change Pre-work/Prerequisites, Contingency Planning, Documentation Revisions |
| Change Requester | 2. Sign and date the Change Request Form. |
| Change Requester | 3. Submit the form to the Change Administrator at least one week prior to an event. (Note that exceptions will be made for emergencies and for problem resolution. In these cases the one-week requirement is waived.) |
| Change Administrator | 4. Add requested change to "IT Change Control Calendar" located in the Exchange Public Folders. Mark as tentative status. |

# Appendix 12-1

## Entire Change Management Document - Review Change Request Form
### (8 of 16)

Procedure:            Review Change Request Forms
Procedure ID:         1002
Version:              04.01.04
Effective Date:       April 01, 2004
*Key Contact:*        *Change Administrator*

Parent Process:

| Process Name: | Process #: |
|---|---|
| Change Management Process | 101 |

Scope:                The purpose of this procedure is to establish the objectives for the weekly meeting of the Change Control Committee. The committee will review all requests for changes and approve or disapprove all change events.

*Functional Participants:*

| Participants: |
|---|
| Change Control Committee |
| Change Control Chairman |

## Procedure Steps:

Materials Needed:          Change Request Form

| Responsible | Task |
|---|---|
| Change Control Committee | 1. Meets on a regular basis (recommend weekly) to review requests. This meeting will take approximately 30 minutes. (Note: this meeting may be eliminated in the future when an electronic process can be established.) |
| Change Control Committee | 2. All current requests will be reviewed during the meeting and a go / no go decision will be made. |
| Change Control Committee | 3. Make suggestions and raise additional issues or questions. May request modifications to dates and times. |
| Change Committee Chairman | 4. Approve/disapprove by completing appropriate sections on I.T. Change Request Form. |
| Change Committee Chairman | 5. Sign and date the request form. |

# Appendix 12-1

## Entire Change Management Document - Communicate Change Event
## (9 of 16)

Procedure:                    Communicate Change Event Calendar
                              Procedure
Procedure ID:                 1003
Version:                      04.01.04
Effective Date:               April 01, 2004
*Key Contact:*                *Change Administrator*
Parent Processes:

| Process Name: | Process |
|---|---|
| Change Management Process | 101 |
| Emergency Change Management Process | 102 |

Scope:                        The purpose of this procedure is outline the
                              tasks involved in communicating Change
                              Events.
                   *Functional Participants:*

| Participant |
|---|
| Change Technician |
| Change Administrator |
| Service Desk |

*Procedure Steps:*

Materials Needed              Change Request Form

Responsible                   Task

Change Administrator          1. Change status of change to "Busy"
                              on the Exchange "IS Change Control
                              Calendar."

Change Administrator          2. Return a copy of the Change
                              Request Form that indicates approval
                              or disapproval to the requester.

Change Technician             3. Confirms scheduling and notifies
                              the Change Administrator of any date
                              and time changes to the scheduled
                              activity.

Change Administrator          4. Resolves scheduling conflicts and
                              notifies Chairperson of all scheduling
                              delays or calendar changes.

Change Administrator          5. Distributes the calendar of change
                              events to the entire enterprise.

Service Desk                  6. Communicates downtime, reduced
                              availability of systems, etc. to the rest
                              of the organization.

## Appendix 12-1

### Entire Change Management Document - Execute Change (10 of 16)

Procedure:                   Execute Change
Procedure ID:                1004
Version:                     04.01.04
Effective Date:              April 01, 2004
Key Contact:                 *Change Administrator*

Parent Processes:

| Process Name: | Process |
|---|---|
| Change Management Process | 101 |
| Emergency Change Management Process | 102 |

Scope:                       The purpose of this procedure is outline
                             tasks that will be performed during a change
                             event.

*Functional Participants:*

| Participant: |
|---|
| Change Technician |

### Procedure Steps:

Materials Needed            Change Request Form

Responsible                 Task

Change Technician           1. The Change Technician is
                            responsible for scheduling vendors
                            and other second level, field support,
                            or construction group members, if
                            needed, for the change event.

Change Technician           2. The Change Technician will provide
                            an ongoing status to Service Desk.
                            He/she will also update the second
                            level support group and/or
                            Infrastructure Construction of
                            unforeseen problems or downtime that
                            could affect production.

# Appendix 12-1

## Entire Change Management Document - Post Change Review (11 of 16)

Procedure:                 Post Change Review
Procedure ID:              1005
Version:                   04.01.04
Effective Date:            April 01, 2004
*Key Contact:*             *Change Administrator*

Parent Processes:

| Process Name: | Process |
|---|---|
| Change Management Process | 101 |
| Emergency Change Management Process | 102 |

Scope:                     The purpose of this procedure is to evaluate
                           the success of the change.

*Functional Participants:*

| Participant |
|---|
| Change Technician |
| Change Control Committee |
| Change Administrator |

## Procedure Steps:

| Materials Needed | Change Request Form |
|---|---|

| Responsible | Task |
|---|---|
| Change Technician | 1. The Change Technician will update page 3 of the Change Request Form after the change is completed indicating any issues or problems with the change event. |
| Change Administrator | 2. The Change Administrator will obtain the Change Request Form from the technician and present it to the Change Control Committee. |
| Change Control Committee | 3. The Change Control Committee will complete the lower portion of page 3 on the Change Request Form indicating overall success or failure of the change. |

# Appendix 12-1

## Entire Change Management Document - Emergency Change (12 of 16)

| | |
|---|---|
| *Process Name:* | *Emergency Change Management Process* |
| *Process ID:* | *102* |
| *Version:* | *04.01.04* |
| Effective Date: | April 01, 2004 |
| *Process Owner:* | *VP IT* |

**Scope:**

The purpose of this process is to control change. It establishes a common methodology that must be used when an emergency technology change is required in the production environment. This process will ensure that changes are communicated within the organization during an unscheduled event that is directly or indirectly affecting production. The process will establish emergency measures that must be followed.

*Definition Of Emergency*

*Change:*

*Emergency changes include remedies required to resolve any adverse impact to production hardware, software, or procedures in the data or voice technologies that have are impacting our external or internal clients.*

Reasons for Emergency Change:

| Reasons for Change Include: |
|---|
| Technology Outage |
| Poor technology performance |
| Technology impacting revenue |
| Reduced technology reliability |
| Client emergencies |

**Supporting Documents:**

| Supporting Documents: |
|---|
| Change Management Process |
| I.T. Change Request Form |
| Change Management Frequently Asked Questions |

# Appendix 12-1

## Entire Change Management Document- Emergency Change (13 of 16)

*Supporting Processes:*

| Process #: | Process Name: |
|---|---|
| 101 | Change Management Process |

*Supporting Procedures:*

| Procedure #: | Procedure Name: |
|---|---|
| 1001 | Declare an emergency |
| 1002 | Research and identify a solution |
| 1003 | Gain approval to proceed |
| 1004 | Execute change |
| 1005 | Document Change |

Roles:

**Change Control Chairperson:**
Approves an emergency change

**Change Control Committee:**
No role.

**Change Technical Advisor:**
Evaluates the emergency solution and Approves the change. Oversees the performance of the emergency change.

**Change Requester:**
The Change Requester identifies an emergency, declares an emergency, researches and identifies a solution, gains approval for an emergency change by contacting the change control chairperson and the technical advisor, and documents the change.

**Change Technician:**
The person who performs the emergency change is the Change Technician. The Change Requester and Change Technician can be the same person.

**Change Administrator:**  A Change Administrator will manage and communicate the emergency change from the declaration of an emergency through the execution of the emergency change.

# Appendix 12-1

## Entire Change Management Document- Emergency Change (14 of 16)

| Responsible party: | Process step: |
|---|---|
| Requester | 1. Declare an emergency.<br>The requester identifies the emergency situation and the need for an emergency change. |
| Requester | 2. Research and identify a solution.<br>The requester contacts the appropriate technical adviser and together they research and identify a solution. |
| Requester | 3. Gain approval to proceed.<br>The requester and the technical adviser contact the change committee chairperson. They explain the situation and the emergency and gain approval to proceed with the emergency change. |
| Change Technician | 4. Execute change.<br>The requester, the technical adviser, and the change technician (if not requester) execute the change. The requester communicates with the change administrator to enable effective communications with the business. |
| Requester | 5. Document change.<br>The requester fills out a Change Request Form to record the change. |

## Appendix 12-1

### Entire Change Management Document - FAQ (15 of 16)

**1. When do I need to fill out a Change Request Form?**
The Change Request Form should be filled out whenever an alteration to production hardware or software is planned. This includes any work that is to be done to any production technology.

**2. What if something breaks and I need to fix it immediately?**
If something breaks that affects production, it should be fixed immediately. This is considered problem resolution and a Change Request Form is not required.

**3. How far in advance should a Change Request Form be submitted?**
The Change Request Form should be filled out as soon as you know a change is necessary. It must be filled out at least one week before the scheduled change.

**4. To whom do I give the Change Request Form?**
The Change Request Form should be given to the Change Administrator. This person is part of the change management committee.

**5. When will I get a decision?**
The Change Control Committee will meet on a weekly basis and will attempt to make a decision on every request that is presented. You should receive the decision within several days from the time you submit the request.

**6. How will I know if the Change is approved?**
The Change Administrator will return the Change Request Form to you after the meeting. The form will indicate approval or disapproval.

**7. Who is on the Change Control Committee?**
The committee includes representation from the business side as well as various members of the IT organization.

**8. What recourse do I have if my change is disapproved?**
If you disagree with a decision, you should contact the Change Control Committee or Change Control Chairperson. The Change Control Committee or Chairperson can escalate the request to the Process Owner if necessary.

**9. Who is responsible for submitting a Change Request Form?**
If you are a technician who is aware of a change that is going to take place, you need to verify that a form has been submitted. Check with the Change Administrator. The technician is responsible for requesting approval for a change.

**10. What happens if I need to postpone a scheduled change?**
If the technician has to postpone a scheduled change, he/she should contact the Change Administrator. The Change Administrator will update the calendar and communicate the change to the Committee Chairman. The schedule change will also be communicated at the next regularly scheduled meeting. It will not be necessary for the technician to submit a new change request form for re-scheduling.

# Appendix 12-1

## Entire Change Management Document - FAQ (16 of 16)

**11. Where can I see the change events?**
All change events will be posted to the event calendar in outlook. You can create a shortcut on the desktop.

**12. When do I have to file the change forms?**
We recommend change forms be filed 24 hours in advance of the committee meeting.

**13. Does the change management process include new clients?**
Yes

**14. Does the change management process include break/fix activities?**
No, those are covered under the emergency change management process.

**15. Does the change management process include vendors?**
Absolutely, yes.

**16. What is the composition of the business representation on the change committee?**
We recommend one business leader from each vertical plus one from the Analytics group.

# Appendix 12-2

## Change Management Request Form and Instructions (1 of 4)

**Overview:**      The purpose of this document is to assist the engineer or second level support analyst in using the change management form to request a change to the production environment. The goal of the process is to assure a stable and safe production environment.

**Intent:**      The intent of the Change Management Form is to document the requested change at such a level of detail that the change management committee can understand and approve the change.

**Inputs:**      Change management schedule, change management form and an understanding of the change desired and the impact on the production environment.

**Mechanisms:**      Microsoft Word and the Change Request Form Template

**Outputs:**      Completed Change Request Form

**Steps:**      To develop a completed project plan:
See the "How to create" section below.

**Controls:**      Engineering or second level support management should be encouraged to sign off on this document to signify approval and acceptance of the change as defined.

### How to create

**Overview:**      Templates and forms are used to increase standardization and efficiencies. Select the change request template and customize for this particular change.

**Change Number Assigned:**      Control number assigned by the change administrator.

**Submitted by:**      Person submitting change request.

**Date Submitted:** Date change request is submitted.

### CHANGE SCOPE SECTION:

**Change Name:**      Descriptive name for the change. The name should be in plain language so it can be used to communicate the change to the business.

**Change Due Date:**      Any deadline associated with the change.

# Appendix 12-2

## Change Management Request Form and Instructions (2 of 4)

**Requested
Change Date:**     Date the change will be made.

**Requested
Start Time:**     Time the change activities will begin.

**Expected
Duration:**     Estimated length of time the change should take under normal
circumstances.

**Change
Technician:**     Technician (engineer, second level support analyst) making the
change.

**Activity
Description:**     Describe the change in detail.  Include the purpose and scope
of the change.

**Completion
Success
Criteria:**     Testing procedures and expected results.  How will the
technician know that the change has been successfully
completed and installed?

**Business
Impact:**     What business or IT operations will be affected and who will be
affected.  Has the change be adequately communicated and to
the proper parties?

**Technology
Impact:**     List the production system that will be affected by the change.
Include all that are impacted.

### RISK ANALYSIS SECTION:

**Business Priority Level**     _____

1 – Non-critical system, minimal financial or business impact
possible.  This is an enhancement to current operations.
2 – Business critical system, significant operational impact
possible.
3 – Mission critical system, significant financial impact possible.

**Risk Level** _____

1 – Fewer than 20 staff members.
2 – At least one entire administrative department (IS, HR, Finance).
3 – One entire business operations center.

# Appendix 12-2

## Change Management Request Form and Instructions (3 of 4)

Complexity　Factor　　　＿＿＿＿＿＿

> 1 – 5 or fewer changes
> 2 – 10 or fewer changes
> 3 – More than 10 changes

### PRE-WORK PREQUISITES SECTION:

**Pre-Work
Description:**　　What preliminary work can be or must be accomplished in order for the change to go smoothly and on schedule?

**Date and Time
Pre-Work
Must be
Completed:**　　What is the latest the pre-work can be completed?

### CONTINGENCY PLANNING SECTION:

**Detail Back-
Out Procedure:**　　Describe what it will take to abort this change and return the production environment to its original state. For example what back-ups need to be made or what work must be undone once the change has started but cannot be completed?

**Estimate Back-
Out Time:**　　How long will it take to back out the procedure if you must abort?

### APPROVAL / DISAPPROVAL SECTION:

**Change
Approved:**　　Yes or No

**Approval Date:**　　Date approved.

**Change
Disapproved:**　　Yes

**Reason for
Disapproval:**　　Description of reasons for disapproval.

**Disapproval
Date:**　　Date disapproved.

**Steps to Gain
Approval:**　　Remediation steps necessary to gain approval.

# Appendix 12-2

## Change Management Request Form and Instructions (4 of 4)

### POST CHANGE REVIEW SECTION:
The following is to be completed by the change technician at the time of the change.

**Actual Change
Date:**          Actual date.

**Start Time:**      Actual start time.

**End Time:**       Actual end time.

**Elapsed Time:**    Change duration.

**Activity
Description:**       Brief description of how change went.

**Completion
Success
Criteria:**          Documentation for testing and assuring change went as
                 planned.

**Business
Impact:**            Expected business impact.

**Unexpected
Business
Impact:**            Any unexpected impacts or occurrences.

# Appendix 12-3

## Change Management Schedule

| System | Monday 0000-2400 | Tuesday 0000-2400 | Wednesday 0000-2400 | Thursday 0000-2400 | Friday 0000-2400 | Saturday 0000-2400 | Sunday 0000-2400 |
|---|---|---|---|---|---|---|---|
| Customer Facing System 1 | | | | | | | |
| Hardware | | | | | | 20:00-07:00 | |
| Software | | | 23:00-07:00 | | | | |
| Customer Facing System 2 | | | | | | | |
| Hardware | | | | | | 20:00-07:00 | |
| Software | 23:00-07:00 | | | | | | |
| Customer Facing System 3 | | | | | | | |
| Hardware | | | | | | 20:00-07:00 | |
| Software | 23:00-07:00 | | | | | | |
| Customer Facing System 4 | | | | | | | |
| Hardware | | | | | | 20:00-07:00 | |
| Software | | | 23:00-07:00 | | | | |
| Financial Systems | | | | | | | |
| Hardware | | | | | | 20:00-07:00 | |
| Software | | | | 23:00-07:00 | | | |
| Accounting Systems | | | | | | | |
| Hardware | | | | | | 20:00-07:00 | |
| Software | | 23:00-07:00 | | | | | |
| Desktop | | | | | | | |
| Hardware | | | | | | 20:00-07:00 | |
| Software | | | | | | | |
| Exchange | | | | | | | |
| Hardware | | | | | | 07:00 | |
| Software | | | | | | 20:00-07:00 | |
| Time Tracking | | | | | | | |
| Hardware | | | | | | 20:00-07:00 | |
| Software | | | | 23:00-07:00 | | | |
| FTP Server | | | | | | | |
| Hardware | | | | | | 20:00-07:00 | |
| Software | | | | | | 20:00-07:00 | |
| Outlook Web Access | | | | | | | |
| Hardware | | | | | | 20:00-07:00 | |
| Software | | 23:00-07:00 | | | | | |
| Internet | | | | | | | |
| Hardware | | | | | | 20:00-07:00 | |
| Software | | | | | | 20:00-07:00 | |
| Intranet | | | | | | | |
| Hardware | | | | | | 20:00-07:00 | |
| Software | | | | | | 20:00-07:00 | |
| Network | | | | | | | |
| Hardware | | | | | | 20:00-07:00 | |
| Software | | | | | | 20:00-07:00 | |

# Appendix 13-1

## Package Evaluation and Selection Process Overview

Here is the recommended process for package evaluation and selection.

| Step | Attachment |
|------|------------|
| 1. Define business and technical requirements | RFI |
| 2. Prepare a package evaluation summary in the form of an | RFI |
| 3. Scope the initiative | RFI |
| 4. Conduct an initial search and identify all potential candidate solutions | Spreadsheet |
| 5. Conduct initial research (buy reports) | |
| 6. Eliminate all but the top 4-6 candidates | |
| 7. Send out the RFI | |
| 8. Evaluate the RFI responses | |
| 9. Narrow the candidate solutions to 3-4 | |
| 10. Schedule and conduct vendor product presentations | |
| 11. Encourage written vendor questions and deliver responses | |
| 12. Conduct vendor client visits and demonstrations | |
| 13. Develop final selection criteria | Sample criteria |
| 14. Map selection criteria to vendors and solutions | Spreadsheet |
| 15. Make selection | |
| 16. Conduct contract negotiations | |
| 17. Purchase | |
| 18. Install | |

## Appendix 13-2

### Sample RFI (Request For Information) (1 of 3)

Company Name

Package Application

### Request for Information
### (Vendor Name)

### Date

This is a business confidential document and may not be reproduced or distributed in any way without written permission from Corporation.

# Appendix 13-2

## Sample RFI (Request For Information) (2 of 3)

# Appendix 13-2

## Sample RFI (Request For Information) (3 of 3)

| | | |
|---|---|---|
| | 5.5 | Database technology |
| | 5.6 | Electronic mail |
| | 5.7 | Internet connectivity |
| | 5.8 | Web presence |

6. RFI response presentation requirements
   - 6.1 Instructions
   - 6.2 Format
   - 6.3 Time frames
   - 6.4 Exceptions
   - 6.5 Non-compliance

7. Other information
   - 7.1 Customization
   - 7.2 Enhancements
   - 7.3 Release strategy
   - 7.4 Upgrades
   - 7.5 Support
     - 7.5.1 Philosophy
     - 7.5.2 Support structure
     - 7.5.3 Support sites
     - 7.5.4 Hours
     - 7.5.5 Fees
     - 7.5.6 Help desk procedures
     - 7.5.7 Problem resolution
     - 7.5.8 Use of third party contractors
   - 7.6 Maintenance
     - 7.6.1 Renewals
     - 7.6.2 Releases
     - 7.6.3 License agreements
   - 7.7 Documentation
     - 7.7.1 List
     - 7.7.2 Updates
     - 7.7.3 On-line help
   - 7.8 Training
     - 7.8.1 Classes and schedules
     - 7.8.2 Train the trainer

8. Confidentiality
   - 8.1 Disclaimers and disclosures

## Appendix 13-3

### Potential Vendor Solution Spreadsheet

| Document Management Project | Vendor 1 - Package 1 | Vendor 2 - Package 2 | Vendor 3 - Package 3 | Vendor 4 - Package 4 | Vendor 5 - Package 5 | Vendor 6 - Package 6 | Vendor 7 - Package 7 | Vendor 8 - Package 8 | Vendor 9 - Package 9 | Vendor 10 - Package 10 | Vendor 11 - Package 11 |
|---|---|---|---|---|---|---|---|---|---|---|---|
| **Print Engine with Bar Coding** | | | | | | | | | | | |
| 8 1/2 X 11 | | | | | | | | | | | |
| 8 1/2 x 14 | | | | | | | | | | | |
| Rxs | | | | | | | | | | | |
| Correspondence | | | | | | | | | | | |
| Envelopes | | | | | | | | | | | |
| Letterhead | | | | | | | | | | | |
| Cards | | | | | | | | | | | |
| **FAX Engine** | | | | | | | | | | | |
| Correspondence | | | | | | | | | | | |
| Claims | | | | | | | | | | | |
| Invoices | | | | | | | | | | | |
| Cards | | | | | | | | | | | |
| **E-mail Internet Engine** | | | | | | | | | | | |
| Correspondence | | | | | | | | | | | |
| Claims | | | | | | | | | | | |
| Invoices | | | | | | | | | | | |
| Cards | | | | | | | | | | | |
| **Electronic Interfaces** | | | | | | | | | | | |
| Correspondence | | | | | | | | | | | |
| Claims | | | | | | | | | | | |
| Invoices | | | | | | | | | | | |
| Cards | | | | | | | | | | | |
| **Requirements** | | | | | | | | | | | |
| Desktop | | | | | | | | | | | |
| Platform | | | | | | | | | | | |
| Database | | | | | | | | | | | |
| Interfaces | | | | | | | | | | | |
| Storage | | | | | | | | | | | |
| Navigation | | | | | | | | | | | |
| Training | | | | | | | | | | | |
| Reports | | | | | | | | | | | |
| Global requirements | | | | | | | | | | | |
| Functional requirements | | | | | | | | | | | |

# Appendix 13-4

## Selection Criteria Mapped to Vendors (1 of 4)

| | | | | | | | Vendor 1 | | Vendor 2 | |
|---|---|---|---|---|---|---|---|---|---|---|
| **Map selection criteria to vendor solutions** | | | | | | | | | | |
| | | | G | General response 0-No or inadequate response | | | | | | |
| | | | | | 1-unknown | 2-adequate, 4-strength | | | | |
| | | | P | Pricing response 0-no bid, 1 through 4 | | | | | | |
| | | | | | (Highest to Lowest) | | | | | |
| | | | B | Binary response 0-False 1-4-True/Yes | | | | | | |
| | | | | | | | | | | |
| | | | | | | | Vendor 1 | | Vendor 2 | |
| | | | | Scoring Category | Section Weight | Weight | Score | Weighted Score | Score | Weighted Score |
| 1 | | DOCUMENT REPOSITORY CAPABILITIES (Store and Retrieve) | | | 0.25 | | | | | |
| | 1.0 | | Ease of document storage | G | | 0.06 | 4 | 0.24 | | 0 |
| | 1.1 | | Ease of document retrieval | | | | | | | |
| | | 1.1.1 | In general | G | | 0.025 | 4 | 0.1 | | 0 |
| | | 1.1.2 | Document indexing capabilities | G | | 0.02 | 4 | 0.08 | | 0 |
| | | 1.1.3 | Ability to establish relationship / links to related docs | G | | 0.015 | 4 | 0.06 | | 0 |
| | 1.3 | | Document printing capabilities | | | | | | | |
| | | 1.3.1 | Individual | G | | 0.03 | 4 | 0.12 | | 0 |
| | | 1.3.2 | Mass / batch | G | | 0.03 | 4 | 0.12 | | 0 |
| | 1.4 | | Document faxing capabilities (sending and receiving) | | | | | | | |
| | | 1.4.1 | Individual | G | | 0.02 | 4 | 0.08 | | 0 |
| | | 1.4.2 | Mass / batch | G | | 0.02 | 4 | 0.08 | | 0 |
| | 1.6 | | OCR capabilities | G | | | | | | |
| | | 1.6.1 | Integrated | B | | 0.02 | 4 | 0.08 | | 0 |
| | | 1.6.2 | Interfaced to other products | B | | 0.01 | | 0 | | 0 |
| | | 1.6.3 | None | B | | 0 | | 0 | | 0 |
| | | | | | | | | | | |
| | | | SECTION TOTAL | | | 0.25 | | 0.96 | | 0 |
| | | | | | | | | | | |
| 2 | | DOCUMENT STANDARDIZATION CAPABILITIES (Design and Implement forms) | | | 0.25 | | | | | |
| | 2.0 | | Is form design and document creation integrated into software | B | | | | | | |
| | | 2.0.1 | Integrated | B | | 0.03 | 4 | 0.12 | | 0 |
| | | 2.0.2 | Interfaced to other products | B | | 0.02 | 4 | 0.08 | | 0 |
| | | 2.0.3 | None | B | | 0 | | 0 | | 0 |

# Appendix 13-4

## Selection Criteria Mapped to Vendors (2 of 4)

| | | | | | | | | | | |
|---|---|---|---|---|---|---|---|---|---|---|
| | 2.1 | | Ease of designing form templates | G | | 0.07 | 4 | 0.28 | | 0 |
| | 2.2 | | Design Tool Integration | | | | | | | |
| | | 2.2.1 | Integrated | B | | 0.04 | 4 | 0.16 | | 0 |
| | | 2.2.2 | Interfaced to other products | B | | 0.03 | 4 | 0.12 | | 0 |
| | 2.3 | | Ease of creating documents from form templates | | | | | | | |
| | | 2.3.1 | Individual | G | | 0.03 | 4 | 0.12 | | 0 |
| | | 2.3.2 | Batch | G | | 0.03 | 4 | 0.12 | | 0 |
| | | | | | | | | | | |
| | | | SECTION TOTAL | | | 0.25 | | 1 | | 0 |
| 3 | DOCUMENT WORKFLOW CAPABILITIES | | | | 0.25 | | | | | |
| | 3.1 | | Does product support document workflow as an integrated standard feature | B | | 0.05 | 4 | 0.2 | | 0 |
| | 3.2 | | Does product support document workflow with the addition of an add on module | B | | 0.04 | | 0 | | 0 |
| | 3.3 | | Does product support document workflow with the addition of a third party product | B | | 0.03 | | 0 | | 0 |
| | 3.4 | | Can product use be modified to provide pseudo document workflow features | B | | 0.02 | | 0 | | 0 |
| | 3.5 | | Ease of document workflow capabilities | G | | 0.03 | 4 | 0.12 | | 0 |
| | 3.6 | | Ability of document workflow capabilities to eliminate external reliance | G | | 0.04 | 4 | 0.16 | | 0 |
| | 3.7 | | Ease of integrating workflows with repository | G | | 0.02 | 4 | 0.08 | | 0 |
| | 3.8 | | Ease of creating and maintaining (modifying) workflows | G | | 0.02 | 4 | 0.08 | | 0 |

# Appendix 13-4

## Selection Criteria Mapped to Vendors (3 of 4)

| | | | | | | | | | | |
|---|---|---|---|---|---|---|---|---|---|---|
| | | SECTION TOTAL | | | | 0.25 | | 0.64 | | 0 |
| 4 | COSTS AND SUPPORT | | | | 0.08 | | | | | |
| | 4.1 | | Cost for base application | P | | 0.015 | 2 | 0.03 | 0 | 0 |
| | 4.2 | | Cost per seat | P | | 0.015 | 3 | 0.045 | 0 | 0 |
| | 4.3 | | Support / Maintenance Costs | P | | 0.015 | 4 | 0.06 | 0 | 0 |
| | 4.4 | | Account Support | | | | | | | |
| | | 4.4.1 | Local account team | G | | 0.005 | 4 | 0.02 | 0 | 0 |
| | | 4.4.2 | Classification | G | | 0.005 | 4 | 0.02 | 0 | 0 |
| | | 4.4.3 | Customer service structure | G | | 0.005 | 4 | 0.02 | 0 | 0 |
| | 4.5 | SLAs | | | | | | | | |
| | | 4.5.1 | IMAC | G | | 0.01 | 2 | 0.02 | 0 | 0 |
| | | 4.5.2 | Problem resolution | G | | 0.01 | 2 | 0.02 | 0 | 0 |
| | | | SECTION TOTAL | | | 0.08 | | 0.235 | | 0 |
| 5 | ARCHITECTURE | | | | 0.1 | | | | | |
| | 5.1 | | Ease of integration | G | | | | | | |
| | 5.2 | | Server OS supported | | | | | | | |
| | | 5.2.1 | NT | B | | 0.005 | 4 | 0.02 | | 0 |
| | | 5.2.2 | 2000 | B | | 0.005 | 4 | 0.02 | | 0 |
| | | 5.2.3 | Linux | B | | 0.003 | | 0 | | 0 |
| | | 5.2.4 | UNIX | B | | 0.003 | | 0 | | 0 |
| | 5.3 | Desktop OS Supported | | | | | | | | |
| | | 5.3.1 | 9x | B | | 0.005 | 4 | 0.02 | | 0 |
| | | 5.3.2 | NT | B | | 0.005 | 4 | 0.02 | | 0 |
| | | 5.3.3 | 2000 | B | | 0.005 | 4 | 0.02 | | 0 |
| | 5.4 | | Database | | | | | | | |
| | | 5.4.1 | SQL | B | | 0.005 | 4 | 0.02 | | 0 |
| | | 5.4.2 | Oracle | B | | 0.001 | 4 | 0.004 | | 0 |
| | | 5.4.3 | Other standard | B | | 0.001 | | 0 | | 0 |
| | | 5.4.4 | Proprietary | B | | 0 | | 0 | | 0 |
| | 5.5 | | Scalability | | | | | | | |
| | | 5.5.1 | Max number of doc limitation | G | | 0.003 | | 0 | | 0 |
| | | 5.5.2 | Max database size | G | | 0.003 | | 0 | | 0 |
| | | 5.5.3 | Max Users (concurrent) | G | | 0.003 | | 0 | | 0 |
| | 5.6 | | Document format(s) supported | | | | | | | |
| | | 5.6.1 | TIF | B | | 0.003 | 4 | 0.012 | | 0 |
| | | 5.6.2 | PDF | B | | 0.002 | 4 | 0.008 | | 0 |
| | | 5.6.3 | Other standard | B | | 0.001 | 4 | 0.004 | | 0 |
| | | 5.6.4 | Proprietary | B | | 0 | | 0 | | 0 |
| | 5.7 | | Scanning capabilities | G | | 0.01 | 4 | 0.04 | | 0 |

# Appendix 13-4

## Selection Criteria Mapped to Vendors (4 of 4)

| | | | | | | | | | | | |
|---|---|---|---|---|---|---|---|---|---|---|---|
| | 5.8 | | Ease of report generation | G | | 0.015 | 4 | 0.06 | | | 0 |
| | 5.9 | | Interface to e-mail (Exchange) | B | | 0.008 | 4 | 0.03 | | | 0 |
| | 5.10 | | Web enabled | B | | 0.01 | 4 | 0.04 | | | 0 |
| | 5.11 | | Server hardware requirements | P | | 0.001 | | 0 | | | 0 |
| | 5.12 | | Interfaces to other products | | | | | | | | |
| | | 5.12.1 | MS Word | B | | 0.001 | 4 | 0.004 | | | 0 |
| | | 5.12.2 | MS Excel | B | | 0.001 | 4 | 0.004 | | | 0 |
| | | 5.12.3 | MS Power Point | B | | 0.001 | | 0 | | | 0 |
| | | 5.12.4 | Visio | B | | 5E-04 | | 0 | | | 0 |
| | | 5.12.5 | Monarch | B | | 5E-04 | 4 | 0.002 | | | 0 |
| | | 5.12.6 | Crystal Reports | B | | 5E-04 | 4 | 0.002 | | | 0 |
| | | | | | | | | | | | |
| | | | SECTION TOTAL | | | 0.1 | | 0.33 | | | 0 |
| 6 | VENDOR PREPAREDNESS | | | | 0.07 | | | | | | |
| | 1.0 | | Response to RFP was received within required timelines | B | | 0.02 | 4 | 0.08 | 0 | | 0 |
| | 2.0 | | Used actual forms in presentation | B | | 0.025 | 4 | 0.1 | 0 | | 0 |
| | 3.0 | | Addressed specific challenges and issues within presentation | B | | 0.025 | 4 | 0.1 | 0 | | 0 |
| | | | | | | | | 0 | | | 0 |
| | | | SECTION TOTAL | | | 0.07 | | 0.28 | | | 0 |
| | | | | | | | | | | | |
| | | | SECTION SUM | | 1.00 | | | 3.445 | | | 0 |

# Appendix 15-1

## Sample Job Descriptions (1 of 2)

**Sample Job Description 1**

**Roles and Responsibilities:** The Technology Support Analyst I contributes to the success of the Information Services Delivery/Support function by installing, supporting, monitoring, testing and troubleshooting the hardware and software pertaining to one or more of the company's voice, data and desktop technology platforms. The Technology Support Analyst I should demonstrate a proficient understanding of at least one technology platform (voice, data, desktop) and easily performs Level I and Level II problem determination on the platform. The position relies on a strong technical aptitude and sound judgment to accomplish goals. The function is expected to perform a variety of tasks concurrently.

**Requisite Skills:**
Technical - Must have a proficient understanding of one of the three technology platforms identified above (voice, data, desktop).
Communication - Must have excellent communication skills, verbal and written.
Management - The Technology Analyst I has no supervisor responsibility.
Mentoring - Must mentor and enrich the professional lives of junior IT associates. Must deal with all employees showing dignity and respect.
**Projects - Must understand standard project management methodology and perform tasks as outlined in project plans.**
Service - Must have a customer service mentality for both internal and external customers.

**Relevant Experience:** Minimum of 1-3 years of experience in a mid size technology diverse, multi-tasking environment. Most recent experience should include one year in a role where the primary responsibility is technology support and implementation.

**Education:** Required         Equivalent industry experience
              Preferred       Technical school diploma, A+ Certification

**Reports To:** Manager Technology Support, Director Technology Support, or VP Technology Support

**Performance Measurements:**
Support –Performance measurements will include the number of service desk tickets resolved, timeliness of resolution, update status of tickets, and quality of problem resolution.
Administration – Performance measurements will include adherence to IT standards and procedures including time recording, and asset management.
Projects - Performance measurements will include implementation of project tasks on time / within budget / and with full functionality, adherence to project management methodology, adherence to documentation and procedures standards.

Process – Performance measurements will include adherence to IT Support policies and procedures including cabling, configuration, tape backups, security, and licensing.

**Allocation of Time:**
| | |
|---|---|
| Construction: | 20% |
| Service/Support: | 70% |
| Project Management: | 10% |

# Appendix 15-1

## Sample Job Descriptions (2 of 2)

**Sample Job Description 2**

**Roles and Responsibilities:**    Responsible for the Delivery/Support function of Information Services. Develops the delivery/support process vision for the organization. Assembles and maintains a team of service desk analysts, systems administrators, and technology support analysts. Designs and constructs the deliver/support processes and procedures to meet the needs of the business.

**Requisite Skills:**
Technical – Must understand and show proficiency with the underlying technology.
Communication – Must have excellent communication skills, verbal and written, and solid presentation skills.
Leadership – Must be able to lead people toward a common goal and develop a team approach.
Management – Must be able to manage numerous delivery/support processes simultaneously without deterioration of service delivery.
Mentoring – Must mentor and enrich the professional lives of employees. Must deal with all employees showing dignity and respect.
Projects – Must understand standard project management methodology and define and document repeatable processes.
Service - Must have a customer service mentality for both internal and external customers.

**Relevant Experience:**    10-12 years in progressive leadership positions.

**Education:**    Required – Associates degree
                  Preferred – Bachelors degree

**Reports To:** SVP Information Services

**Performance Measurements:**
Administration – Performance measurements will include development and communication of the delivery/support process vision, leadership and team building, mentoring and employee development, understanding and projection of a service mentality.
Projects – Performance measurements include technical delivery/support of service solutions, delivery of projects on time / within budget / and with full functionality, adherence to project management methodology, adherence to documentation and procedures standards.
Process – Performance measurements will include ability to standardize, document, and develop means for institutionalizing repeatable processes and instilling a process approach within the team.

**Allocation of Time:**
    Construction:               10%
    Service/Support:        80%
    Project Management:    10%

# Appendix 16-1

## Sample Roles and Responsibilities (1 of 2)
### Infrastructure Engineering

### Process Responsibilities:

Core process responsibilities for Infrastructure Engineering are:
- Define technology infrastructure strategy
- Define technology solutions
- Implement technology solutions

### Roles

Primary roles for Infrastructure Engineering are:
- Consulting services
- Project management
- Professional development
- Third tier support

### Responsibilities

Primary responsibilities for Infrastructure Engineering are:
- Implement a scalable, reliable and cost effective backbone that provides connectivity both internally an externally.
  - Identify voice, data and video technology needs that provide the infrastructure that links the SMB together into a virtual company and provides for adequate excess growth capacity.
  - Identify and implement enterprise management solutions.
  - Research and present infrastructure in support of business needs.
  - Select technologies that meet defined business requirements.
  - Assist in strategy development.
  - Define tactics to implement strategies.
  - Issue RFP/RFI documents.
  - Prepare financial analyses and ROI calculations.
  - Lead product and vendor selection committees.
- Engineer current and future technology to support client needs. Research and design enterprise wide voice, data and video solutions.
  - Identify hard and soft technology that solves specific business challenges.
  - Define scalable fault-tolerant and repeatable solutions that meet existing and future business requirements.
  - Issue RFP/RFI documents for specific business challenges.
  - Prepare financial analyses and ROI calculations for specific business challenges.
  - Lead product and vendor selection committees for specific business challenges.
- Implement the highest quality reliable technical solutions for our business partners including testing, documentation, and knowledge transfer.
  - Install defined technology solutions.
  - Define test and acceptance criteria.
  - Attain customer sign off and acceptance.
  - Define site documentation standards.
  - Define turnover and knowledge transfer standards.

# Appendix 16-1

## Sample Roles and Responsibilities (2 of 2)
### Infrastructure Engineering

- Provide expert technical solutions to our business partners.
    - Partner with the sales and marketing teams to provide professional consultative advice to our customers and clients.
    - Set realistic expectations for new business solutions delivery.
    - Provide training and knowledge transfer for deployed technology.
    - Present engineered solutions to customers and clients.
    - Act as a technology liaison between the IT team, vendors, business users, customers and clients.
    - Provide input to the development project scope and project plan documents.
- Define and implement work management processes and project management methodologies that will enhance the effectiveness and success of the team.
    - Single point of contact for all new project engineering activities for the team.
    - Develop infrastructure project management methodology and templates.
    - Conduct work load management and scheduling.
    - Interface with project management office to develop scope and project plans.
    - Update project plans.
    - Complete capital appropriations documents.
    - Manage project activities and infrastructure portion of project budgets.
    - Manage project resources that relate to infrastructure activities.
    - Prioritize infrastructure tactical activities.
    - Define infrastructure work flow process.
- The infrastructure team will pursue excellence by ongoing education and training.
    - Attain Microsoft certifications.
    - Attain Cisco certifications.
    - Attain Network certifications.
    - Attain PMI certifications.
    - Cross train.
- Provide third tier support for mission critical infrastructure to maintain maximum production computing systems availability.
    - Provide technical guidance and support on problems escalated from two lower tiers.
    - Provide 24X7 on call support.
    - Exceed the SLA for tier three support.

# Appendix 16-1

## Sample Roles and Responsibilities (1 of 2)
### Computer Operations

**Process   Responsibilities:**

Core process responsibilities for Computer Operations are:
- Run installed mainframe infrastructure components
- Run installed mainframe software components
- Generate agent calls
- Generate corporate correspondence
- Run electronic client communications

### Roles

Primary roles for Infrastructure Engineering are:
- Scheduling
- Computer operations
- Monitoring
- Quality assurance

### Responsibilities

Primary responsibilities for Computer Operations are:
- Run the processes residing on the mainframe infrastructure components.  The components are defined below.
  - Mainframe hardware
  - High speed color laser printers
  - Telecommunications equipment
  - Outbound predictive dialers
  - PBX and telephony
- Run the processes residing on the mainframe infrastructure in the form of the software components to support the business.
  - Back office components
    - Finance suite of applications
    - Accounting suite of applications
    - Sales force management
    - Customer relationship management
    - Faxing
    - E-mail
  - Customer facing components
    - Marketing applications
    - Sales order entry
    - Reorder processing
    - Shipping
    - Web orders
    - Customer mailers
    - Customer correspondence
- Generate agent calls.
  - New business entry
  - File transfer processing
  - File / database maintenance
  - Nightly batch processing
  - Build agent call queues

# Appendix 16-1

## Sample Roles and Responsibilities (2 of 2)
### Computer Operations

- o   Present agent call queues
- Generate corporate correspondence
  - o   New business entry
  - o   File transfer processing
  - o   File / database maintenance
  - o   Nightly batch processing
  - o   Build correspondence queues
  - o   Print corporate correspondence
- Run electronic client communications
  - o   Maintain FTP site
  - o   Run client new business file acquisition
  - o   Run client return file processing
  - o   Run client financial file processing
  - o   Run client demographic file processing
- Scheduling
  - o   Develop and maintain production schedules
  - o   Record start, stop and duration times for all jobs
  - o   Record job failures
- Computer operations
  - o   Monitor daily production
  - o   Assure all production runs and in a timely manner
  - o   Provide communication and corrective action on all job failures
  - o   Print all reports and correspondence
  - o   Transfer all electronic files
- Monitoring
  - o   Monitor all production
  - o   Monitor all back-ups and restores
  - o   Monitor system performance
  - o   Monitor disk, memory, and CPU usage
- Quality assurance
  - o   Assure all production finishes as required
  - o   Assure system is available for online usage each day
  - o   Assure completeness and quality of all printed output
  - o   Assure completeness and quality of all electronic files
  - o   Assure system performance

# Appendix 16-2

## Sample Employee Performance Review Form (1 of 2)

| Employee Name:<br>POSITION TITLE<br>DATE                              REVIEW | Position Title: | Review Date: |
|---|---|---|
| **Notable achievements / Goals accomplished / Special strengths:** | | |
| **Performance Measurements:** | **Rating:** | **Comments (Continue on separate page if needed):** |
| A. Support | | |
| B. Projects | | |
| C. Process | | |
| D. Administration | | |
| **Requisite Skills:** | **Rating:** | **Comments (Continue on separate page if needed):** |
| 1. Technical | | |
| 2. Communication | | |
| 3. Management | | |
| 4. Projects | | |
| 5. Service | | |
| 6. Mentoring | | |
| 7. Leadership | | |

# Appendix 16-2

## Sample Employee Performance Review Form (2 of 2)

| Summary Rating: | | Rating legend - U = Unacceptable, BE = Below Expectations, ME = Meets Expectations, EE = Exceeds Expectations |
|---|---|---|
| Rate By (name & signature of reviewer) & Date of Review: | % Merit Increase | Dept. Head Approval : |
| | | |
| Suggestions For Growth / Development | | |
| | | |
| Employee Comment Section (I have read the performance review and discussed it with my supervisor.) | | |
| EMPLOYEE'S SIGNATURE:           DATE: | | |

# Appendix 16-3

## Department Scorecard (1 of 2)

| Department | Role and responsibility | Staff members | Monthly Goal | Key Measure | Performance | Possible | Score |
|---|---|---|---|---|---|---|---|
| Planning and Project Management | Project management | Project managers | Completed projects | Number completed on time, within budget, and with requisite functionality over total number completed. | 4 of 6 | 10 | 7 |
| Infrastructure Construction | Construction | Engineers | Completed projects | Number completed on time, within budget, and with requisite functionality over total number completed. | 5 of 5 | 10 | 10 |
| Back Office Software Applications | Construction | Relationship managers | Completed projects | Number completed on time, within budget, and with requisite functionality over total number completed. | 3 of 3 | 10 | 10 |
|  | Support |  | Systems Availability / Meeting SLAs | Performance against SLAs based on numerical score percentages | 99.3% availability against 99.999% target | 10 | 9 |
| Customer Facing Software Applications | Construction | Relationship managers | Completed projects | Number completed on time, within budget, and with requisite functionality over total number completed. | 4 of 5 | 10 | 8 |
|  | Support |  | Systems Availability / Meeting SLAs | Performance against SLAs based on numerical score percentages | 99.999% availability against 99.999% target | 10 | 10 |

# Appendix 16-3

## Department Scorecard (1 of 2)

| | | | | | | | |
|---|---|---|---|---|---|---|---|
| Systems Administration | Support | Systems Administrators | Systems Availability / Meeting SLAs | Performance against SLAs based on numerical score percentages | 99.999% availability against 99.999% target | 10 | 10 |
| Service Desk | Support | Service Desk Analysts | Problem support through work tickets | Work tickets closed over work tickets opened. | 275 out of 300 work tickets closed | 10 | 9 |
| Field Support and Desktop Support | Support | Field Support and Desktop Analysts | Problem support through work tickets | Work tickets closed over work tickets opened. | 58 out of 60 work tickets closed | 10 | 9 |
| Second Level Support | Support | Second Level Support Analysts | Problem support through work tickets | Work tickets closed over work tickets opened. | 37 our of 40 work tickets closed | 10 | 9 |
| Department | All | All | All | All | | 100 | 91 |

454172

Made in the USA